Vital Stein

Vital Stein

Gertrude Stein, Modernism and Life

Sarah Posman

Edinburgh University Press

Edinburgh University Press is one of the leading university presses in the UK. We publish academic books and journals in our selected subject areas across the humanities and social sciences, combining cutting-edge scholarship with high editorial and production values to produce academic works of lasting importance. For more information visit our website: edinburghuniversitypress.com

© Sarah Posman, 2022, 2024

Edinburgh University Press Ltd
The Tun – Holyrood Road
12(2f) Jackson's Entry
Edinburgh EH8 8PJ

First published in hardback by Edinburgh University Press 2022

Typeset in 11/13 Adobe Sabon by
IDSUK (DataConnection) Ltd, and
printed and bound by CPI Group (UK) Ltd,
Croydon, CR0 4YY

A CIP record for this book is available from the British Library

ISBN 978 1 4744 2535 3 (hardback)
ISBN 978 1 4744 2536 0 (paperback)
ISBN 978 1 4744 2537 7 (webready PDF)
ISBN 978 1 4744 2538 4 (epub)

The right of Sarah Posman to be identified as the author of this work has been asserted in accordance with the Copyright, Designs and Patents Act 1988, and the Copyright and Related Rights Regulations 2003 (SI No. 2498).

Contents

Acknowledgments: A ~~Novel~~ Page and a Half of Thank Yous   vi

Clear as Mud, by Way of Introduction   1

Part I   Beginning with Evolution

1. Life's Story   33
2. Complete Understanding   60

Part II   The Cinema, or Beginning Again

3. Generation   87
4. Tradition   112
5. Cinematic Collectivities   141

Part III   And Again, Naturally

6. Landscapes   173

Now That Is All   209

Bibliography   212
Index   230

Acknowledgments

A ~~Novel~~ Page and a Half of Thank Yous

I often read acknowledgement sections in scholarly books with the same joy I feel on starting on a novel, simply because I love it when the details, names, lists and distractions that make up the nebulous context of writing come into view, all neatly introduced by a narrative voice cleansed of the doubts and fatigue that also accompanied the writing process. This is my attempt at a thank you.

Thanks to all my former colleagues at Ghent University, where I began writing about Stein, and in particular to Marysa Demoor and Bart Keunen, who supervised my dissertation, and to Birgit Van Puymbroeck and Elke Gilson for our conversations about modernism and research. My deepest gratitude goes to Charles Altieri and Sascha Bru for their feedback on the chapters that make up this book. Thanks also to Lyn Hejinian, Marjorie Perloff, Joshua Clover, Juliana Spahr, Kate Briggs, Moosje Moti Goosen, Lisi Schoenbach, Steven Meyer, Adam Frank, Sjoerd Van Tuinen, Stijn De Cauwer, Charles Wolfe, Eric Bennett, Marius Hentea, David Ayers, David Herd, Ariane Mildenberg, Michel Delville, David Caplan, Hélène Aji, Ulla Haselstein, Franziska Gygax, Tania Ørum, Laura Luise Schultz, Solveig Daugaard, Mia You, Isabelle Alfandary, Charles Bernstein and the Gertrude Stein network for meaningful encounters, dialogue and advice. I am obliged to the Special Research Fund at Ghent University, the Belgian American Educational Foundation and the Flemish Research Fund for funding my research projects and I am very grateful to the team of Edinburgh University Press for bringing this manuscript to life.

I started writing this book as an academic researcher and finished it as a teacher. How I wish I could be both. I hope that my continued enthusiasm for Stein's work enlivens its pages and makes up for any flaws. A key moment in my writing process was a visit to the town of Belley and its surroundings in 2019. Taking in the landscape and spending time in Stein's garden taught me that it is really true: for all the beautiful plenitude, "there is no there there."* I could begin again.

Fortunately, my family and friends have been truly there. Thanks to my wonderful parents, Rosa and Dirk, for their help, encouragement and love. Merci, also, to Willem, Hanne, Jesper and Erik for their warm presence, to Eddy and Lucrèce for countless dinners made with kindness, to Sarah and Nicolas for lovely summer evenings in our garden, to Tom and Katrien for music and parties, to Jonathan and L'Abri for their much-appreciated help in creating beautiful spaces to live in, to Manu and Ingrid for conversations and stories, to Isabel and Bernd for laughter and epic rides to southern coordinates, to Iannis for comradeship, to my running friends for hundreds of happy kilometers, to Karen, Elena, Debora and Sofie for lovingly dissecting life and to Éireann for a lifeline of letters. Hanne, Lien, Angelique and Fran: I cherish our long friendship. Els, Hans, Johan, Samuel, Koen, Matthijs, Kila, Koen, Laurens, Jeroen, Carl, Siebe, Daniël, and Tom and Staša: thank you for reminding me that I like writing.

I want to tell my secondary school students that their open-minded outlook, quick feedback and brisk intelligence mean the world to me. While teaching does not facilitate writing (so many children and so little time!), their energy has kept me in touch with the liveliness of thought processes. In an important sense, that is what Stein's work is all about.

Vital Stein is for Christophe, Jacob and Helena. I consider myself such a lucky one that I can do this thing living with you – forever thank you for the difference in me.

A part of the introduction was previously published as the entry "Life" in *50 Key Terms in Contemporary Cultural Theory*, ed. Joost de Bloois, Stijn De Cauwer and Anneleen Masschelein. Kalmthout: Pelckmans Pro, 2017.

---

* Gertrude Stein, *Everybody's Autobiography* (New York: Exact Change, 1993), 298.

Clear as Mud, by Way of Introduction

I said in the beginning of saying this thing that if it were possible that a movement were lively enough it would exist so completely that it would not be necessary to see it moving against anything to know that it is moving. This is what we mean by life and in my way I have tried to make portraits of this thing always have tried always may try to make portraits of this thing.

Gertrude Stein

[D]ifference is not a determination but, in its essential relation to life, a differentiation. Differentiation certainly comes from the resistance life encounters from matter, but it comes first and foremost from the explosive internal force which life carries within itself.

Gilles Deleuze

For Gertrude Stein, life is what literature should portray. Life, of course, is literature's perennial problem, but what sets a modernist understanding of life apart is an interest in life itself – not the good life or someone's life, but life as ongoing, all-encompassing movement. That is how I read the quotation above, which I take from Stein's lecture "Portraits and Repetition."[1] What "we," or Stein and her modernist contemporaries, mean by life is a movement that is "lively enough" not to be dependent on something else ("not [. . .] to see it moving against anything to know that it is moving"). A movement, in short, that "exists completely." That deceptively straightforward statement counts as the prompt for this book. I wanted to know what it meant for Stein as a modernist author to think of life as this complete and lively thing.

While, initially, the parameters of *Vital Stein* seemed clear – it was to be a book about Stein, modernism and life – the ground these terms covered and the relations between soon revealed themselves to be "clear as mud," to quote Stein's generously ironic description of her own work.² But mud is not a bad place to start when you are dealing with life.³

Who, first, is Stein's modernist "we"? Stein may have hosted a famous salon frequented by the *crème de la crème* of the early twentieth-century Parisian artistic scene and in her work she often strategically spotlights her ties with Picasso, but she was also very eager to distinguish her work from what others were doing. There were many complicated friendships and some collaborations, but she never joined a collective project – no magazine, no society, no brothers or sisters in poetical arms. There are, in fact, conspicuously few instances of "we" in her essays, even if she was fascinated by the figure of everyone.

Much of her work, second, strikes readers as too long and repetitive to make for lively reading. Even Stein's most supportive readers have felt inspired by the question "How not to read Gertrude Stein?"⁴ How, then, should we interpret the liveliness she was after, if she makes it so hard for us to feel it?

Life and vitality, third, come with distinct romantic and vanguard overtones, not modernist. If Shelley concludes "The Triumph of Life" with the question "Then, what is life?," Yeats responds a century later with the claim that "Man has created death."⁵ Modernism favored the impersonal truths of science – think of Eliot's platinum, oxygen and sulfur dioxide in "Tradition and the Individual Talent" – over the lyrical analogies between a living nature and poetic genius we find in romantic projects, from Wordsworth's lonely cloud to Coleridge's theory of organic form. Life in the early twentieth century was claimed by the avant-gardes, and they were less interested in answering the question "What is life?" than in living it, in and through art. Tristan Tzara, for example, trumpeted an "I-don't-give-a-damn attitude of life" in the Dada Manifesto and even the Vorticists shouted "WE ONLY WANT THE WORLD TO LIVE, and to feel its crude energy flowing through us."⁶ Stein never set out to write a manifesto, which is the genre that embodies the vanguard ambition to intervene in life, and she was never on any barricades shouting out against the status quo. She loved a bourgeois lifestyle and her texts often testify to the joy she felt in buying nice things and having dinner parties. She furthermore ridiculed some of the avant-garde's key figures. Her 1917 text "Marry Nettie," for example, can be read as a poignant critique on the rhetoric of Marinetti's Futurist Manifesto, and in *Paris France* (1940), she diagnoses "the sur-realist[s]" as a bunch of crowd-pleasers.[7] How does Stein's interest in life relate to theirs?

If, returning to our Stein quotation, life means movement, why not, finally, go with time, or process? These concepts, as many critics have shown, have helped us understand how the unruly forms of both canonically modernist and avant-garde expression relate to developments in the sciences, psychology and philosophy.[8] Why insist on life? And why trust Stein when she refers to life as "this thing"? Is her work not too muddy, too full of all sorts of things, to hold one answer to the question?

The quotation that I have been able to use as the cover for this book, "Thank you for the difference in me" from Stein's 1929 text "Saving the Sentence," is my first answer.[9] Although, as will become clear, new technologies of movement and the early twentieth-century debate about time and process as philosophical ideas help me map Stein's understanding of life, the concept of difference connects all of her attempts to portray life. How, Stein asked herself again and again, can we think of life as one "thing" creating so much difference? This does not mean that life is some kind of source, out of which different life forms flow, or a mere container for different species. For Stein, life means that things can be things while also always differing from themselves and entering into relations with other things, or beings. Those endless relations make up the movement of life.

Stein perhaps most famously voiced her fascination with difference in the opening poem of *Tender Buttons*:

> A carafe, that is a blind glass.
> A kind in glass and a cousin, a spectacle and nothing strange a single hurt color and an arrangement in a system to pointing. All this and not ordinary, not unordered in not resembling. The difference is spreading.[10]

I will return to this poem and explain why a life-obsessed writer devotes a book to inanimate things, but for now what matters is that Stein tells us that we cannot consider a single object like a carafe as one thing only. As soon as we look at it, it becomes many things, including a "blind glass" and "[a] kind in glass and a cousin, a spectacle and nothing strange a single hurt color and an arrangement in a system to pointing." This enumeration is not a matter of mere resemblance. Rather, it tells us about the various lives a carafe can lead in different constellations, from the everyday to the linguistic and the poetic. Odd as it may sound, a carafe will not stay put. The more you look at it, the more you see that the difference is spreading, moving.

Stein's fascination with life as difference is not an idiosyncrasy. I argue that it connects her writing to a number of late nineteenth- and twentieth-century thinkers, working in different contexts and not necessarily familiar with each other's work, who also conceived of life as a single, open system. In the chapters that make up *Vital Stein*, I will focus on Wilhelm Dilthey, Henri Bergson, Walter Benjamin and A. N. Whitehead. As I outline below, life as Stein's "thing" is bound up with a modern construction of life and with the counter-reactions that construction triggered. I consider the "we" in Stein's phrase "what we mean by life," then, as a heterogeneous constellation of modernist thinkers tackling the problem of life. Before I explain what makes life into a problem of modernity, I want to pause at the question of whether the writers I engage with can be considered vitalists.

Vitalism

If we look for the term vitalism in the work of the writers I bring together here, then the answer to the above question is no. Stein made it clear that "[t]he question always is about that anything, how much vitality has it [. . .]," but she did not think of herself as a vitalist. Dilthey is often associated with the tradition of *Lebensphilosophie*, but that is considered a distinct project from the early twentieth-century vitalism that has become almost synonymous with Bergson's name.[11] Benjamin thought Bergson's vitalist project unforgivably naïve and Whitehead also distinguished himself from it. Bergson himself, notably, pointed to the "stumbling-block of the vitalist theories" of his era, and never positioned his work as vitalist.[12] If, however, we take our cue from Gilles Deleuze, who, as my second opening quotation announced, was fascinated by "the explosive internal force which life carries within itself" – and wanted his work to be considered "vitalistic" because of that – then, yes, this book brings together early twentieth-century vitalist thinkers.[13] All of them wrote about life as a differentiating force.

Vitalism comes in many forms and especially its connotations with either bad science or a fascist eugenics agenda explain why some scholars have recoiled from the concept.[14] I will explore early twentieth-century vitalism in more detail in the chapters to come, but for now I want to point out that, in the most general sense, vitalism refers to theories that posit an invisible living principle. In the early twentieth century, notably, the German biologist Hans Driesch published *Der Vitalismus als Geschichte und als Lehre* (1905), arguing that there is a "suprapersonal entelechy" at work in life, which determines every biological and historical form.[15] Despite his own reservations, the second major vitalist figure of the early twentieth century was Bergson. He can be seen to bridge the biological fascination with a life force and the era's interest in the then novel domain of psychology. Bergson's *élan vital*, translated as impetus of life or vital impetus, is rooted in his concept of a cosmic memory, which we can only tap into if we enter a particular state of mind. Among modernist writers and thinkers, these vitalist projects were hailed or ridiculed. C. K. Ogden, for example, applauded the work of Driesch, and was responsible for its translation in 1914, while Wyndham Lewis, famously, repented his early fascination with vitalism and derided what he refers to as the "time-cult" in *Time and Western Man*. Interestingly, Lewis stages Stein as one of its prominent representatives:

> He who understands fully what Miss Stein means by "time" [. . .] (not the Miss Stein that is the *faux-naïf* literary performer, but the old pupil of James and follower of Bergson) will possess the key to the "transitional" chaos, which he can then open at will, inform himself at his leisure of the true value of its highly-advertised interior, and then close it again, and lock it on the outside. The more people able to shut and lock that door the better.[16]

While the door on vitalism closed when philosophy took an analytic turn, the ongoing popularity of Gilles Deleuze and Michel Foucault has turned vitalism into one of the most pervasive isms of twenty-first-century theory.[17]

Looking at contemporary theory, Benjamin Noys observes a "hegemony of vitalism." He frames the situation as follows:

> The neo-Nietzschean and neo-Spinozan coding of what I have called "affirmationism", the turn to an initial affirmation coded as productive, inventive and constructive, is often propped on an affirmation of the exalted powers of life. On the one side we have a series of signifiers oriented by this excessive "life": production, creativity, becoming, invention, affirmation, construction, the immeasurable, and the antonyms on the other side tell their own story: death, consumption, destruction, stasis, negation . . . And yet the hegemony of vitalism is attested to by the fact that even these antonyms are the sites for new vitalisms: the vitalisms of contagion, viral vitalisms, the exploit, undead vitalism, "dark vitalism", etc.[18]

The fact that vitalism is everywhere tends to erode what it means. In tune with Noys's diagnosis, Claire Colebrook's "distinction between a contemporary vitalism that is overwhelmingly organic and committed to meaning and a wilder vitalism that considers life beyond the membrane of the organism" sums up just how contradictory contemporary vitalisms can be. They can claim that life is ours – it is our brain, our milieu, our being that produces meaning – or demand we take our conception of life beyond living beings, which is what Colebrook does, drawing on the work of Deleuze.[19] Yet vitalism's omnipresence also points to a very real concern. Because we feel stuck in political, social, ecological, sanitary crises, we experience the need to protect life. In order to understand our contemporary fascination with vitalism, and make some progress when it comes to the question of how to live in the company of others on this planet, we need to look back and engage with the work of earlier thinkers tackling the problem of life in response to the intellectual, institutional and environmental concerns of their time. Their networks are no longer ours, but we are connected to them still.

In a sense, *Vital Stein* deepens a Deleuze-inspired vitalism focused on difference by engaging in detail with the work of thinkers important to Deleuze, but it is not a book about Deleuze. Stein's work and the problems she encountered in it have determined the connections I establish. That explains the presence of Wilhelm Dilthey, who conspicuously does not fit the Deleuzean line-up. While Dilthey may seem an equally odd Steinian figure, his project, as I will explain, enables me to ground Stein's beginnings as a writer. In staging a dialogue between a body of theoretical work and Stein's writings, I furthermore show that theoretical reflection, or "thought" as Deleuze and Guattari refer to it in *What Is Philosophy?*, is not restricted to philosophy. Although I have my doubts about their sketch of the three domains in which thought happens – they see thought happening in philosophy, science and art, whereas I think we need a thousand plateaus of thinking – I very much agree that "[t]he three thoughts intersect and intertwine."[20] All of Stein's literary work is about thought, is a form of thought. Or, as Audrey Wasser puts it,

> [i]t is as if Stein would suspend the process of concept formation [. . .] while holding on to its constituent elements, retaining the integrity of the process as a creative and living activity, but distributing its elements across the static landscape of an aesthetic composition.[21]

The making visible of intersections between various modes of thinking is key to the work we do as literary scholars.

Curiously, scholars of modernism have seemed to hold back in engaging with vitalism. While there are studies on, for example, modernism and mediated life, sexual life, and the (im)possibility of a utopian life, life per se seems all but absent from the field.²² Some critics have, of course, engaged with individual writers and thinkers for whom life was a central theme and there is quite some work on Bergson's influence, but vitalism as a framework is largely unexplored terrain.²³ In *Out of Character: Modernism, Vitalism, Psychic Life*, Omri Moses notes that while "[t]he influence of vitalism as a discourse on modernism was enormous," it may be considered a wonder that "[it] has until the last decade received so little attention as an intellectual framework for understanding the climate in which literary modernism developed."²⁴ *Vital Stein* is different from the framework Moses erects, in that my focus is not on the mind. In mapping Stein's shifting understanding of life, I show how her initial interest in psychology evolves into a project in which the mind is one part of, rather than the gateway to, a network of relations. What *Vital Stein* thus makes apparent is that the tendency of contemporary vitalisms to deny the subject a central position not only is informed by a mid-twentieth-century philosophical climate, in which a nascent (post)structuralism enthusiastically discarded any remnants of idealism, but is very much a part of a modernist vitalist framework.

Furthermore, while Moses "linger[s] longest on moments of interpersonal intimacy as a site for vitalizing exchange," an important part of my story concerns Stein's question of how to relate to "everybody," from all possible Americans in *The Making of Americans* in the early 1900s over the mass audience of the cinema in the 1910s, to the question of who and what inhabits a landscape in the 1920s.²⁵ Stein's interest in the figure of everybody aligns with the very real concerns of Dilthey, Benjamin, Bergson and Whitehead for a collective life. Benjamin's political commitment to the possibilities that life holds may need little explanation, but we do not readily think of Dilthey, Bergson or Whitehead as engaged thinkers. All three, however, took to heart the idea of a society working towards freedom. For Dilthey, the unending and shared work of interpretation, transforming the historical tradition in which it takes place, is what creates freedom. Freedom is not, then, a given or a category, but a practice of endless revision. Bergson's *The Two Sources of Morality and Religion* is responsible for launching the idea of a creative open society, later taken up by Karl Popper. For Bergson, "[t]he open society is the society which is deemed in principle to embrace all humanity," and as such represented a tendency that runs counter to the human instinct to live in small communities.²⁶ He tried to help build such an open society by serving as the first president of the International Committee on Intellectual Cooperation, set up by the League of Nations. Like Bergson, Whitehead worked in the margins of the political system, serving as a high administrator promoting educational reform and supporting women's suffrage. Criticizing the tendency to define freedom in negative terms, as in freedom *from* censorship, he wanted us to consider a freedom for something, serving the common good, in answer to basic human needs. Prometheus's taming of fire, he points out, did not "bring to mankind freedom of the press."[27] The vitalist framework I propose, then, brings into view a modernism focused on collective life rather than on the individual mind.[28] But what makes life into a modern problem?

Modern(ist) and Avant-Garde Life

Life, Michel Foucault wants us to see, is a relatively recent thing. In *The Order of Things* he argues that "[u]p to the end of the eighteenth century [. . .] life does not exist: only living beings."[29] Foucault does not deny that, for centuries, life has been philosophy's key problem. But the problem of life in, for example, Aristotle is the problem of the good life, and that is not what Foucault is interested in in *The Order of Things*. Thinkers tackling "the good life" pose the question of how individuals and societies can attain a happy existence. In the *Nicomachean Ethics*, for example, Aristotle explores the meaning of eudaimonia, which we tend to translate as "happiness," even if the notion refers less to a feeling than to the project of perfecting one's soul so as to "live well" and "do well." What Foucault understands by life in *The Order of Things* is life as a concept above and beyond living beings, or what nineteenth-century life philosophers would often refer to as life itself.

The late eighteenth century is a pivotal moment, for Foucault, because up until then natural historians conceived of life as a container concept for different classes and species. Whereas philosophers and scientists hardly sidestepped the question of how to classify, they did not call into question that the process of classification, via observing, describing and naming, led to knowledge. That changed when Kant fundamentally altered the way in which we think about knowledge. If, before Kant, to know was to represent, then his work radically problematized representation. Knowledge based on representation implies that an idea, as a mental representation rooted in intellectual or sensory intuition, tells us what a thing is. Language, in this view, is an instrument for thinking. Kant, however, poses the questions of how ideas represent their objects and of how thinking relates to language. For Foucault, this situation sets in motion modernity, which comes down to the falling apart of the classical framework that made it seem possible for the whole of the universe to be known by the same method. Components of that once coherent framework now become structures on their own, demanding to be known on their own terms. Language is no longer seen as an instrument but as an independent system (for a modernist writer like Mallarmé, language itself could speak); humanity, analogously, is no longer considered the locus of representations but their source (with the Kantian transcendental mind creating them); and life is no longer the sum of living beings. Life, Foucault writes, "escapes."[30]

Life escaping into modernity implies several things. It means that life becomes an object of knowledge rather than some kind of background against which classification takes place. Developments in the fields of chemistry and physics in the eighteenth and nineteenth centuries led scientists to see biological life in terms of chemical processes and mechanisms. Life appeared explicable; in the nineteenth century, it seemed only a matter of time before the essential mechanisms would be mapped and codes cracked. Furthermore, modern developments in agriculture and politics diverted the threat of unforeseeable death, whether through famine or a tyrannical monarch, and thus had an impact on demographic life. Concomitantly, knowledge production sped up, and developments in the fields of economics, statistics and medicine resulted in better living conditions. Life, in other words, became manageable on different fronts and in different domains. Such a system is what Foucault refers to as bio-power, which forms the core of his views on bio-politics. Importantly, this modern tendency to explain and control life also triggered a counter-reaction.

Reacting against the tendency to approach life as a scientific object of study, writers and thinkers working in various traditions started arguing that life cannot be known by scientific methods since those fail to account for the experience of living. In the eighteenth century, the romantics voiced a polyphonic anti-materialism and yearned for a return to nature. Wordsworth, notably, critiques our "meddling intellect" and, at the end of "The Tables Turned," cries out "Enough of science and of art."[31] In the nineteenth and early twentieth centuries, a number of thinkers tackled the issue of how to conceptualize life in terms different from the sciences. Some have been labeled life philosophers or vitalists, although they were not necessarily familiar with each other's work and had often little to do with those vitalist theories seeking to isolate a living principle or animating force that distinguishes animate beings from inanimate things.[32] More important than a label that unites their efforts is the questions they asked themselves in rethinking and reorganizing the life that modernity has created. Those, I argue, were also Stein's.

For some of these thinkers, such as Friedrich Nietzsche and Henri Bergson, the way in which societies organize knowledge about life was connected to power and violence. "Freeing" life from those scientific and/or moral frameworks was the goal of their projects. Others focused on an institutional reorganization of the disciplines devoted to the study of life. Wilhelm Dilthey, for example, wanted to match the advance of the natural sciences by establishing a new discipline, the *Geisteswissenschaften*, or human sciences. Dilthey considered life to be synonymous with history, as the sum of human experience and expression. Where the natural sciences were concerned with describing outer experience, the human sciences, with history as the flagship discipline, had to offer a rich understanding of inner experience. Dilthey's proposed hermeneutic method implies the act of self-reflexively re-experiencing the life of others, which, via an open-ended dialogue between the psychological and social contexts of both the interpreter and the object of study, was to result in rich historical knowledge, open to change as experience fluctuates. When Stein quit her scientific training and turned to literature in the early 1900s, the question of how to understand inner experience, or what she calls character or bottom nature, became her key problem. Her project comes with far more friction than Dilthey's – the impossibility of understanding everyone and oneself triggers writerly despair – but that friction is testament to her attempts to approach life in a way she was not trained to do.

Bergson's project of a creative life amounts to a very different life philosophy. Although Bergson, like Dilthey, was fascinated by the past, he had very little to say about history. Life, for the French philosopher, amounts to something like a bio-psychological force, which he referred to as the *élan vital*. And where Dilthey wanted to match the natural sciences, Bergson was very critical of them. The central aim of his book *Creative Evolution* (1907), for instance, is the refutation of a mechanist scientific framework. "Life," he argues, "is no more made of physico-chemical elements than a curve is composed of straight lines." What life is made of, rather, is differentiating energy: "Life [. . .] is undoubtedly creative, i.e. productive of effects in which it expands and transcends its own being." In always effectuating change, on all possible levels, from that of the individual human mind to the universe, life collects a multitude of variations, which make up a cosmic memory. The method by which we can access that memory, Bergson argued, is intuition. Contrary to Dilthey's re-experiencing, which is a situated self-reflective act and a method correlative to that of the sciences, Bergson wants us to think of intuition as an almost meditative state, which demands we put our intellectual habits on hold. By Bergson's account, the intellect "feels at home among inanimate objects," which it can observe, describe and name, but fundamentally fails to make sense of the process of change or differentiation, which can be grasped only through intuition.[33] He furthermore holds the intellect responsible for creating closed societies, in *Two Sources of Morality and Religion*. If, for Nietzsche, life needed to be freed from the shackles of morality through struggle, then Bergson pictures an open society generated by a mystical creative emotion.

Although the humanist specifics of Dilthey's project have been criticized by many twentieth-century thinkers, and his method of understanding sits uneasy with contemporary humanities research that is often data-focused, the problems he addressed – how to understand life as an open-ended process with a manifold of expressions, and how to institutionalize that process of understanding – are issues we, as so-called lifelong learners in a globalized world, cannot afford not to think about. For Bergson, what life is comes down to the biological tendency of organic matter to change – not merely to increase or decrease, but to change in nature, to become different. That focus on differentiation, Deleuze argues in his famous essay "Bergson's Conception of Difference," is exactly what makes Bergson into a key thinker of the twentieth century. For Deleuze, Bergson offers a way out of the logic of the dialectic, which has dominated philosophy since Plato, because he does not need for something to correspond to something else.[34] That is also how I read Stein's lively movement, existing "so completely that it would not be necessary to see it moving against anything to know that it is moving."

Another response to life's escape, and its alleged manageability in different domains, is the project of a radical empiricism, introduced by William James and elaborated on by Alfred North Whitehead. Both are sometimes seen as process philosophers akin to Bergson, but their work comes with very different sets of scopes and ambitions. In general terms, both react against the tendency of specialization that modernity, as Foucault understands it, fostered. For James, traditional empiricism was too focused on "the disjunctions," too intent on seeing things "as 'loose and separate' as if they had 'no manner of connection.'" He wanted to be able to see the connections between supposedly very different modes of experience and proposed a radical empiricism, by which he wanted to find "a real place [. . .] for every kind of thing experienced, whether term or relation." Hardly a static worldview, James's theory of a radical empiricism is akin to that of Bergson in embracing the difference at work in experience. He calls his philosophy "a mosaic philosophy, a philosophy of plural facts." Although he is wary of making too much of the mosaic analogy and refuses the idea of a "bedding" for the mosaic, or a container concept that holds together the different factors and relations in experience, he frames life as a dynamic unity. "Life," James writes, "is in the transitions as much as in the terms connected." The image of the mosaic works well to highlight the pluralism of James's project, but it cannot do justice to the movement of experience. "The tissue of experience," or life, moves. "It is 'of' the past, inasmuch as it comes expressly as the past's continuation; it is 'of' the future in so far as the future, when it comes, will have continued *it*."[35]

If James left his theory of a radical empiricism unfinished, with the hope of it "grow[ing] into a respectable system [. . .] by the contributions of many cooperating minds," then Whitehead can be considered one of the leading cooperating minds.[36] Whitehead was fascinated by the idea of a dynamic unity and, in much greater depth than James, he tackled the issue of how the new (the future) can be considered a continuation of the old (the past). His work is not, however, founded on the idea of process or continuation. Whitehead practiced philosophy to correct an error. The whole of his metaphysical system springs from his "protesting against [. . .] the bifurcation of nature," which he considered the core problem of western philosophy:

> What I am essentially protesting against is the bifurcation of nature into two systems of reality, which, in so far as they are real, are real in different senses. One reality would be the entities such as electrons which are the study of speculative physics. This would be the reality which is there for knowledge; although on this theory it is never known. For what is known is the other sort of reality, which is the byplay of the mind. Thus there would be two natures, one is the conjecture and the other is the dream.[37]

James's radical empiricism grew out of his work as a psychologist, but Whitehead moved towards philosophy as a mathematician and high-ranking administrator. For Whitehead, the "bifurcation of nature," which the French philosopher and sociologist of science Bruno Latour sums up as "the strange and fully modernist divide between primary and secondary qualities," is one of the most powerful modern constructions, which has exerted a gigantic influence on the way in which we see the world, organize knowledge production and run schools and universities.[38] In thinking about how to theorize the two allegedly distinct realities as part of one nature, Whitehead also tackled the question of "the order" of that nature and the processes of growth or creativity at work in it. In contrast to the theory of efficient causality, which, as Steven Shaviro sums up, "refers to the naturalistic chain of causes and effects, or the way that an entity inherits conditions and orientations from 'the immortal past,'" Whitehead makes room for novelty, or difference.[39] This novelty is what he defines as life: "an organism is 'alive' when in some measure its reactions are inexplicable by *any* tradition or pure physical inheritance."[40] The relationship between Whitehead and Stein, and James and Stein, has been documented by scholars. Steven Meyer, notably, has positioned Stein as a radical empiricist in his erudite *Irresistible Dictation*.[41] I hope I can add to their work by spotlighting Stein's concern with nature as "a thing existent in itself" that refuses to be defined by one particular framework or tradition.[42] "Nature," for Stein, "is not natural and that is natural enough."[43]

Vital Stein, in sum, argues that Stein's work intersects with these theoretical projects, which react against the modern tendency to organize and manage life, or aspects of life, in distinct disciplines. That organizational ardor, the tendency to situate, know and control every aspect of our world and lives, Bruno Latour has shown, undergirds modernity; it is the purifying tendency that feeds the modern critical stance.[44] In one way or another, Stein was always refusing that stance. She wanted to "include everything every day" and sought for ways to work against purification - the only clarity she could accept was that of mud.[45]

In focusing on Stein's interest in an impure life, this book also contributes to ongoing work in the field of avant-garde studies, even if I steer clear of vanguard collectives. Perhaps surprisingly, the field of avant-garde studies initially more or less overlooked the concept of life. Peter Bürger's *Theory of the Avant-Garde*, first published in 1974 and translated into English in 1984, set the parameters for the field. He famously distinguishes between modernism, which he considers to continue a nineteenth-century bourgeois aesthetic program, and the avant-garde, which he sees as wanting to break with that bourgeois scheme and bring about a new collective life or "social praxis." In making that distinction, he pits "whole" against "fragmented," "organic" against "non-organic," and "living" against "lifeless" material. The former qualities are modernist, the latter vanguard:

> Artists who produce an organic work [...] treat their material as something living. They respect its significance as something that has grown from concrete life situations. For avant-gardistes, on the other hand, material is just that, material. Their activity initially consists in nothing other than in killing the "life" of the material, that is, in tearing it out of its functional context that gives it meaning.[46]

Life, in *Theory of the Avant-Garde*, is either a smothering present to escape from, or a future that is yet to arrive. "Only an art the contents of whose individual works is wholly distinct from the (bad) praxis of the existing society," he argues, "can be the center that can be the starting point for the new organization of a new life praxis."[47] That new life praxis, however, was never made. For Bürger, the avant-garde is essentially a failed project. "Now that the attack of the historical avant-garde movements on art as an institution has failed and art has not been integrated into the praxis of life," he concludes, "art as an institution continues to survive as something separate from the praxis of life."[48]

An important response to Bürger's anatomical approach and the rigid life/death opposition that underpins his scheme is Hal Foster's *Return of the Real*. Foster disagrees with Bürger's presentation of (the death of) the avant-garde as a given. He reminds us that events, even failed events, do not disappear off of the face of the earth after they have occurred; their effects resonate, the memories of them linger and change as we work through them. Although *Return of the Real* is largely concerned with the neo-avant-gardes, the questions it poses concerning temporality, anticipation and reconstruction make an important point about the narratives we construct to make sense of art and writing, or indeed the past. Reading Foster, it becomes clear how much Bürger's story is part of the modern critical stance, intent on marking clean breaks. This is Foster on Bürger:

> [T]he aim of the avant-garde for Bürger is to destroy the institution of autonomous art in order to reconnect art and life. Like the structure of heroic past and failed present, however, this formulation only seems simple. For what is art and what is life here?[49]

Bürger's scheme sets up the avant-garde for failure and makes a caricature out of (the desired) life "as if it were simply there to rush in like so much air once the hermetic seal of convention is broken." What it misses, Foster points out, is an engagement with the contextual and performative dimensions of avant-garde art; the avant-garde's dialogue with the web of "languages, institutions and structures of meaning, expectation and reception" it sought to reform.⁵⁰

Studies of modernism and the avant-garde of the last two and a half decades have taken up Foster's cue and delved into those languages, institutions and structures. Of key importance in this renewed impulse to historicize has been the concept of everyday life. Ben Highmore, for example, critiques *Theory of the Avant-Garde* for sidestepping the ambiguous character of the relationship between life and avant-garde art. For Highmore too, Bürger's dialectic lacks dynamics, as he can only see everyday life as inauthentic, in the grip of a capitalist machinery of which the instrumental logic alienates us from what is good and real. For avant-garde artists, by contrast, everyday life "was something to be decried and denounced, yet it was also the possibility of salvation."⁵¹ Highmore grounds his understanding of the everyday in the work of the French theorists Henri Lefebvre and Michel de Certeau, who wanted to conceptualize everyday life as the field in which instrumental reason affects our thoughts and actions, and as the arena in which we can rebel against that process. Art, in this logic, does not need to magically make available a new mode of living. Making art and making life, rather, interlock. Lefebvre, for example, called for everyday life to "become a work of art," taking the burden away from the individual composition and imbuing the ongoing creative transformations that make up everyday life with aesthetic potential.⁵²

Building on feminist theory of the everyday, Stein scholars have noted how the concept of everyday life intersects with Stein's project.⁵³ Bryony Randall, Liesl Olson and Lisi Schoenbach have, in different ways, shown that Stein's literary experiment takes her into the paradoxes, and the politics, of the everyday. Where Randall incorporates Stein into a tradition of innovative modernist writing by women that finds a new sense of agency in their engagements with daily time, Olson makes us see the importance of habit for Stein in a world heading for destruction in the 1930s. Both call for a nuanced and complex gendered construction of everyday life. Randall, for example, points out that some feminist work "risk[s] staying within structures of power which construct gender in a binary fashion, by simply changing the polarisation of 'everyday life,' making it a good thing rather than a bad thing."[54] Schoenbach addresses the question of how Stein's engaging with the everyday relates to her take on understanding. For Schoenbach, Stein's thinking on habit intersects with James's and John Dewey's theories of experience and makes us see a pragmatic modernism, which she sets apart from a vanguard discourse of rupture and revolution.

With *Vital Stein* I have wanted to move beyond the much-explored affinities between Stein and James, and shift the emphasis from the importance of everyday experience to that very Steinian abstraction of "every day." There are hundreds of instances of "every day" in Stein's texts and I think she very much enjoyed the paradox of the phrase. She wondered if she could "complete every day" and "[be] naming every day" and "include everything every day."[55] Like life, "every day" is an open system – no one is counting – and one that stretches beyond routine. My engaging with Stein's love of abstractions is not a turn away from the feminist work on Stein that has tended to ground her writing in her living, and that first triggered my interest in her work. In my readings I hope to show that Stein's mode of theorizing refuses that clichéd contrast between, on the one hand, the overlooked feminine realm of the concrete, embodied and personal, and, on the other, the normative masculine world of the abstract, cerebral and political. Stein being Stein, she not only relentlessly makes visible the contours, tastes, smells and voices of the former, she also works against obsolete, patriarchal structures of meaning by making it clear that the two are one. Stein's take on "the personal is the political," if you like, is that the concrete is the abstract.

There is, returning to Stein's ambition to "include everything every day," something distinctly unpragmatic about her interest in that every day. While I agree with Schoenbach that the idea of rupture, avant-garde gesture par excellence, is not part of Stein's toolbox, Stein's love of the idea of radical inclusion nevertheless infuses her work with a distinct avant-garde energy. She insists on a new system – for reading and thinking and living – and she makes it very clear that she wants us to join.[56] This, in fact, is where the liveliness of reading Stein comes in. Reading Stein asks for a new way of reading, rather than a non-reading. Her work invites you to "be in it" and experience its ambience, as Joshua Schuster has pointed out.[57] In declaring that you can "do as you please, write the name, change it, declare that you are strong, be annoyed," Stein demands we engage.[58] And when she writes that "[c]omposition is the thing seen by every one living in the living they are doing, they are the composing of the composition [...]," she tells us that the text we are reading, or seeing, is as much a product of her living as it is of ours.[59] Stein worked out her theory of composition, furthermore, in a text that reads conspicuously like a manifesto, even if she did not publish it as a manifesto. In tune with the tradition of the manifesto, Stein's 1926 "Composition as Explanation" combines oratory and writing, speaks for its present (the 1920s working through the trauma of World War One), stages a collectivity (Stein's beloved "everyone") and is rife with apparent contradictions (in, for example, stressing both the shared experience of modernity and unique individual creation).[60] Perhaps most importantly, it captures the energy of the historical avant-gardes by constantly stressing that life and writing collapse into each other.

But what, finally, to make of Stein's avant-garde energy? In "Composition as Explanation," Stein's absolute belief that everything changes – "[t]he composition is different and always going to be different everything is not the same" – is radically modified by her warning that change does not simply happen. There is no new order waiting in the wings. "Nothing changes," she tells us again and again, "except composition," and the how and what of the composition is down to us, to the living we are doing.[61] I read Stein's avant-gardism as a comment on the avant-garde, much as I read Bruno Latour's unlikely manifesto, "An Attempt at a Compositionist Manifesto," as a witty engaging with the genre's legacy. Both draw on the avant-garde's dynamics while refusing to accept the system that underpins it, which is that of a supposedly ever more efficient modernity dangling the carrot of progress while eroding our capacity to compose our lives. Both focus our attention on the importance of compositions in which "[e]ach part is as important as the whole" and "one human being is as important as another human being and you might say that the landscape has the same values, a blade of grass has the same value as a tree."[62]

Composing

Latour uses the idea of composition as an alternative to critique, which is too focused on discovering a true reality behind a veil of appearances. Composition makes for a more earth-bound alternative not least because, he quips, it comes with "the pungent but ecologically correct smell of 'compost'" – or, indeed, mud.[63] Composition also crops up in the work of one of Latour's intellectual *compagnons de route*, the Belgian philosopher of science Isabelle Stengers. I want to pause briefly at her take on composition here, because it enables me to explain how this book works.

By making a composition, or by "composing with the world," Stengers understand the creation of an assemblage, or a constellation of forces, in which world and self constitute each other and in which care is a more important principle than truth. A composition asks for an additive logic, not one that strips in search of a naked truth or one that refuses all ground and dwells in high analytical skies. "Composing with," Stengers explains, demands we engage in "[a]dding, not deconstructing." That means that the person doing the composing – the critic, theorist, poet or composer – "interpret[s] conjointly, (that is, without opposition, hierarchy or disconnection), what we usually describe in mutually contradictory terms, for example, freedom and determination, or cause and reason, or fiction and reality, or mind and matter."[64] For Stengers, as for Latour, the process of thinking together is both an ethical project – it starts where universalism and relativism have failed us, in either glossing over differences or making it impossible to find common ground – and a way of reading and writing.[65]

In her astute *Thinking with Whitehead*, Stengers explains her approach to Whitehead's project as follows:

> Unlike the portraitist, whose task is to make the viewers feel, to transfer what was lived and created, but without personally taking over from it, my approach to Whitehead cannot be dissociated from the importance of his work in my life. In this sense, I am part of the motley crew of "Whiteheadians," of those ecologists, feminists, educators, theologians, and so on, who have discovered that Whitehead helped them to imagine and to fight against "ready-made" models, and above all, not to despair.[66]

My inspiration is more Stengersian than strictly Whiteheadian and I can only aspire to belong to that motley crew, but I have taken my cue from Stengers's approach to construct a narrative that lets itself be guided by the work it writes in response to, which, in odd ways, has grafted itself on the rhythm of my life. For Stengers, thinking with Whitehead means she sets out on an adventure, with adventure as key Whiteheadian concept. The concept of adventure implies "that all continuity is questionable," that every step of the story has to be carefully considered and constructed.[67] My Steinian version of that adventure is beginning again and again.

"Beginning again and again," Stein tells us in "Composition as Explanation," "is a natural thing."[68] More than effortlessness or spontaneity, that means it has to be dealt with, given shape, composed. I started writing about Stein as a PhD student; I began again when I was working on additional research projects and then again when I was working as a teacher. Each of these beginnings demanded I took seriously Stein's processes of beginning again. So, I have tried to follow Stein in her observation that "there was an inevitable beginning of beginning again and again and again" by dividing this book into different beginnings.[69] Each shows Stein tackling the problem of life through a different prism. These prisms are history, the cinema and nature. It may sound contradictory that I have mapped Stein's interest in life itself via other concepts, but these, again, are not gateways to a hidden life. As Latour makes clear, mediations are not there to be discarded; they are part and parcel of being – there is no being-as-being without being-as-other.[70] For Stein, history, cinema and nature are the others that make it possible for her to think about life. Each concept is very much "of her time" and also prompts her to break with an established way of doing things; each makes it possible for her to think about life as a creative fostering of myriads of connections.

I have constructed an arc of beginnings, starting with Stein's early history projects over her interest in the cinema in the 1910s, to her 1920s work on the notion of landscape. This means I have spotlighted three instances of Stein looking back on her work: her claim that she "began with evolution," her statement that she "was doing what the cinema was doing" and her realization that she "lived in a landscape that made itself its own landscape."[71] Each of *Vital Stein*'s beginnings has a composition modeled on Stein's approach to writing. The chapters on history come with a panoramic angle because Stein was writing in response to a nineteenth-century *Zeitgeist*. The work she was writing was big in scope: she wanted to write a complete history. Stein's 1910s writings tend to be much shorter, concrete and focused – more lively, even. The chapters on cinema respond to that move by zooming in, both conceptually and contextually. I explore the concept of generation in relation to a biological vitalist discourse and sketch the era's fascination with early film as a device able to portray life itself. In the 1920s, Stein's writing changes again when a stillness creeps in. Her focus shifts to nature, as a composition or landscape. Stein's is not, or at least not first, an environmentalist focus. Her interest, rather, is in the question of how, in a composition, the abstract and the concrete exist together, like in a Cézanne painting. I argue that her literary thinking in this period is entwined with the project of Whitehead, in which the relation between abstract and concrete is one of the key questions, and I attempt to trace Stein's abstract/concrete entanglements.

While it is in the nature of writing to go on and of compositions to become implicated in other compositions, *Vital Stein* does not go beyond Stein's sprawling opera, *Four Saints in Three Acts*, and the portraits she wrote in the late 1920s. Quite a few of the texts Stein wrote in the 1930s and 1940s have found their way into this book because in them she looks back on her earlier work, but Stein's work from the 1930s onwards no longer has one central idea, or thing, via which she tackles life. Her interest in life does not, of course, suddenly evaporate. It leads to a number of texts in which she tackles the related issues of creativity and identity: *Four in America* (written in 1933), the lecture "What Are Masterpieces and Why are There So Few of Them?" (1935) and *The Geographical History of America or The Relation of Human Nature to the Human Mind* (1936). But she also starts doing very different things. She sets up a dialogue with literary history and genre. *Stanzas in Meditation* (1932), for example, shows her responding to Wordsworth's "long dull" poems, and in *Dr. Faustus Lights the Lights* (written in 1938) she reworks Goethe's *Faust*.[72] In *The Autobiography of Alice B. Toklas* (1932) and *Everybody's Autobiography* (1937), she explores the conventions of life writing, *Blood on the Dining Room Floor* (1933) counts as her experiment with a murder mystery, and with *The World Is Round* (1939) Stein wrote a children's book.[73] What unites all of these projects is Stein's interest in audiences. Quite a few scholars have addressed the figure of the audience in relation to Stein, but I would love to read a book on the different ways in which Stein conceives of that figure in her late writings.[74]

Undoubtedly, my story is not how it happened. Stein's story is not how it happened. For Stein's work to go on living in our time, we need to create a composition that enables us to see new things in her work. That implies we stick closely to her texts and work with an awareness of our own horizons. To return to Stengers, Stein's claims about her own work have spurred me to look beyond the ready-made contexts and have helped me to imagine a story that is not only about Stein, but also, inevitably if implicitly, about our life in the twenty-first century. Stein's work does not have answers to the questions of how to find a common ground or history, of how to make sense of life and life-forms not ruled by the powers that be, or of how to live in and with nature. But reading Stein and Dilthey and Bergson and Benjamin and Whitehead and Deleuze and Latour and Stengers may just help us see our problems differently.

Notes

1. Gertrude Stein, *Lectures in America*, in *Writings: 1932–1946*, ed. Harriet Scott Chessman and Catharine R. Stimpson (New York: Library of America, 1998), 290.
2. Gertrude Stein, *Everybody's Autobiography* (New York: Exact Change, 1993), 126.
3. "For thousands of years, before any scientific explanation was available, humans have linked soil and life. In the second chapter of the Book of Genesis, we are told: 'The Lord God formed man of the dust of the ground.' Appropriately, in this Bible story the name of the first person to roam the Garden of Eden was Adam, a name based on the Hebrew name for soil or clay, *adama*." David W. Wolfe, *Tales from the Underground: A Natural History of Subterranean Life* (Cambridge, MA: Basic Books, 2001), 25.
4. In 1957 John Ashbery noted that Stein's *Stanzas in Meditation* "is a general, all-purpose model which each reader can adapt to fit his own set of particulars" (*Selected Prose*, ed. Eugene Richie (Ann Arbor: University of Michigan Press, 2004), 12). Ulla Dydo compares Stein's text "Business in Baltimore" to "a decorative wallpaper" that "does not require understanding" (*Stein Reader* (Evanston, IL: Northwestern University Press, 1993), 481). See also Craig Dworkin, *Reading the Illegible* (Evanston: Northwestern University Press, 2003).
5. Percy Bysshe Shelley, *Selected Poems and Prose*, ed. Jack Donovan and Cian Duffy (London: Penguin, 2016), 587; W. B. Yeats, *The Collected Poems of W. B. Yeats*, ed. Richard J. Finneran (New York: Scribner, 1996), 234.
6. Vassiliki Kolocotroni, Jane Goldman and Olga Taxidou, eds, *Modernism: An Anthology of Sources and Documents* (Edinburgh: Edinburgh University Press, 1998), 278, 291.
7. Gertrude Stein, *Paris France* (New York: Liveright, 1970 [1940]), 59.
8. See, for example, Stephen Kern's classic, *The Culture of Time and Space 1880–1918* (Cambridge, MA: Harvard University Press, 1983), Ronald Schleifer's *Modernism and Time: The Logic of Abundance in Literature, Science and Culture 1880–1930* (Cambridge: Cambridge University Press, 2000) or Enda Duffy's *The Speed Handbook* (Durham, NC, and London: Duke University Press, 2009). Of particular interest is Juliana Chow's article "Motion Studies: Vitalism in Gertrude Stein's Work," *Arizona Quarterly: A Journal of American Literature, Culture and Theory* 69.4 (2013): 77–109. Chow establishes a firm connection between Stein's interests in movement and life.
9. Gertrude Stein, *How to Write*, ed. Patricia Meyerowitz (New York: Dover Publications, 1975 [1931]), 21. The graffito on the cover adds a "forever." It is a photograph taken on the island of Lesbos.

10. Gertrude Stein, *Tender Buttons*, ed. Seth Parlow (San Francisco: City Lights Books, 2014), 11.
11. Stein, *Lectures in America*, 226.
12. Henri Bergson, *Creative Evolution* (Mineola: Dover Publications, 1998 [1911]), 42.
13. Gilles Deleuze, "Bergson's Conception of Difference," *Desert Islands and Other Texts, 1953–1974*, ed. David Lapoujade and trans. Michael Taormina (Los Angeles: Semiotext(e), 2004), 40.
14. An important study that traces the entanglements between racial discourses and vitalist theory is Donna V. Jones's *The Racial Discourses of Life Philosophy: Négritude, Vitalism and Modernity* (New York: Columbia University Press, 2010).
15. Hans Driesch, *The History and Theory of Vitalism*, trans. C. K. Ogden (London: Macmillan, 1914), 237.
16. Wyndham Lewis, *Time and Western Man*, ed. Paul Edwards (Santa Rosa, CA: Black Sparrow Press, 1993), xiv–xv.
17. Scott Lash distinguishes between "two vitalist genealogies." One is Deleuzian and stretches back to Bergson and the French sociologist Gabriel Tarde; the other is Foucauldian and goes back to Nietzsche and George Simmel. As he sees it, "[t]he Bergsonian tradition focuses on perception and sensation while the Nietzschean tradition focuses on power." See Scott Lash, "Life (Vitalism)," *Theory Culture & Society* 23 (2006): 323–9.
18. Benjamin Noys, "The Poverty of Vitalism (and the Vitalism of Poverty)," paper presented at To Have Done with Life: Vitalism and Anti-vitalism in Contemporary Philosophy Conference; June 17–19, MaMa, Zagreb, Croatia. Available at: <https://www.academia.edu/689255/The_Poverty_of_Vitalism_and_the_Vitalism_of_ Poverty_> (last accessed September 3, 2021).
19. Claire Colebrook, *Deleuze and the Meaning of Life* (London: Continuum, 2010), 3.
20. Gilles Deleuze and Félix Guattari, *What Is Philosophy?*, trans. Hugh Tomlinson and Graham Burchell (New York: Columbia University Press, 1994), 198.
21. Audrey Wasser, *The Work of Difference: Modernism, Romanticism and the Production of Literary Form* (New York: Fordham University Press, 2016), 159. On Stein as a theoretical writer, see also: Ryan Tracy, "Writing in Cars with Gertrude Stein and Jacques Derrida, or, The Age of Autotheory," *Arizona Quarterly: A Journal of American Literature, Culture, and Theory* 76.1 (2020): 15–37.
22. See, for example: Mark Goble, *Beautiful Circuits: Modernism and the Mediated Life* (New York: Columbia University Press, 2010); Benjamin Kahan, *Celibacies: American Modernism & Sexual Life* (Durham, NC: Duke University Press, 2013); David Ayers, Benedikt Hjartarson, Tomi Huttunen and Harri Veivo, eds, *Utopia: The Avant-Garde, Modernism and (Im)possible Life* (Berlin: Walter de Gruyter, 2015).

23. On Bergson and modernism, see, for example: Mary Ann Gillies, *Henri Bergson and British Modernism* (Montreal: McGill University Press, 1996) and S. E. Gontarski, Paul Ardoin, Laci Mattison, eds, *Understanding Bergson, Understanding Modernism* (London: Bloomsbury, 2013).
24. Omri Moses, *Out of Character: Modernism, Vitalism, Psychic Life* (Stanford, CA: Stanford University Press, 2014), 19, 200.
25. Ibid., 205.
26. Henri Bergson, *The Two Sources of Morality and Religion*, trans. R. Ashley Audra and Cloudesley Brereton, with the assistance of W. Horsfall Carter (Garden City: Doubleday & Anchor, 1954), 267.
27. A. N. Whitehead, *Adventures of Ideas* (Cambridge: Cambridge University Press, 1933), 84.
28. On modernist poetry and collective life, see Joel Nickels's *Poetry of the Possible: Spontaneity, Modernism and the Multitude* (Minneapolis and London: University of Minnesota Press, 2012).
29. Michel Foucault, *The Order of Things: An Archaeology of the Human Sciences* (London: Routledge, 2002), 175.
30. Ibid., 177.
31. William Wordsworth, *The Major Works*, ed. Stephen Gill (Oxford: Oxford University Press 2008), 131. Interestingly, Whitehead focuses on Wordsworth in *Science and the Modern World* (New York: The Free Press, 1967 [1925]), 77, in which he offers a diagnosis of modern (scientific) thought. He writes: "Wordsworth in his whole being expresses a conscious reaction against the mentality of the eighteenth century. [. . .] He felt that something had been left out, and that what had been left out comprised everything that was most important." The epistemic divide that Whitehead argues against, and for which he summons Wordsworth, is at the heart of Amanda Jo Goldstein's *Sweet Science: Romantic Materialism and the New Logics of Life* (Chicago: University of Chicago Press, 2017), which details a Lucretian materialism at the heart of romantic life writings.
32. For a good overview of eighteenth- and nineteenth-century vitalist theory, see the introduction to Denise Gigante's *Life: Organic Form and Romanticism* (New Haven, CT: Yale University Press, 2009). For more in-depth philosophical explorations, see Sebastian Normandin and Charles T. Wolfe's edited collection, *Vitalism and the Scientific Image in Post-Enlightenment Life-Science, 1800–2010* (Dordrecht: Springer, 2013); Scott M. Campbell and Paul W. Bruno, eds, *The Science, Politics, and Ontology of Life-Philosophy* (London and New York: Bloomsbury, 2013) and Mariam Fraser, Sarah Kember and Celia Lury, eds, *Inventive Life: Approaches to the New Vitalism* (London: Sage, in association with *Theory, Culture & Society*, 2006).
33. Bergson, *Creative Evolution*, 31, 52, ix.
34. Deleuze, "Bergson's Conception of Difference," 32. The Bergsonist idea of life as a self-differentiating multitude, furthermore, informs

the work of Michael Hardt and Antonio Negri, two contemporary thinkers who engage with bio-politics in relation to capitalism. Their much-debated book *Empire* proposes the multitude as the creative resistance to capitalism – like Bergson's life, it "expands" and "transcends" its own forms – yet also shows capitalism to parasitize on the multitude's creativity. If capitalism used to function through labor, it has now moved on to what Negri and Hardt call "biopolitical production": it has entered and "produces" our minds and bodies. On the Bergsonist discourse of virtuality they note that it is "insufficient," as they "need to insist on the reality of the being created, its ontological weight, and the institutions that structure the world, creating necessity out of contingency" (*Empire* (Cambridge, MA: Harvard University Press, 2000), 468).
35. William James, "A World of Pure Experience," in *Writings: 1902–1910*, ed. Bruce Kuklick (New York: Library of America, 1987), 1160, 1181.
36. Ibid., 1182.
37. Alfred North Whitehead, *The Concept of Nature* (Cambridge: Cambridge University Press, 2015 [1920]), 21.
38. Bruno Latour, "What Is Given in Experience?," Foreword to Isabelle Stengers's *Thinking with Whitehead: A Free and Wild Creation of Concepts* (Cambridge, MA: Harvard University Press, 2011), xii.
39. Steven Shaviro, *Without Criteria: Kant, Whitehead, Deleuze and Aesthetics* (Cambridge, MA: MIT Press, 2009), 86.
40. Alfred North Whitehead, *Process and Reality: An Essay in Cosmology*, ed. David Ray Griffin and Donald W. Sherburne (New York: The Free Press, 1978), 104.
41. There is a lot of work on Stein and James, often with a focus on his psychology and pragmatism. See, for example: Lisa Ruddick, *Gertrude Stein: Body, Text, Gnosis* (Ithaca, NY: Cornell University Press, 1990), Dana Cairns Watson, *Gertrude Stein and the Essence of What Happens* (Nashville: Vanderbilt University Press, 2005), Joan Richardson, *A Natural History of Pragmatism: The Fact of Feeling from Jonathan Edwards to Gertrude Stein* (Cambridge: Cambridge University Press, 2007) and Lisi Schoenbach, *Pragmatic Modernism* (Oxford: Oxford University Press, 2012). A study that opens up to James's radical empiricism is Claudia Franken's *Gertrude Stein, Writer, Thinker* (Münster: LIT, 2000).
42. Gertrude Stein, *The Autobiography of Alice B. Toklas*, in *Writings: 1932–1946*, ed. Harriet Scott Chessman and Catharine R. Stimpson (New York: Library of America, 1998), 880.
43. Gertrude Stein, *Ida: A Novel*, ed. Logan Esdale (New Haven, CT: Yale University Press, 2012), 116.
44. Bruno Latour, *We Have Never Been Modern*, trans. Catherine Porter (Cambridge, MA: Harvard University Press, 1993), 11.
45. Gertrude Stein, "Natural Phenomena," in *Painted Lace and Other Pieces, 1914–1937*, vol. 5 of *The Yale Edition of the Unpublished*

Writings of Gertrude Stein (New Haven, CT: Yale University Press, 1955), 228.
46. Peter Bürger, *Theory of the Avant-Garde*, trans. Michael Shaw (Minneapolis: University of Minnesota Press, 1984), 70.
47. Ibid., 50.
48. Ibid., 57.
49. Hal Foster, *The Return of the Real: The Avant-Garde at the End of the Century* (Cambridge, MA: MIT Press, 1996), 15.
50. Ibid., 16.
51. Ben Highmore, "Awkward Moments: Avant-Gardism and the Dialectics of Everyday Life," in Dietrich Scheunemann, ed., *European Avant-Garde: New Perspectives* (Amsterdam: Rodopi, 2000), 249. See also Highmore's *The Everyday Life Reader* (London: Routledge, 2002) and *Ordinary Lives: Studies in the Everyday* (London: Routledge, 2011).
52. Henri Lefebvre, *Everyday Life in the Modern World*, translated by Sacha Rabinovitch (New Brunswick: Transaction, 1984 [1968]), 204, quoted in Ben Highmore, *Everyday Life and Cultural Theory: An Introduction* (London: Routledge, 2002) 119.
53. Lefebvre claimed that women are "incapable of understanding the everyday" (quoted in Highmore, *Everyday Life and Cultural Theory*, 126). Laurie Langbauer addressed this issue in her essay "Cultural Studies and the Politics of the Everyday," *Diacritics* 22.1 (1992). See also the work of Rita Felski: introduction to special issue, "Everyday Life," *New Literary History* 33.4 (2002) and "The Invention of Everyday Life," in *Doing Time: Feminist Theory and Postmodern Culture* (New York: New York University Press, 2000).
54. Bryony Randall, *Modernism, Daily Time and Everyday Life* (Cambridge: Cambridge University Press, 2007), 19.
55. Gertrude Stein, "Nest of Dishes," in *Painted Lace and Other Pieces*, 101; Gertrude Stein, "An Acquaintance with Description," in *Writings: 1903–1932*, 532; Stein, "Natural Phenomena," 228.
56. See also Harriet Scott Chessman, *The Public is Invited to Dance: Representation, The Body and Dialogue in Gertrude Stein* (Stanford, CA: Stanford University Press, 1989).
57. Joshua Schuster, *The Ecology of Modernism: American Environments and Avant-Garde Poetics* (Tuscaloosa: University of Alabama Press, 2015), 48.
58. Gertrude Stein, "If You Had Three Husbands," in *Geography and Plays* (Mineola: Dover Publications, 1999), 385.
59. Gertrude Stein, "Composition as Explanation," in *Writings: 1903–1932*, ed. Harriet Scott Chessman and Catharine R. Stimpson (New York: Library of America, 1998), 523.
60. On the genre of the manifesto, see Janet Lyon, *Manifestoes: Provocations of the Modern* (Ithaca, NY: Cornell University Press, 1999).
61. Stein, "Composition as Explanation," 528.

62. Stein, *A Primer for the Gradual Understanding of Gertrude Stein*, edited by Robert Bartlett Haas (Santa Barbara, CA: Black Sparrow Press, 1971), 16.
63. Bruno Latour, "An Attempt at a 'Compositionist Manifesto,'" *New Literary History* 41.3 (2010): 474.
64. Isabelle Stengers, "A Constructivist Reading of *Process and Reality*," in *The Lure of Whitehead*, ed. Nicholas Gaskill and A. J. Nocek (Minneapolis: University of Minnesota Press, 2014), 52–3.
65. As Latour puts it in his "An Attempt at a Compositionist Manifesto" (474): "[f]rom universalism it takes up the task of building a common world; from relativism, the certainty that this common world has to be built from utterly heterogeneous parts that will never make a whole, but at best a fragile, revisable, and diverse composite material."
66. Isabelle Stengers, *Thinking with Whitehead: A Free and Wild Creation of Concepts*, trans. Michael Chase (Cambridge, MA: Harvard University Press, 2011), 10–11.
67. Ibid., 14.
68. Stein, "Composition as Explanation," 522.
69. Ibid., 525.
70. See the "Being-as-being, being-as-other" entry on Latour's collaborative website, An Inquiry into Modes of Existence (AIME). Available at: <http://modesofexistence.org/inquiry/#a=SET+VOC+LEADER&c[leading]=VOC&c[slave]=DOC&i[id]=#vocab-3&i[column]=VOC&s=0&q=being-as-other> (last accessed September 6, 2021).
71. Gertrude Stein, *Wars I Have Seen* (London: Brilliance Books, 1984), 61; Stein, *Lectures in America*, 294, 262.
72. In a 1932 letter to Louis Bromfield, Stein wrote that she was "trying to write a long dull poem like the long ones of Wordsworth and it is very interesting to do" (quoted in Ulla Dydo with William Rice, *Gertrude Stein: The Language that Rises, 1923–1934* (Evanston, IL: Northwestern University Press, 2003), 493). On Stein and Wordsworth, see Rebecca Ariel Porte, "Long Dull Poems: Stein's *Stanzas in Meditation* and Wordsworth's *The Prelude*," in *Primary Stein: Returning to the Writings of Gertrude Stein*, ed. Sharon J. Kirsch and Janet Boyd (Lanham, MD: Lexington Books, 2014). On Stein and Faust, see Sarah Posman, "'More Light! – Electric Light': Stein in Dialogue with the Romantic Paradigm in *Doctor Faustus Lights the Lights*," also in *Primary Stein*.
73. On Stein's writing for children, see, for example: Kimberley Reynolds, *Radical Children's Literature: Future Visions and Aesthetic Transformations in Juvenile Fiction* (Basingstoke: Palgrave Macmillan, 2007).
74. Juliana Spahr's *Everybody's Autonomy: Connective Reading and Collective Identity* (Tuscaloosa: University of Alabama Press, 2001) is relevant here, as is Adam Frank's multi-angled project Radio Free Stein, available at: <https://radiofreestein.com/> (last accessed

September 6, 2021). See also: Kirk Curnutt, "Inside and Outside: Gertrude Stein on Identity, Celebrity, and Authenticity," *Journal of Modern Literature* 23.2 (1999): 291–308; Karen Leick, *Gertrude Stein and the Making of an American Celebrity* (New York: Routledge, 2009); and Roy Morris Jr, *Gertrude Stein Has Arrived: The Homecoming of a Literary Legend* (Baltimore: Johns Hopkins University Press, 2019).

PART I

BEGINNING WITH EVOLUTION

When the French philosopher Jean Wahl wrote a piece on Gertrude Stein for the *New Republic* in 1945, he concluded his article by calling her "a Heraclitan in the nineteenth century."[1] To picture Stein as a pre-Socratic in the nineteenth century, at the end of her career, is a bit of an unfair move. Like most modernists, Stein had spent her life trying to break with the nineteenth century, pronouncing it "dead dead dead" in her memoir *Wars I Have Seen*.[2] Whenever she explained her poetics, she highlighted that it was to be considered a twentieth-century project, that her "idea of a whole thing" corresponded to "the Twentieth Century conception of a whole."[3] Yet Wahl has a point. The key problem that Stein explored in her writing is one that we tend to trace back to Heraclitus and that, because of ground-breaking work across intellectual domains and epitomized by Darwin, became a key issue in the nineteenth century: *panta rhei*, or everything moves.

Evolution is, by Stein's own account, where she "began."[4] The following chapters argue that Stein's response to the evolutionary framework and the paradigm of neo-Darwinism that dominated late nineteenth-century science intersects with the tradition of the life philosophy that peaked in the late nineteenth and early twentieth centuries. Critical of the nineteenth century's mechanist scientific climate, life philosophers, in different ways, tried to think about life in a way that went beyond typologies of different species. Philosophically, they reacted against the tradition of idealism. In both a scientific and an idealist framework, they objected, life was severed from lived experience. Taking from the sciences a concern for the empirical and from idealism an interest in structures surpassing the individual mind, they tried in different ways to conceptualize life as a collective experience. William James, for example, suggested the concept of pure experience, Wilhelm Dilthey proposed the idea of an objective mind, and Henri Bergson coined several concepts that gesture towards a dynamic, felt life unity, going from *élan vital* to the notion of the virtual as real yet not actual substratum. In spotlighting the lived experience of the thinker, life philosophers also objected to the methods of the natural sciences and the pristine schemes of idealist philosophy, which eclipsed experience and left little room for the context in which the research was taking place. As a way to integrate experience in research, James radicalized empiricism, Dilthey advocated a new discipline, the *Geisteswissenschaften* or human sciences, and Bergson, somewhat reluctantly, chose intuition as the name for a new way of thinking.

Stein's early writings, *Q.E.D.*, *Three Lives* and *The Making of Americans*, breathe a concern for the twofold concern central to life philosophy: how to conceptualize the unity of life, from lived experience? This question problematizes both the experience of knowing, which is subject to ongoing change, and the object of study, which is impossible to grasp in its finitude. As I have pointed out in the introduction, Stein was fascinated by the idea of "a movement [. . .] lively enough it would exist so completely that it would not be necessary to see it moving against anything to know that it is moving."[5] That is what she meant by life and was always trying to portray. How to know and portray such a life that exists completely yet escapes complete understanding? Stein would grapple with this issue for decades, but the way in which she tried to solve it in her early texts aligns her project with the focus on the relation between individual and context in work by late nineteenth-century life philosophy. All of Stein's early pieces explore the relation between individual lives and the larger constellations, or collective life, that these are part of. Where many critics have explored the ways in which Stein's approach to the experience of knowing draws on William James, much less attention has been devoted to Stein's concern for understanding the larger shape of life – her "idea of a whole thing" or her plan, in *The Making of Americans*, to write a "whole history."[6]

I start by unpacking Stein's "beginning with evolution." Stein's relationship to the Darwinian framework was ambiguous. "Evolution," she writes in *Wars I Have Seen*, "opened up the history of all animals vegetables and minerals, and man, and at the same time it made them all confined, confined within a circle, no excitement of creation any more."[7] While Darwin's work raised many profound epistemological and methodological issues that opened up the Newtonian scientific template, post-Darwinian evolutionary theory tended to construct closed rather than open models for development. Nineteenth-century philosophers of history, by contrast, answered the prompt of the natural sciences to think empirically by moving in the direction of both an open-ended conceptualization of history and open modes of understanding. That, I argue, is the context in which we need to read Stein's early texts, which are all, in one way or another, "histories." One of the key figures in the late nineteenth-century theoretical debate on history is Wilhelm Dilthey, for whom life was synonymous with history. I read Stein in dialogue with Dilthey and unpack the echoes of a hermeneutical framework in Stein's early texts; the title of the short story "Melanctha: Each One as She May" refers to the name of the Renaissance hermeneutical thinker Melancthon, and in writing *The Making of Americans* Stein was fascinated by Otto Weininger's *Sex and Character*, which draws on Dilthey's theory of understanding. In engaging with hermeneutics, I also nuance a constructivist approach to Stein, which tends to eclipse Stein's early fascination with understanding and meaning.

Notes

1. Jean Wahl, "Miss Stein's Battle," in *Critical Essays on Gertrude Stein*, ed. M. J. Hoffman (Boston: G. K. Hall, 1986), 83.
2. Stein, *Wars I Have Seen*, 21.
3. Gertrude Stein, "How Writing Is Written," in *How Writing is Written. The Previously Uncollected Writings of Gertrude* Stein, ed. R. B. Haas, vol. 2 (Los Angeles: Black Sparrow Press, 1974), 153.
4. Stein, *Wars I Have Seen*, 61.
5. Stein, *Lectures in America*, 290.
6. Gertrude Stein, *The Making of Americans: Being a History of a Family's Progress* (Normal, IL: Dalkey Archive Press, 1995), 182.
7. Stein, *Wars I Have Seen*, 61.

Chapter 1

Life's Story

When Stein looks back on her nineteenth-century background in her memoirs she repeatedly points to the importance of Darwin and the evolutionary paradigm. When she began "knowing everything," she reflects in *Everybody's Autobiography*, Darwin's influence was pervasive.[1] In *Wars I Have Seen*, she confides that the natural scientists Huxley, Agassiz and Darwin "made the difference of before and after."[2] In attributing to Darwin a key role in the marking of a new era, Stein echoes many of her contemporaries. John Dewey, for example, held Darwin responsible for the "intellectual revolt" and "new intellectual temper" of the second half of the nineteenth century in the title essay of *The Influence of Darwin on Philosophy* (1910). Darwin, Dewey claimed, had brought change to the "conceptions that had reigned in the philosophy of nature and knowledge for two thousand years, the conceptions that had become the familiar furniture of the mind, [and that] rested on the assumption of the superiority of the fixed and final."[3] Dewey's point is something we do not often think through today. The framework we tend to credit for pulling the rug from under our feet and installing difference where before we had truths and certainties is post-structuralism. Yet it is Darwin, Elizabeth Grosz has shown, who "uncannily anticipates Derridean *différance*" when he inquired into the origin of species.[4]

Darwin famously never really answered the question of the origin of species. Yet his broaching the issue, Grosz points out, opened up fundamental questions about the object of scientific inquiry.[5] With Darwin, the scientific object of study, life, became an epistemological and methodological problem. What is its unit? How to integrate the study of the individual, the group and the species and a concern for life in its totality? In providing the prompt for such questions, Darwin compromised his own plan to transpose the largely Newtonian framework from physics into the field of natural history. Darwin's methodological legacy is not so much a system of laws as the insight that precise prediction or calculation is impossible, that we have to work with tendencies and broad principles rather than universal laws. For Grosz, Darwin "introduced a new understanding of what science must be to be adequate to the reality of life itself, which has no real units, no agreed upon boundaries or clear-cut objects, and to the reality of time and change that it entails."[6] At the heart of the "intellectual revolt" triggered by Darwin, then, we find the shift from a coherent system of concepts and theories, regulated by Newton's laws, to that of an open system, "never caught and whirled about in the vortex of infinite forces," as Henry Adams put it in his autobiography.[7] The very structures used for making sense of life became subject to what was seen as the prime characteristic of life: movement, or time.

This epistemological turning point is aptly summed up by Bergson, when, in *The Creative Mind* [La Pensée et le mouvant (1934)], he sketches how he came to realize the central flaw in the project of Herbert Spencer. Spencer, like Darwin a nineteenth-century evolutionary scientist, took evolution in the opposite direction of the indeterminacy we can read in Darwin. Spencer propagated evolution as the key principle to explain the development of all life, from natural life to the workings of the mind and the development of nations. For the young Bergson, Spencer's work promised the level of precision he found wanting in philosophical systems and he felt confident that any flaws in the Spencerian would soon be smoothed out.[8] It is upon embarking on that task as a student, he reflects, that he

> was very much struck to see how real time, which plays the leading part in any philosophy of evolution, eludes mathematical treatment. Its essence being to flow, not one of its parts is still there when another part comes along. Superposition of one part on another with measurement in view is therefore impossible, unimaginable, inconceivable. [. . .] Ever since my university days I had been aware that duration is measured by the trajectory of a body in motion and that mathematical time is a line; but I had not yet observed that this operation contrasts radically with all other processes of measurement, for it is not carried out on an aspect or an effect representative of what one wishes to measure, but on something which excludes it. The line one measures is immobile, time is mobility.[9]

The problem central to life philosophy is that of how to configure a method for knowing about life as mobility without losing that sense of movement, of time. For all life philosophers the experience of time was an epistemological issue – they wanted to know how to go about knowing time – even if they approached it in different ways.

Evolutionary theorists, by contrast, were not very concerned with the dynamics of evolution, or time as mobility. "Darwin himself," as James Guthrie points out, "did not attach any particular importance to time."[10] In the chapter on "Natural Selection, or The Survival of the Fittest" of *The Origin of Species*, Darwin denies the claim that time plays a formative role in natural selection:

> The mere lapse of time by itself does nothing, either for or against natural selection. I state this because it has been erroneously asserted that the element of time has been assumed by me to play an all-important role in modifying species, as if all the forms of life were necessarily undergoing change through some innate law. Lapse of time is only so far important, and its importance in this respect is great, that it gives a better chance of beneficial variations arising and of their being selected, accumulated and fixed.[11]

Time, in *The Origin of Species*, is an all-encompassing matrix much more than any kind of dynamic force, as it is in the classic Newtonian framework. By Darwin's account, change takes place in time, through what we perceive to be intervals or lapses, but time itself is not affected by change and neither is it to be considered the motor of change.

In studies on the modern understanding of time, accordingly, Darwin's evolutionary theory is not of prime importance. In his book on the concept of time in American philosophy, Bertrand Helm, for example, argues that the nineteenth-century criticism leveled against a teleological understanding of time was "due neither to mere institutional changes nor to the increasing prestige of scientific theories, including the Darwinian version of biological evolution."[12] Rather, the debate on time in nineteenth-century America was catalyzed by many different factors, including Darwinism, but also informed by theological debate stirred by the new biblical criticism and hermeneutics imported from Germany. Similarly, Stephen Toulmin and June Goodfield read *The Origin of Species* as part of a vast intellectual operation. Darwin's century, they point out, was also Hegel's and Comte's and Marx's. Those thinkers, they explain, built on the tradition of historical thinking initiated by Herder in the late 1700s. Whereas Enlightenment thinkers tended to interpret the waning of past societies as so many faltering social machines, and understood progress as the application of all that Reason dictated to society, Herder's romantic vision conceived of history as a development.[13] Although romantic philosophers of nature stressed the singular course and teleological direction of history, their take on nature as a developing force made possible a radically new historical consciousness in the nineteenth century. The work of historians and geologists digging up a past they found difficult to make tally with biblical design, as well as the intellectual debates on historical methodologies and truth claims, spurred by Nietzsche, caused the main road of history to give way to a manifold network of temporalities. Time, it became clear, stretched back infinitely longer than theology could account for and moved in ways that were visibly not the work of God. This revolution, for Toulmin and Goodfield, intersects with Darwin's work but owes little to Darwin per se.[14]

And yet, Darwin came to symbolize the nineteenth-century encounter with time and history. His work on the slow progress of evolution confirmed the immense specter of geological time, stretching out to hundreds of millions of years, that Charles Lyell had proposed. The impact of Darwin's theories on nineteenth-century culture, moreover, was huge, on both sides of the Atlantic. Darwin himself may not have written *The Origin of Species* with human experience in mind, but when he reflected "How fleeting are the wishes and efforts of man! How short his time! And consequently how poor will his products be, compared with those accumulated by nature during whole geological periods!," he robbed "man" of his privileged place in the chain of being and hurled him into the vastness of geological time – adding that the chances for apprehending the extensions of change in the natural world look slim.[15] After Darwin, "man" could no longer be considered the sovereign singularity in Nature he had been for the romantics. As Gillian Beer has shown, Darwin's major narrative of natural history established that "it was possible to have plot without man - both plot previous to man and plot even now regardless of him."[16]

Excitement of Creation

Stein's encounter with Darwin's work, as she remembers it in the early 1940s, was both exhilarating and disappointing. "Evolution," she writes:

> was as exciting as the discovery of America, by Columbus quite as exciting, and quite as much an opening up and a limiting, quite as much. By that I mean that discovering America, by reasoning and

then finding, opened up a new world and at the same time closed the circle, there was no longer any beyond. Evolution did the same thing, it opened up the history of all animals vegetables and minerals, and man, and at the same time it made them all confined, confined within a circle, no excitement of creation any more.[17]

What Stein found fascinating about Darwin's work is that "it opened up the history of all animals vegetables and minerals, and man." The history of "man," Stein suggests, should become the history of men, in the plural, like animals, vegetables and minerals. Darwin's idea, as he formulates it in *The Descent of Man*, that instead of separate orders there exist "numberless gradations [. . .] between the highest men of the highest races and the lowest savages," and that "[t]herefore it is possible that they might pass and be developed into each other," makes it possible to think about life as an open system, of which we cannot predict the possible variations and developments.[18] In such a scheme, history needs to be rewritten. Instead of trying to understand "man," we should try to grasp the variation of subject formations that the "passing and developing into each other" of different lives have led to. That, as we will see, is what Stein attempts in her "complete history," *The Making of Americans*.[19]

In the quotation Stein relates evolution to the discovery of America because, for her, America symbolized an open system. In *The Autobiography of Alice B. Toklas*, for example, she refers to America as "the oldest country in the world" and explains that "because by the methods of the civil war and the commercial conceptions that followed it America created the twentieth century."[20] The post-war democratic system and the abolishment of slavery in the nineteenth century had united Americans in one nation and made possible – in idea more than in practice – the "developing into each other" of individuals. Commerce played an important role in that unifying process. The link between natural history and economics is not random. Both, as Grosz points out, concern "relatively self-contained but fundamentally open-ended systems that function in specific context and of which the dynamics are difficult to grasp by means of a fixed set of laws."[21] Stein's idea of America as one open territory for people to relate to one another and practice exchange is what, by her account, returns it to the organizing principles of life itself and hence what makes it both the "oldest" country and the first to follow up on the Darwinian impulse and create the twentieth century, which implies "assembling the whole thing out of its parts."[22]

Yet evolution, for Stein, also confines and rules out "excitement of creation." After Darwin, life increasingly came to be seen as no longer the work of an outsider God or creator, but as a historical process that "confines" us to a single life, on a round, or circular, world. By many critical accounts, this new worldview can be seen as the trigger for modernist experimentation and a new function of meaning – meaning was no longer to be found in the hereafter, it was to be made here and now.[23] Yet it also underlined that individual life at a certain point just stops. And that was a disconcerting insight for many, Stein included. In *The Geographical History of America or The Relation of Human Nature to the Human Mind*, for example, she confides that while she knew where she was going, she "[did] not like it like that."[24] But that is not all that explains the sense of closure that sounds through Stein's reflection on evolution. Darwin's work on evolution also led to a scientific climate in which exploration gave way to what Stein, in *Lectures in America*, refers to as ongoing description. Science as endless description is a closed game. "If this can really be done the complete description of everything," she wonders, "then what else is there to do. We may well say nothing."[25] What Stein considers to be "exciting" is what she refers to in the context of the discovery of America by Columbus as "reasoning and then finding." Columbus's reasoning, as is well known, did not lead him to find what he thought he would; seeking a westward route to Asia, he mistook the Antilles, where he landed, for islands on the coast of India, the West Indies. Yet his reasoning led to the discovery or finding of "the new world." *What* you find, in an open system, cannot be calculated by logic. The new is new precisely because it differs from preconceived patterns and plans, because it excites or calls (*ciere*) you out of (*ex*) what you already know – excitement of creation. Evolution put a stop to exciting discoveries because, in the naturalist climate of the late nineteenth century, it seemed as if the key to solve the secret of all life, "the riddle of the universe" as the German evolutionist Ernst Haeckel phrased it, was within reach.[26]

Stein's ambivalence towards evolution, as an intellectual event that both "opened up" history and then "closed" it, runs parallel to Nietzsche's ambiguous relationship to Darwin. Nietzsche's concept of "genealogy" owes something to Darwinian insights in that it enables him to trace the origins and development of moral values in human behavior, man-made systems and concrete environments rather than in an ideal design. But where Darwin highlights the role of the material environment, demanding species to react, Nietzsche turns the tables and stresses the active force internal to life, the will to power that seeks to overcome matter. It is hard not to recognize Nietzschean echoes in Stein's spotlighting of creativity and excess. In "Many Many Women," written just after *The Making of Americans*, she affirms, for example, that "being one being creative she is creating being one who is not a kind of a one," and one way of reading her dynamic 1911 portrait of Picasso is to see it as a text about an *Überman*-artist: charismatic, prolific and with a train of followers.[27] When, in the early 1930s, the behavioral psychologist B. F. Skinner claimed to have discovered Stein's "secret" by claiming that, as a writer, she drew on the work she did in a psychology laboratory as a medical student, selling us "automatic writing" as literature, Stein rebuked him.[28] "No," she wrote to Ellery Sedgwick, the editor of the *Atlantic Monthly* in which sections of *The Autobiography of Alice B. Toklas* had appeared, "it is not so automatic as he thinks . . . If there is anything secret it is the other way . . . I think I achieve by xtra consciousness, excess."[29] Stein's excessive poetics takes established forms and practices beyond themselves; what interests her is not how different parts make up a whole but how parts and whole change each other.[30]

In order to be able to work on her excessive projects, Stein needed to "kill what was not dead, the nineteenth century which was so sure of evolution and prayers, and Esperanto and their ideas."[31] Stein's putting evolution on a par with religion here resonates with Nietzsche's comparison of scientists to priests in *On the Genealogy of Morality*; both are "slaves" of an ascetic truth ideal. The reference to Esperanto, furthermore, hints at a contrast between an artificially constructed "universal language," devised as an efficient, closed system, and the incessant variation and indeterminacy that natural languages are subject to. Darwin actually used the development of languages as a model to think about the development of species, describing languages as "genealogical systems."[32] It is in such differentiating development, rather than the closed mechanist templates of evolutionary theorists such as Herbert Spencer, that Stein invests her hope for the twentieth century. In the twentieth century, she continues in *Wars I Have Seen*, "there is no Esperanto, no universal knowledge."[33] Stein's denying the twentieth century any closed frameworks – which, when she was working on *Wars I Have Seen* in the middle of World War Two, counted as much as an expression of hope as it was an elucidation of her poetics – implies that "coincidences" can be "real again," and not "a law of chance" as they had been in the nineteenth century.[34] The paradoxical phrase "a law of chance" here resonates with the difficulties Darwin experienced in trying to make sense of randomness. As Curtis Johnson explains, Darwin, throughout his career, "was up against the idea [...] that some of the weirdest adaptations in nature must be haphazard, without rhyme or reason."[35] That insight, that nature ultimately defies calculation, is what Stein found exciting about evolution and what she considered to have "opened up the history of all animals vegetables and minerals, and man."

By means of a conspicuous comma, Stein distinguishes between the project of opening up, on the one hand, "the history of all animals vegetables and minerals" and, on the other, that of opening up "the history of man." The creative, open historical impulse that Stein associates with Darwin may not have galvanized thinking about time and change in nineteenth-century evolutionary theory, but in the field of theoretical history, the German Historical School was reacting against closed frameworks, and paving the way for Dilthey's open hermeneutics of life. The work done on "the history of man" in that context had a huge impact on intellectual life in both Europe and the US. While Stein does not relate her work to a German intellectual context, echoes of the latter can be found in her writings. In what follows I unfold how we can see Stein's approach to an open history in relation to what is sometimes referred to as the crisis of historicism in the nineteenth century.

A Hermeneutics of Life

When, from the late 1930s onwards, Stein starts looking back on her work and life, she often mentions William James. Oddly, she repeatedly connects James to the concept of the will to live, which is not a Jamesian concept. In *Wars I Have Seen*, for example, Stein remembers James as "always [saying] there is the will to live without the will to live there is destruction, but there is also the will to destroy, and the two like everything are in opposition."[36] And in *Lectures in America* she relates her theory of insistence, or repetition with a difference, to "what William James calls the Will to Live."[37] "[W]hat makes life," she explains, is "that the insistence is different, no matter how often you tell the same story if there is anything alive in the telling the emphasis is different."[38] It is Arthur Schopenhauer who first argued the world should be conceived of as will, with will as foundational, irrational force. Steven Meyer, who understands Schopenhauer's concept of will to live as referring to "the instinctual life of the body, the ceaseless and monotonous repetition of its pulses and desires," argues that Stein's understanding of the differential force of "the Will to Live" sets her apart from Schopenhauer.[39] Yet Schopenhauer's will to live concerns more than repetitive instinct. As Robert Wicks explains, Schopenhauer approached the will as an objectified form, as "a constant presence that permeates the biological world and is the inner drive of all living things, past present and future [. . .] the eternal chorus of life, whenever and wherever there are living things."[40] The will to live, then, is that out of which all variation, all actual life, emerges – or one story told differently many, many times.

It is remarkable that Stein puts the concept will to live in the mouth of William James because it does not crop up in his writings. James's phrase "the will to believe," as Meyer notes, is the closest echo of it.[41] James was not even particularly fond of or even interested in Schopenhauer.[42] Yet the idea of one drive or flux out of which all variation emerges is central to James's late thinking. While James steers clear of Platonism, refusing any absolute or "bedding" for the "mosaic" of experience, he does approach life or experience as a creative unity. "Experience itself, taken at large," he writes in "A World of Pure Experience" (1904), "can grow by its edges."[43] In the essay "Does 'Consciousness' Exist?" (1904) he suggests that "there is only one primal stuff or material in the world, a stuff of which everything is composed," which he refers to as "pure experience."[44] This experience is "pure" because it only exists as a virtual assemblage and cannot be experienced as a totality. "[T]here is no *general* stuff of which experience at large is made," James modifies, "[t]here are as many stuffs as there are natures in the things experienced."[45] In *A Pluralistic Universe*, published in 1909, he defines pure experience as "the immediate flux of life which furnishes the material to our later reflection with its conceptual categories [. . .] a *that* which is not yet any definite *what*, tho ready to be all sorts of whats."[46] If will, in Schopenhauer's *The World as Will and Representation*, is what the world is for us, how we feel it as opposed to how we represent it, then pure experience, for James, is "but another name for feeling or sensation."[47] Although James worked on these ideas right before his death, when Stein was in Paris starting on her literary projects, he was already moving towards them in his lectures of the late 1890s, when Stein was still his student.[48] But perhaps even more remarkable than Stein using the will to live for what we can understand as James's pure experience – one flux of life out of which concrete variations materialize – is that she relates "what William James calls the Will to Live" to a historical sensibility and to the idea of expression.

After telling her audience that "no matter how often you tell the same story if there is anything alive in the telling the emphasis is different," Stein shares the experience of when she first "became conscious of these things."

> I became conscious of these things, I suppose anybody does when they first really know that the stars are worlds and that everything is moving, that is the first conscious feeling of necessary repetition, and it comes to one and it is very disconcerting. Then the second thing is when you first realize the history of various civilizations, that have been on this earth, that too makes one realize repetition and at the same time the difference of insistence. Each civilization insisted in its own way before it went away.[49]

What she understands here as "necessary repetition" relates to a confrontation with deep time, both cosmological and historical. As a child, Stein was struck by the insight that her world was not *the* world, that her life was a detail in ongoing cycles of creation and destruction, rise and fall. Life, in other words, is given form again and again but looks different each time. Another experience that made her realize that repetition is impossible, she tells us, was when she was living in Baltimore "with a whole group of very lively little aunts who had to know anything." Here she spotlights expression. Living in an environment where "everything [was] said often," Stein found out that nothing was ever told in the same way.[50] Exact repetition is impossible, then, since the way in which we give expression to life, both on a macro scale (civilizations) and a micro scale (everyday experience), is always different. That she sums up this anecdote by stating that "[t]his is what William James call the Will to Live" is surprising because James was not very interested in theories either of history or of expression.

Nevertheless, as James Kloppenberg has shown, William James contributed to a new historical sensibility. In *Principles of Psychology* James urged his students to study "by way of history."[51] History, here, is opposed to static analysis and implies that facts can change over time because experience changes. Such a dynamic stance is central to James's radical empiricism. When, in his work on psychology, James underlined that identical repetition of a phenomenon is impossible, that "we *must* think of it in a fresh manner, see it under a somewhat different angle, apprehend it in different relations from those in which it last appeared," he helped shape a changing understanding of history, in which present experience became the ground for reflection about the past.[52] The dominant nineteenth-century theories of history sought to offer narratives of directionality and purpose, in response to discoveries about the origin of the world and man in the natural sciences.[53] In Hegel's philosophical historicism, society developed in accordance with Reason, and in Ranke's positivist scheme history answered a providential design. In both positivist and idealist frameworks, history was conceived of as a closed system, in which the past held a truth that could be unlocked. Implicit in such approaches to history is what Walter Benjamin called a "homogeneous, empty time" by which the past can be divided in sections and by which one can trace, in Rankian fashion, with impartial eyes the progress of universal history.[54] James's focus on experience as a "stream of consciousness," in which "*no state once gone can recur and be identical with what it was before*," makes such an understanding of time untenable.[55] Because we live time, time is radically open-ended. In a letter to Henry Adams he once remarked, criticizing Adams's deterministic outlook on society, that "unless the future contains genuine novelties, unless the present is really creative of them, I don't see the use of time at all."[56] Applied to the study of history, James's view asks for a subjective approach, grounded in the historian's experience.

James addressed the relativism that seems inherent to his position when, in *The Will to Believe*, he wrote that "there is indeed nothing which someone has not thought absolutely true, while his neighbor deemed it absolutely false."[57] Although, in *A Pluralistic Universe*, he programmatically positioned himself as "knit up with the finite world *as such*, and with things that have a history," he did not engage with the problem of what a focus on changing and individual truths means for the study of history.[58] He criticized a certain line of historical thinking. In essays like "The Importance of Individuals" and "Great Men and their Environment," for example, he discards Herbert Spencer's format of a determinist history in which all human actions are predestined by standing up for individual genius. And in "Hegel and his Method," he targets Hegel and posits a pluralistic metaphysic as an alternative for an absolutist take on history that propagates the rationality of the universe. The idea that "at bottom all is well with the cosmos," James writes, may be rationally satisfying on the grounds of beauty, intellect and morals, but it is not so practically. The idea of "a static eternal," he points out, is incompatible with "the finite world of change and striving" in which we actually live.[59] What this Darwinian "world of change and striving" implies for the study of history is left unanswered by James. The issue was at the heart of the late nineteenth-century "crisis of historicism," however, a debate that determined German intellectual life and quickly spread internationally.

The Crisis of Historicism

At stake in the crisis of historicism is the triangular relationship between science, philosophy and history. Hegel had proclaimed the goal of philosophy to be "the scientific knowledge of truth," and by his account the science of philosophy, which included the philosophy of nature and the philosophy of spirit, was the absolute science.[60] Hegel's idealist scheme, however, clashed with developments in the natural sciences and the increasing materialist and empiricist orientations of the nineteenth century. Science not only divorced itself from philosophy but took its place as "absolute" framework for making sense of the world. This development left history, in a sense, unmoored. Whereas, in Hegel, history is the materialization of Spirit, post-Hegelian thinkers of history wanted to approach history outside of an idealist system, and started exploring how to approach it as a science. Leopold von Ranke's Historical School departed sharply from Hegel. In contrast to Hegel's deductive approach, this group of thinkers focused on the particular and the individual. Although they distinguished history from the natural sciences, in that they considered the former to be concerned with individual and hence interpretable decisions and actions instead of "natural" developments, they wanted to translate the ideal of objectivity associated with the natural sciences to their field. This led Ranke to famously pronounce that the good historian should uncover history "as it actually happened," that he should "extinguish his self and let history speak through him" and that "every epoch is immediate to God."[61] The latter criterion, while not excluding the notion of progress, demands we appreciate an era for itself and not, as in a progressive scheme, on the basis of what it has progressively given rise to. In terms of method, this meant that the intellectuals affiliated with the Historical School, in Burckhardt's manifesto-like formulation,

> are content with observation; we make cross-sections through history, and in as many directions as possible; above all, we do not provide a philosophy of history. That is a centaur, a *contradictio in adjecto*: for history, that is, coordination, is not philosophy, and philosophy, that is, subordination, is not history.[62]

By subordination, Burckhardt here understands the hold of a closed system, the shaping of facts into an existing grid or Hegelian worldscheme. Their agenda was to "free" history of such a template and deal with the past per se.

In zooming in on the individual, and thus distinguishing their project from Hegel's objective idealism, the Historical School in a sense returns to a romantic framework. The methodological principles of observation and coordination tally with the romantic focus on the individual since any pre-established frameworks and "subordination" would rob the individual of its individuality.[63] The combination of these romantic echoes and the impulse to graft history on the rapidly developing natural sciences, which had proved so successful in explaining the universe, explains the international success of the German Historical School. In the US the newly founded American Historical Foundation, for example, elected Ranke, "the father of scientific history," as its first honorary member in 1885.[64] The German project resonated with the stress on the individual in nineteenth-century American intellectual life, central to the project of the Transcendentalists, while at the same time promising a scientific, objective approach to the study of history.

A key figure in the nineteenth-century American debate on history is Ralph Waldo Emerson. In his 1840s essay, "History," Emerson argued that the whole of history can be explained "from individual experience."[65] History, for Emerson, constituted the unity of all experience. "There is one mind common to all individual men," he writes and "[o]f the works of this mind history is the record." This implies that "the whole of history is in one man" and that "it is all to be explained from individual experience."[66] Although Emerson's belief in a transcendental mind appears to clash with the scientific ideals of the German Historical School, they too conceptualized a supra-individual historical consciousness, which led them to deal with nations, states, ethics, cultures and the concept of class. While they did not project an absolute mind, their holistic approach can be considered in line with Hegel's idealism and Emerson's transcendentalism. Ranke, Georg Iggers points out, was ultimately committed to unveiling the transcendent forces steering history, "spiritual, life-giving, creative forces" determining the concrete and individual facts.[67] He called on the researcher's intuition, furthermore, to fathom these forces, which of course compromises the impartiality he prescribed. In Emerson the subjective, intuitive approach to the past is manifest. "Every mind," he writes in "History," "must know the whole lesson for itself, - must go over the whole ground. What it does not see, what it does not live, it will not know." Because we can only know the past "in our private experience," Emerson concludes that "[a]ll history becomes subjective [. . .] there is properly no history; only biography."[68]

Stein was, of course, familiar with Emerson and in her *Narration* lectures she expresses her admiration for his writing. Elaborating on her essay "What Is English Literature?," she distinguishes between an American and an English literary tradition. What makes the two traditions different is their relationship to life. Whereas English writing, for Stein, operates in close connection to "daily living," she posits that there is no daily living, no predictable routine, in America. What American writing expresses is the flux of life, or life as creativity, before it materializes into concrete forms and things:

> Those same words that in the English were completely quiet or very slowly moving began to have within themselves the consciousness of completely moving, they began to detach themselves from the solidity of anything, they began to feel themselves as if they were anywhere or anything, think about American writing from Emerson, Hawthorne Walt Whitman Mark Twain Henry James myself Sherwood Anderson Thornton Wilder and Dashiell Hammitt [sic] and you will see what I mean, [. . .] words left alone more and more feel that they are moving and all of it is detached and is detaching anything from anything and in this detaching and in this moving it is being in its way creating its existing.[69]

American writing, in other words, is concerned with the creation of life rather than with the description of life forms or patterns. Stein, in tune with Emerson, focused on her own mind, on her own creative talents, in tackling history.[70]

That Stein engaged with the problem of history writing is not often acknowledged. And yet, when, in the early 1900s, she left the Johns Hopkins laboratories in order to write, she set about composing histories, with a strong autobiographical focus.[71] The first story she wrote, *Q.E.D.*, can be read as an autobiographical account of an unhappy love affair, and her two consecutive projects, *Three Lives* (originally titled *Three Histories*) and *The Making of Americans: Being a History of a Family's Progress*, relate to her immigrant background and to her experience of living in Baltimore. Stein's literary concern with history was not extraordinary. Any writer, Henry James had argued, in his famous 1888 essay "The Art of Fiction," should write as a historian. For James, the position of historian was the only "standing room" for the novelist. Where it is taken for granted, James argues, that history represents life, novels are all too often looked upon as mere make-believe. Nevertheless, "the only reason for the existence of a novel," James claims, "is that it does attempt to represent life," and should it stop doing that, literature "will have arrived at a very strange pass."[72] Stein admired Henry James but not because his work, in any straightforward way, "represent[s] life." For Stein, the life his writing knew how to express had a transcendental appeal. Applauding James's writing, she writes: "over it all something floated not floated away but just floated, floated up there."[73] This, by Stein's account, could be made felt only by "detaching" life, as force or energy, from the solidity of particular things and reliving its impulse.

Such a creative approach to history clashes with the scientific ambitions of the discipline of history. That is an issue Stein addresses in her 1930s lectures, *Narration*. History, here, is a problem because it had turned out not to be the scientific discipline some historians thought it was. She writes that "the only comfort" to a historian, the idea that the past repeats itself and that there is thus a degree of predictability and hence of scientific footing to history, "has been taken away from the historian."[74] The solution for the historian, Stein suggests, "is that any one must amuse himself with anything and not think to recognize anything beside this thing, beside playing with what he is playing with as he is writing what he is recognizing while the writing is being written by him."[75] It is in writing as it is "being written," a personal engagement with something particular, rather than in recognition, or making sense of something by relating it to an already existing form, that life can be shown. Yet history, of course, typically seeks to find patterns and meaning in sequences of events, and that, to Stein, is "a burden a burden of everything, a burden of so many days which are days one after the other." In the *Narration* texts Stein returns to a problem that had occupied her for much of the 1900s: the idea that history "really ought to be literature."[76]

Emerson's insistence on living the past, recreating it in our own individual experience in order to understand it, George J. Stack argues, amounts to "a very rudimentary form of Wilhelm Dilthey's conception of historical understanding."[77] Dilthey was a major figure in the German debate on history after Ranke and an all-round intellectual whose affinity with William James is often touched on yet rarely explored in any great depth.[78] Born a generation after Ranke, he tried to move beyond the Historical School's focus on the particular to the larger "objectivations" of history without reverting to idealism or Kantian transcendentalism. Stein's approach to knowing the past, I argue, takes Emerson's focus on reliving the past in a direction similar to Dilthey's project. Like Dilthey, Stein was fascinated by the idea that life "expresses" itself in countless variations. When she explains her take on expression in her *Lectures in America*, furthermore, her spotlighting of "talking and listening" moves in the direction of a hermeneutical understanding of life. The idea that life is hermeneutical counts as one of Dilthey's major insights. It means that the process of making sense of life is part of being alive, instead of an activity that gets added to a primary reality. As Michael Ermarth explains, for Dilthey, "interpretation is the original condition of life itself, not the subsequent refraction of an antecedent reality."[79] This is what Stein discovered when she was living with her aunts in Baltimore. By "listen[ing] to what anybody was saying and what they did say while they were saying what they were saying," she reflects, "I began to find out then [. . .] the difference between repetition and insisting and it is a very important thing to know. You listen as you know."[80] Knowing runs parallel to listening to a story's different versions. Knowing, like listening, is processual. Knowing, furthermore, requires a subjective response: talking. Taking in the stream of life's variations and responding to them is what Stein understands as "talking and listening." This is an activity that, for Stein, is emphatically connected to life: "it is necessary if you are to be really and truly alive it is necessary to be at once talking and listening."[81] Complete and "lively" movement, after all, "is what we mean by life and in my way I have tried to make portraits of this thing always have tried always may try to make portraits of this thing."[82] Before I explore how Stein portrays life in her early history projects, I zero in on Dilthey's hermeneutics of life.

Understanding Life on its Own Terms

The intellectual trajectory of Wilhelm Dilthey in many ways runs parallel to that of William James. While both recognized the affinities between their respective projects, they addressed different problems. History was a key concern for Dilthey throughout his career, with, as Frederic Jameson puts it, "the supreme mystery of the historiographical act" the pivot of his voluminous writings.[83] Dilthey was also, however, very much interested in psychology, and in his essay "Ideas for a Descriptive and Analytic Philosophy" [Ideen über eine beschreibende und zergliedernde Psychologie] (1894), he draws on James's psychology.[84] He famously moved on from a Jamesian descriptive approach, however. He uses what he considered the prime blind spot of psychology – the impossibility of knowing a feeling not analytically but as a feeling – to argue for a theory of expression and understanding. For Dilthey, the translation of sensation or lived experience into language does not by definition alienate us from it, as it did for James, but can provide a way into it. "The antinomy in psychology," Dilthey wrote,

> has been pointed out by James: that one can never grasp a feeling as such in self-observation. Such a feeling is always something very complex and compacted, which can be partially reduced to its parts but not taken whole. However, one can overcome the standpoint of James through the relation of expression and understanding.[85]

As an alternative to the scientific description of lived experience, Dilthey proposed a hermeneutics of life.

Dilthey's attempt to move beyond James and work with the whole, rather than take it apart, can be seen to correspond to Stein's relationship to her former teacher. Much has been written about the influence of James's descriptive psychology on Stein, in particular with respect to her typological project *The Making of Americans*.[86] Stein herself captured the dynamics as follows:

> When I was working with William James I completely learned one thing, that science is continuously busy with the complete description of something, with ultimately the complete description of anything with ultimately the complete description of everything. [. . .] When I began The Making of Americans I knew I really did know that a complete description was a possible thing, and certainly a complete description is a possible thing. But as it is a possible thing one can stop continuing to describe this everything. That is where philosophy comes in, it begins when one stops continuing describing everything.[87]

Stein loves using the phrase "one thing," but it rarely means one element. "One thing," in Stein, refers to a qualitative unity rather than a quantitative unit. "Complete description," then, does not come with a neat definition. She uses the phrase to show that when she was working with William James, she was working in a largely mechanist scientific context in which scientists were progressively mapping uncharted terrain and thus approaching the condition of complete knowledge.⁸⁸ But she also distinguishes such a scientific approach from complete description as she understands it when she was writing *The Making of Americans*. In the context of *The Making of Americans*, complete description makes it possible to "stop continuing to describe this everything." Complete description, in other words, becomes a project that is more philosophical and less scientific. *The Making of Americans*, as we will see in Chapter 2, can be read as an exercise in hermeneutics, with the narrator increasingly troubled by the question of what it means to completely understand and express or describe something.

The key ingredients of Dilthey's hermeneutics are experience, expression and understanding. All three are essential to the task he set himself, which was that of "understanding life on its own terms," a phrase he uses again and again. In response to the natural sciences, which, in Dilthey's account, were concerned with outer experience, Dilthey argued for a new discipline: the *Geisteswissenschaften*, or human sciences. Encompassing philology, history, sociology and psychology, the human sciences had to offer a rich understanding of inner experience, of the ways in which human beings live and give expression to their worlds.⁸⁹ Inner experience, for Dilthey, constitutes what he called the "fundamental cell" of the human, historical world.⁹⁰ This is an awkward biological metaphor for a thinker devoted to constructing a specifically human domain of knowledge, but the tension between biology and history allows us to grasp the relation between what Dilthey referred to as "life itself" and "objectificated life." For Dilthey, as Ilse Bulhof explains, life itself amounts to energy, which finds expression or objectification in history.⁹¹ In Dilthey's words: "History is the domain of life, apprehended both as its objectification in the sequence of time and as its formation in accordance with temporal and productive relationships. History is a whole that is never possible to complete."⁹² History, in other words, is the framework in which we, human individuals and groups, make something of the energy that is life. We live (experience) and give form to (express) our time while trying to understand what has come before us and what the future may look like.

The method of Dilthey's hermeneutics is understanding. Dilthey draws on the romantic philosopher Friedrich Schleiermacher, who had reconfigured the discipline of hermeneutics by shifting its focus from "the Word" to human life, and understands hermeneutics to work across disciplines, incorporating insights from logic, rhetoric, dialectic, philology and psychology. Hermeneutics, then, does not constitute one systematic framework, and understanding, as a working method, calls for a creative, broadly narrative approach: to make your own or rediscover "the I in the thou."[93] Like Emerson, Dilthey considered biography the key historical genre. In approaching the development of an individual life as a story, Dilthey moves away from both a mechanist and an organic template, the dominant nineteenth-century models of development, according to which man is understood to function as either a machine or a purposive organism.[94] Life-as-story spotlights the unpredictable course of development; each event, each experience can change the course of an individual's life. The biographer's task of narrating the life of someone else, furthermore, demands that one try to re-experience their experiences: not to copy them but to approach them from one's own living and thinking, which also is always already historically mediated.[95] For Dilthey, the act of self-reflexively re-experiencing leads to historical knowledge. It makes us see individual actions and decisions as embedded in larger contexts and opens up for us not the workings of Spirit but history as a "productive nexus," a system in which, on different levels, meaning is made.

While Dilthey considered the individual "[t]he fundamental form" in which a productive system arises, his late writings shift focus from individual life to life as objective spirit, by which he understands the whole network of objectifications or expressions making up history.[96] Expression, then, is an imprint not of a particular experience, but of life beyond the individual. What this "life beyond" amounts to, for Dilthey, can be seen to hold mid-way between the concrete and the abstract. Dilthey repeatedly refers to art in order to elucidate what he means by expression, and it is in his aesthetics that he moves away from history per se and veers towards an understanding of life that Paul Ricoeur calls "logical." "In Dilthey's late works," Ricoeur writes,

> the inner connection (*Zusammenhang*) which gives to a text, to a work of art, to a document, its capacity to be understood by another and to be fixed by writing is something similar to the ideality which Frege and Husserl recognized as the meaning of a proposition. If this comparison holds, then the act of *verstehen* is less *geschichtlich* and more *logisch* than the famous article of 1900 "Die Entstehung der Hermeneutik" had claimed it was.[97]

Given Dilthey's outspoken concern for the historical, I think that what Ricoeur calls logic can be seen in line with what Deleuze calls a logic of sense. Sense, for Deleuze, is what lies beyond and below individual expression and intentional meaning but is still part of the empirical world. A "logic" of sense, then, does not refer to an ideal system but to the tendency of relations to form, events to take place. Of course, where for Deleuze this leads back into a chaosmos, a chaotic state of possibility, for Dilthey it revealed *das Wesenhafte*, or the essential: an intuitive understanding of the complex formations making up a life nexus.[98]

Dilthey's spotlighting of the supra-individual quality of expression in his texts written after 1900 is an important modification of his focus on the individual, but it does not constitute a break with his earlier work. His *Life of Schleiermacher* (1871), for example, reconfigured the genre of biography precisely because it had shown that the "whole being" of Schleiermacher implied an excursion into the historical and intellectual context in which Schleiermacher lived and worked. Furthermore, when, in the 1890s, Dilthey was fascinated by descriptive psychology, he understood empirical observation and description of the particular as bound up with a generalizing "seeing typically."[99]

The concept of the type, in Dilthey, holds a function that falls in between that of the laws of the natural sciences and the ideas of metaphysics. Seeing typically, as he understood it, made it possible to appreciate a more intense mode of lived experience because it brought to light a particular, new formation of life. The type, he wrote, functions as "a way to overcome experience by means of experience, so that it is felt more intensely than in the truest copy of reality."[100] It reveals, in other words, an empirical configuration that is new to one's understanding of reality. Critics have tended to relate Dilthey's understanding of type to the morphological theory of type as it was developed in the natural sciences. While Dilthey's definition of the type – he explains types as "certain basic forms, which [...] recur over and over again amid all variation" – clearly draws on the natural sciences, we cannot lose sight of his core ambition to distinguish the human sciences from the natural sciences.[101] "Seeing typically" is, for Dilthey, first a form of artistic creativity. In his 1895–6 essay "Contributions to the Study of Individuality," he writes, for example, that "[n]o scientific mind can ever exhaust, and no progress in science can ever approximate, what the artist has to say about the content of life."[102] Jos De Mul argues that, in the course of the 1890s, Dilthey can be seen to return to his earlier writings on aesthetics, in which he had set artistic creativity apart from analytical toil, claiming, for example, that "[t]he writer does not arrive at his representation of the typical by intellectually comparing an individual with dozens of other individuals, but by representing him in his irreducible individuality."[103] The typical as the irreducibly individual may sound paradoxical, but should be understood as a particular formation, a particular combination of elements, making possible individual expression. In "Contributions to the Study of Individuality," Dilthey sketches the development of life as arising out of uniformity and attaining an ever more complex degree of "connectedness": "[t]he typical connectedness of characteristics increases in the universe in an ascending sequence of forms of life and reaches its pinnacle in organic and then in psychic life."[104] Hermeneutics as a form of higher understanding, in other words, always concerns a singular expression or a particular combination of psychological and historical nexuses.

Although Dilthey often spotlights the figure of the artist as a romantic genius, a seer, he also moves in the direction of a modernist, formalist understanding of art. Works of art, for Dilthey, come with a particular, formal truth that transcends the artist and that cannot be accessed through the scientific processes of observation, reflection and theory:

> No truly great work of art can [. . .] want to put forward a spiritual content that misrepresents its author; indeed, it does not want to say anything about its author. Truthful in itself, it stands – fixed, visible, and abiding – and it is this that makes possible a methodically reliable understanding of such works. Thus there arises in the confines between knowing and doing a sphere in which life discloses itself at a depth inaccessible to observation, reflection, and theory.[105]

Taking this into account, Dilthey's early twentieth-century hermeneutics is not only, as it is so often taken to be, at the tail end of a romantic, subjectivist project, but also part of a budding modernism in which the composition, as system, gains in importance. Where Dilthey's "fixed, visible, and abiding" aesthetic form may trigger associations with the New Criticism's figure of the well-wrought urn, his approach was much more open to historical contingencies than the New Criticism. It is ultimately in lived experience, which is changeable and fickle, that life discloses itself.

Notes

1. Stein, *Everybody's Autobiography*, 250.
2. Stein, *Wars I Have Seen*, 61.

3. Dewey, *The Influence of Darwin on Philosophy and Other Essays in Contemporary Thought*, 1.
4. Elizabeth Grosz, *The Nick of Time: Politics, Evolution and the Untimely* (Crows Nest: Allen and Unwin, 2004), 21.
5. Ibid., 20.
6. Ibid., 21.
7. Henry Adams, *The Education of Henry Adams* (Boston and New York: Houghton Mifflin Company, 1918), Chapter 34, available at: <https://openlibrary.org/books/OL13446110M/The_education_of_Henry_Adams> (last accessed September 3, 2021).
8. Bergson's background was in mathematics and the sciences. His decision to study philosophy at the École Normale disappointed his teacher, Desboves, who wrote to him "you will only be a philosopher and have missed your vocation." At the École Normale, where he was in the same class as Emile Durkheim and Jean Jaurès, Bergson worked on the theories of Herbert Spencer. See Keith Ansell Pearson, Introduction, in *Henri Bergson: Key Writings*, ed. Keith Ansell Pearson and John Mullarky (New York: Continuum, 2001), viii.
9. Henri Bergson, *The Creative Mind: An Introduction to Metaphysics*, trans. Mabelle L. Andison (New York: Citadel Press, 1992), 12.
10. James R. Guthrie, *Above Time: Emerson's and Thoreau's Temporal Revolutions* (Columbia: University of Missouri Press, 2001), 39.
11. Charles Darwin, *The Origin of Species by Means of Natural Selection; or, The Preservation of Favored Races in the Struggle for Life* (New York: Hurst, 1872), 91, available at: <https://openlibrary.org/books/OL7230649M/The_Origin_of_Species_by_Means_of_Natural_Selection> (last accessed September 3, 2021).
12. Bertrand Helm, *Time and Reality in American Philosophy* (Amherst: University of Massachusetts Press, 1985), 3.
13. For more on Herder's impact on the practice of history, see, for instance: Donald R. Kelley, *Fortunes of History: Historical Inquiry from Herder to Huizinga* (New Haven, CT: Yale University Press, 2003).
14. Stephen Edelston Toulmin and June Goodfield, *The Discovery of Time* (Chicago: University of Chicago Press, 1982), 238.
15. Darwin, *The Origin of Species by Means of Natural Selection*, 73.
16. Gillian Beer, *Darwin's Plots: Evolutionary Narrative in Darwin, George Eliot and Nineteenth-Century Fiction* (Cambridge: Cambridge University Press, 2000), 17.
17. Stein, *Wars I Have Seen*, 61.
18. Charles Darwin. *The Descent of Man and Selection in Relation to Sex* (New York: D. Appleton and Company, 1872), 34, available at: <https://openlibrary.org/books/OL6586780M/The_descent_of_man_and_selection_in_relation_to_sex> (last accessed September 3, 2021). See also Elizabeth Grosz, *Becoming Undone: Darwinian Reflections on Life, Politics and Art* (Durham, NC: Duke University Press, 2011), 17.

19. Stein, *The Making of Americans*, 284.
20. Stein, *The Autobiography of Alice B. Toklas*, 739.
21. Grosz, *The Nick of Time*, 33.
22. Stein, "How Writing is Written," 152.
23. On this, see, for example, George Steiner, *Real Presences: Is There Anything in What We Say* (London: Faber, 1989) and Ronald Schleifer, *Rhetoric and Death: The Language of Modernism and Postmodern Discourse Theory* (Urbana: University of Illinois Press, 1990).
24. Gertrude Stein, *The Geographical History of America or The Relation of Human Nature to the Human Mind*, in *Writings: 1932–1946*, ed. Harriet Scott Chessman and Catharine R. Stimpson (New York: Library of America, 1998), 391.
25. Stein, *Lectures in America*, 283.
26. From 1895 until 1899, Haeckel worked on *Die Welträtsel* (1895–9), which came out in English in 1901 as *The Riddle of the Universe*.
27. Gertrude Stein, "Many Many Women," in *Matisse, Picasso and Gertrude Stein, with Two Shorter Stories* (Mineola, NY: Dover Publications, 2000), 159.
28. See B. F. Skinner, "Has Gertrude Stein a Secret?," *Atlantic Monthly* 53 (1934), Available at: <https://www.bfskinner.org/publications/pdf-articles/> (last accessed September 3, 2021).
29. Stein quoted in Steven Meyer, *Irresistible Dictation: Gertrude Stein and the Correlations of Writing and Science* (Stanford, CA: Stanford University Press, 2001), 227.
30. This, as Sianne Ngai has shown in *Ugly Feelings* (Cambridge, MA: Harvard University Press, 2005), is what makes Stein's texts so important, since reading Stein demands we open up the collection of categories by which we make sense of (aesthetic) experience.
31. Stein, *Wars I Have Seen*, 21.
32. Grosz, *The Nick of Time*, 27.
33. Stein, *Wars I Have Seen*, 2.
34. Ibid., 21.
35. Curtis Johnson, *Darwin's Dice: The Idea of Change in the Thought of Charles Darwin* (Oxford: Oxford University Press, 2015), 90.
36. Stein, *Wars I Have Seen*, 63.
37. Stein, *Lectures in America*, 289.
38. Ibid., 288.
39. Meyer, *Irresistible Dictation*, 213.
40. Robert L. Wicks, *Schopenhauer's 'The World as Will and Representation': A Reader's Guide* (London: Continuum, 2011), 114.
41. Meyer, *Irresistible Dictation*, 213.
42. In his biography Robert Richardson shows that James's early delight in Schopenhauer changed into loathing (Robert D. Richardson, *William James: In the Maelstrom of American Modernism* (New York: Houghton-Mifflin, 2006, 14)).

43. James, "A World of Pure Experience," 1180.
44. William James, "Does 'Consciousness' Exist?," in *Writings: 1902–1910*, ed. Bruce Kuklick (New York: Library of America, 1987), 1142.
45. James, "Does 'Consciousness' Exist?," 1153.
46. William James, "The Thing and Its Relations," in *Writings: 1902–1910*, ed. Bruce Kuklick (New York: Library of America, 1987), 782–3.
47. Ibid., 783.
48. Meyer, *Irresistible Dictation*, 248.
49. Stein, *Lectures in America*, 289.
50. Ibid., 289.
51. James quoted in James Kloppenberg, *Uncertain Victory: Social Democracy and Progressivism in European and American Thought, 1870–1920* (Oxford: Oxford University Press, 1986), 109.
52. William James, *Psychology: Briefer Course*, in *Writings: 1878–1899*, ed. Gerald E. Myers (New York: Library of America, 1992), 156.
53. Charles Bambach, *Heidegger, Dilthey and the Crisis of Historicism* (Ithaca, NY: Cornell University Press, 1995), 6.
54. Walter Benjamin, "On the Concept of History," in *Selected Writings: 1938–1940*, vol. 4, ed. Howard Eiland and Michael W. Jennings (Cambridge, MA: Belknap Press of Harvard University Press, 2006), 395.
55. James, *Psychology: Briefer Course*, 154.
56. James quoted in Kloppenberg, *Uncertain Victory*, 107.
57. William James, *The Will to Believe and Other Essays in Popular Philosophy*, in *Writings: 1878–1899*, ed. Gerald E. Myers (New York: Library of America, 1992), 468.
58. William James, *A Pluralistic Universe and Other Essays in Popular Philosophy*, in *Writings: 1902–1910*, ed. Bruce Kuklick (New York: Library of America, 1987), 651.
59. James, *A Pluralistic Universe*, 681.
60. Hegel quoted in Bambach, *Heidegger, Dilthey and the Crisis of Historicism*, 22.
61. Ranke quoted in Georg G. Iggers, "The Intellectual Foundations of Nineteenth-Century 'Scientific' History: The German Model," in *The Oxford History of Historical Writing*, vol. 4: *1800–1945*, ed. Stuart Macintyre, Juan Maiguashca and Attila Pók (Oxford: Oxford University Press, 2011), 42.
62. Burckhardt quoted in Herbert Schnädelbach, *Philosophy in Germany 1831–1933*, trans. Eric Matthews (Oxford: Oxford University Press, 1984), 42. Schnädelbach quotes from Jakob Burckhardt, *Weltgeschichtliche Betrachtungen*, ed. R. Marx (Stuttgart: Kröner, 1955), 4.
63. Schnädelbach, *Philosophy in Germany*, 45.
64. Iggers, "The Intellectual Foundations of Nineteenth-Century 'Scientific' History," 41.
65. Emerson, "History," in *Essays and Lectures*, ed. Joel Porte (New York: Library of America, 1983), 237.

66. Emerson, "History," 237.
67. Ranke quoted in Iggers, "The Intellectual Foundations of Nineteenth-Century 'Scientific' History," 48.
68. Emerson, "History," 240.
69. Gertrude Stein, *Narration: Four Lectures* (Chicago: University of Chicago Press, 2010), 10.
70. On Stein in relation to Emerson, see Meyer, *Irresistible Dictation*, 137–8. Meyer zooms in on Stein's comma after Emerson in the *Narration* quotation.
71. For discussions of Stein's experiment with writing history across her career, see for example: Phoebe Stein Davis, "'Even Cake Gets to Have Another Meaning': History, Narrative, and 'Daily Living' in Gertrude Stein's World War II Writings," *MFS: Modern Fiction Studies* 44.3 (1998): 568–607; Laura Doyle, "The Flat, the Round, and Gertrude Stein: Race and the Shape of Modern(ist) History," *Modernism/modernity* 7.2 (2000): 249–71; Kelley Wagers, "Gertrude Stein's 'Historical Living.'" *Journal of Modern Literature* 31.3 (2008): 22–43.
72. Henry James, "The Art of Fiction," in *Literary Criticism*, ed. Leon Edel, vol. 1 (New York: Library of America, 1984), 46.
73. Stein, *Lectures in America*, 222.
74. Stein, *Narration*, 58.
75. Ibid., 58.
76. Ibid., 58–9.
77. George J. Stack, *Nietzsche and Emerson: An Elective Affinity* (Athens: Ohio University Press, 1992), 110.
78. Dilthey and James met once, in 1867, at the home of Herman Grimm, and although Dilthey fell asleep during the dinner, James was very much impressed by his erudition. In a letter James described Dilthey as "overflowing with information with regard to everything knowable and unknowable. He is the first man I have ever met of a class, which must be common here, of men to whom learning has become as natural as breathing." Although they never saw each other again, they would continue to read each other's work. I have found this quotation in Michael Ermarth's study, *Wilhelm Dilthey: The Critique of Historical Reason* (Chicago: University of Chicago Press, 1978), 32.
79. Ermarth, *Wilhelm Dilthey*, 347.
80. Stein, *Lectures in America*, 289.
81. Ibid., 290.
82. Stein, *Lectures in America*, 290.
83. Fredric Jameson, translator's note to "The Rise of Hermeneutics," by Wilhelm Dilthey, trans. Fredric Jameson, *New Literary History* 3.2 (1972): 229.
84. Wilhelm Dilthey, *Ideas for a Descriptive and Analytic Psychology*, trans. Rudolf A. Makkreel and Donald Moore, in *Understanding the Human World*, ed. Rudolf A. Makkrcel and Frithjof Rodi, vol. 2 of *Selected Works* (Princeton, NJ: Princeton University Press, 2010), 142.

85. Dilthey quoted in Ermarth, *Wilhelm Dilthey*, 213. The quotation is from the Berlin Nachlass (Literatur-Archiv der deutschen Akademie der Wissenschaften, Berlin).
86. See, for example: Ruddick, *Gertrude Stein: Body, Text, Gnosis*, and Meyer, *Irresistible Dictation*.
87. Stein, *Lectures in America*, 283–4.
88. See also Steven Meyer's introduction to Stein's *The Making of Americans*.
89. Martin Jay notes that Dilthey was not rigorous in his distinction between the two and that, especially in his earlier work, he can be seen to use them interchangeably. See *Songs of Experience: Modern American and European Variations on a Universal Theme* (Berkeley: University of California Press, 2005), 224.
90. Wilhelm Dilthey, *Drafts for a Critique of Historical Reason,* trans. Rudolf A. Makkreel and William H. Oman, in *The Formation of the Historical World in the Human Sciences*, ed. Rudolf A. Makkreel and Frithjof Rodi, vol. 3 of *Selected Works* (Princeton, NJ: Princeton University Press, 2002), 265.
91. Ilse Bulhof, *Wilhelm Dilthey: A Hermeneutic Approach to the Study of History and Culture* (The Hague: Martinus Nijhoff, 1980), 164.
92. Dilthey, *Drafts for a Critique of Historical Reason*, 260.
93. Ibid., 213. On the phrase "the re-discovery of the I in the Thou," Ermarth (*Wilhelm Dilthey*, 249) explains: "Originally coined by Wilhelm von Humboldt this formulation reflected the humanistic premises of idealism concerning the ultimate community of all persons. The community of human subjects engenders a special cognitive relation which cannot be resolved into the dichotomous subject-object model of conventional epistemology – though of course there is an 'object' for *Verstehen*."
94. Jos De Mul, *The Tragedy of Finitude: Dilthey's Hermeneutics of Life*, trans. Tony Burrett (New Haven, CT: Yale University Press, 2014), 176.
95. Jacob Owensby, *Dilthey and the Narrative of History* (Ithaca, NY: Cornell University Press, 1994), 155.
96. Dilthey quoted in the introduction to Dilthey, *The Formation of the Historical World in the Human Sciences*, 4.
97. Paul Ricoeur, *Interpretation Theory: Discourse and the Surplus of Meaning* (Fort Worth: Texas Christian University Press, 1976), 90–1.
98. Ermarth (*Wilhelm Dilthey*, 263) quotes the following excerpt from Dilthey's "Briefe von und an Hegel" (*Archiv für Geschichte der Philosophie* 1 (1888), 291): "Artistic creation produces types which raise and intensify [*steigern*] the manifold of experiences to an image and thus represent it. Thus, the opaque and mixed experiences of life are made comprehensible [*verständlich*] in their meaning through the powerful and clear structure of the typical. That which is elevated and connected in the type, what is seen to be necessary to the coherence of life from the vantagepoint of the life of the creator – that we can call the essential [*das Wesenhafte*]."

99. Ermarth (*Wilhelm Dilthey*, 177) quotes from Wilhelm Dilthey, *Die Geistige Welt: Einleitung in die Philosophie Lebens. Erste Hälfte: Abhandlungen zur Grundlegung der Geisteswissenschaften*. Gesammelte Schriften 5, ed. G. Mische, 2nd edn (Stuttgart: B. G. Teubner / Göttingen: Vandenhoeck & Ruprecht, 1957).
100. Ermarth (*Wilhelm Dilthey*, 263) quotes from Wilhelm Dilthey, *Die Geistige Welt: Einleitung in die Philosophie Lebens. Zweite Hälfte: Abhandlungen zur Poetik, Ethik und Pädagogik*. Gesammelte Schriften 6, ed. G. Mische, 3rd edn (Stuttgart: B. G. Teubner / Göttingen: Vandenhoeck & Ruprecht, 1958), 172.
101. Wilhelm Dilthey, *Contributions to the Study of Individuality*, trans. Erdmann Waniek, in *Understanding the Human World*, ed. Rudolf A. Makkreel and Frithjof Rodi, vol. 2 of *Selected Works* (Princeton, NJ: Princeton University Press, 2010), 238.
102. Dilthey, *Contributions to the Study of Individuality*, 242.
103. De Mul (*The Tragedy of Finitude*, 183) quotes from *Die Geistige Welt*, Gesammelte Schriften 5, 282.
104. Dilthey, *Contributions to the Study of Individuality*, 239.
105. Dilthey, *Drafts for a Critique of Historical Reason*, 228.

Chapter 2

Complete Understanding

Contemporary literary criticism has largely turned away from hermeneutics to a constructivist approach. Stein's work, which tends to be used as a test case for new critical perspectives, has been at the heart of this development. Astrid Lorange, in her wonderful *How Reading Is Written: A Brief Index to Gertrude Stein*, for example, wants to liberate Stein from a hermeneutical framework. "The problem [. . .] with hermeneutical modes of interpretation," Lorange quotes Steven Shaviro, "is that they reduce the unknown to already-known, the already determined."[1] For Stein, Lorange outlines, this has meant a history of criticism that either highlights the polysemy of her texts, locating meaning in (indeterminate) language, or decodes, locating meaning in her life and world. The constructivist approach of Lorange's book draws on the affinity between the projects of A. N. Whitehead and Stein to argue for a mediated readerly engagement with Stein's writings. Via a whole list of other writers, from Epicurus to Tan Lin, she explores not what Stein's texts mean, but how they can be read expansively, in connection with a range of other texts and experiences. Her approach can be seen as part of a new critical practice, and the new understanding of reading central to it, of which Franco Moretti's distant reading project is the most famous example. In "Ways of Not Reading Gertrude Stein," Natalia Cecire, for example, connects Stein's praxis of writing illegible texts to present-day debate about digital ways of "not-" or "distant" reading.[2] The only way to engage with an illegible text, she points out, is to not-read it. As Tanya Clement has done, we might come up with an algorithm that maps the dynamics of *The Making of Americans*.[3]

Lorange, Cecire and Clement draw on the network logic of Stein's poetics to counter a closed model of reading.[4] At its most basic, what they do is radically expand the function of "context." Context is no longer what a text refers to but what enables us, its readers, to construct a text. And that "text" might then consist of an index of abstractions to use, as in Lorange's Whitehead-informed reading, or of digital patterns, as in Clement, or of a not-to-be-read text as protest, as in Cecire. Meaning is not found, these critics show. Meanings, rather, are made. I am hugely impressed by their work, but their creative readings, intent on countering literary criticism's closed hermeneutics, leave little room to engage with either Stein's obsession with meaning or with the late nineteenth-/early twentieth-century context in which creative, open-ended meaning was the central problem: life philosophy and its project of reconfiguring hermeneutics as an alternative to mechanist science and idealist philosophy.

In many of her texts, Stein emphasized the importance of reading and being read. Meaning and understanding, furthermore, stand out as key concepts in her early writings. The 1911 text "G.M.P," for example, locates an open understanding of creation in meaningful expression, or talk: "if creating is not exhausting and if not exhausting is allowing saying what is saying when talking is enlarging what enlarging is meaning when meaning has expression."[5]

Talk, for Stein, is meaning in its state of expression. This is a creative process because it adds to our understanding of a closed, quantitative logic. It enlarges what enlarging means. Second, our post-modernist understanding of interpretation is more in line with hermeneutics as it featured in life philosophy than we have taken it to be. Ironically, some of the famous interventions in post-modernist literary criticism that have urged us to move away from interpretation echo early twentieth-century concerns with a rich, open-ended meaning. Susan Sontag's 1960s claim, for example, that "interpretation is the revenge of the intellect upon art" resonates with life philosophy's attempt to counter an intellectualist climate by spotlighting intuition early in the century.[6] Similarly, contemporary affect studies can be seen to bring into focus what life philosophy wanted to deal with as central to processes of knowing: embodiment and the production of moods.

In studies such as Lorange's, hermeneutics tends to be associated with New Criticism, which is blamed for enslaving literary criticism to closed meaning. The New Criticism approach to literary texts can be seen as part of what Latour calls the clichéd modern stance: the quest for purity. As such, it is an extension of that nineteenth-century scientific context in which the key to solving the riddle of the universe seemed within reach. Post-structuralism rediscovered the Nietzschean line of life philosophy, in which meaning gets endlessly made and is radically open. Yet the post-structuralist focus on discourse has, by and large, left Dilthey and Bergson, life philosophers more than language-philosophers, out of the picture. The contemporary post-post-structuralist speculative turn, in which the question of ontology gains ground over language, is tentatively bringing their work back into focus. For Stein, re-engaging with their work means that we get to see her work as deeply invested in questions of meaning and understanding. As scholars investing in constructing open meanings, we cannot, I think, take it for granted that all hermeneutical modes of interpretation reduce the unknown to the already known. Hermeneutics is not what keeps us from appreciating the wide range of what Stein's modernism can be, but a blind spot in Stein research.

"Melanctha": Understanding Others

Many of Stein's early texts are rife with comments on the difficult issue of understanding and making oneself understood. For example, only a couple of lines into *Q.E.D.*, Stein's thinly veiled autobiographical account of an unhappy triangular love affair, the character Adele, alter ego of Stein, faces a difficult journey of understanding. "Heigho," she sighs, "its [sic] an awful grind; new countries, new people and new experience all to see, to know and to understand; old countries, old friends and old experiences to keep on seeing knowing and understanding."[7] "Melanctha: Each One as She May," the central story in *Three Lives*, echoes not only the romantic plot of *Q.E.D.*, but also the fraught process of understanding steering the plot, and features a protagonist in the grip of learning to understand.[8] And *The Making of Americans*, Stein's most ambitious project of the early 1900s, presents us with a narrator in search of "completed understanding."[9] How to understand Stein's conception of "understanding"? Given Stein's penchant for etymology, we can read the many instances of "understanding" in her stories as attempts at "standing," or being, "inter," or among, others. The many troubled instances of understanding in Stein's early texts, then, point to what Dilthey called the "nexus," the larger structure enabling relations between individuals.[10]

In *Q.E.D.*'s static account of a character clash, the process of individuals trying to understand each other amounts to "a dead-lock."[11] The three protagonists share an American identity but their different backgrounds thwart togetherness. As the narrator puts it:

> All three of them were college bred American women of the wealthier class but with that all resemblance between them ended. Their

appearance, their attitudes and their talk both as to manner and to matter showed the influence of different localities, different forebears and different family ideals. They were distinctly American but each one at the same time bore definitely the stamp of one of the older civilisations, incomplete and frustrated in this American version but still always insistent.[12]

By having "insistently" different backgrounds frustrate friendship, Stein thwarts the American ideology of differences merging or melting into each other. *Three Lives* elaborates on that issue by exploring the lives of others. The book tells the life stories of three young women: the German immigrant servants Anna and Lena, and Melanctha, "a graceful, pale yellow, intelligent, attractive" Black woman.[13] As in *Q.E.D.*, understanding concerns the issue of a shared American context intersected by different traditions. But in "Melanctha," Stein's project is less deterministic. Instead of on the past, she focuses on the present and on the dynamic process of understanding that constitutes the present.

Stein wrote *Three Lives* in 1905–6, and meant the stories to be read as histories. She considered various titles for the project, from "The Making of an Author being a History of one woman and many others," to "The Progress of Jane Sands, being a History . . ." and, her favorite, "*Three Histories* by Jane Sands." The Grafton Press, who published the book, did not like the title, however, and asked her to change it to *Three Lives*, fearing *Three Histories* would cause the book "to get confused with [their] real historical publications."[14] Richard Bridgman finds it inexplicable that Stein did not object to the title change, but *Three Lives* may well have suited Stein.[15] Like Dilthey, Stein puts life and history on the same level. What was to be *Three Histories*, notably, starts with a comment on life. The epigraph Stein chose for the collection is one she ascribed to the French symbolist writer Jules Laforgue: "Donc je suis un malheureux et c'est ni ma faute ni celle de la vie."[16] The quotation is usually explained as an indication of Stein's somewhat misguided discovery of the French context she was working in – misguided because the line most probably is not Laforgue's.[17] We should also, however, look into why Stein would opt for what she took for a Laforgue quotation: why, in other words, she related her project to French symbolism. Such questions, Charles Altieri has pointed out, paradoxically tend to be sidestepped as old-fashioned in an explicitly transnationalist academic climate.[18] What Stein, like many others, found in French symbolism was a critique on "exteriority," as Arthur Symons phrases it in *The Symbolist Movement in Literature* (1899).[19] Laforgue, Symons shows, trumpeted "la vie" over categories and ideals, "exterior" devices that fail to get at the essence of life: "Il n'y a pas de type, il y a la vie."[20] Stein's reference to Laforgue in *Three Lives*, then, can be read as a poetic cue. She too wants to write about life itself. Yet where, as Symons pointed out, French symbolist life amounted to spirit, Stein, in tune with the German Historical School, equates life with history.

While the combination of American context, French symbolism and the German Historical School may seem a stretch, it makes good sense to look at *Three Lives* from the vantage of different intellectual traditions intersecting. The intersecting of traditions is, on one level, precisely what the book is about. The stories "The Good Anna" and "The Gentle Lena" by their titles hint at the genre of hagiography. The outcome of the encounter between the old-world genre of the saint's life and the new American immigrant story is, in both cases, an alienating combination of "firm fixed" habits and a context that did not create them.[21] *Three Lives* shows Stein exploring her German immigrant background. Although the middle story, "Melanctha," is set in a Black community, where any German references are far off, it nevertheless echoes the framework of its accompanying stories that move German habits or tradition into America. Here, however, Stein tackles it with a greater sense of dynamics. The peculiar name of Stein's protagonist, Melanctha, hints at the name of Philipp Melancthon (sometimes also spelled Melanchthon), the German Reformist theologian and theorist of hermeneutics.[22] Stein's Black Melanctha, who is characterized as in the grip of two opposing forces – the desire to understand, to be among others, and the desire to wander – embodies the hermeneutic problem that comes with any immigrant experience: how to understand "other" forms of life? How to make yourself understood?

In his famous essay "The Rise of Hermeneutics" (1900), Dilthey lauds Schleiermacher for surpassing Melancthon. While Melancthon liberated text interpretation from Catholic dogma, he insisted on a closed system underpinning (biblical) texts. "For Melancthon [. . .]," Dilthey points out, "each written work is composed according to rules, and is afterwards understood according to rules. It is a kind of logical automaton, clothed with style, images and figures."[23] Stein's "Melanctha" can be read as a comment on that tradition, with Stein transposing the German tradition to a very different context, a Black community in the fictional American town of Bridgepoint. What if you do not know the rules?, this story asks. Dilthey's answer to that question, via Schleiermacher, is the double, open-ended process of grammatical (or formal) and psychological (or empathic) understanding.[24] With reference to the process of interpreting a written text, he writes:

> Grammatical exegesis works its way up through the text from individual connections to those larger relationships that dominate the whole. Psychological exegesis begins by a projection into the creative inner process, and proceeds onward to the outer and inner forms of the work and beyond that to an intuition of its unity with the other works in the spiritual stance of its creator.[25]

In other words, for Dilthey, following Schleiermacher, grammatical and psychological understanding intertwine in an ongoing, circular hermeneutic process. It is necessarily "partial" and open, yet still makes communion possible. For Dilthey, the "re-experiencing of an alien form of life" is possible because we all share one "general human nature."[26]

Stein complicates the processes of psychological and grammatical understanding; she gives us a wandering protagonist and subverts formal rules, in terms of both genre and language. Early twentieth-century readers testified to feeling "immured" in Melanctha's life with little sense of how to process what they were reading.[27] Reading "Melanctha" is not the same as grasping Melanctha. Stein allows her protagonist to gain "understanding" while growing up, for example, but there is little *Bildungs*-logic at work in the story. Melanctha neither is embraced by society at large nor ends up as an outcast. Instead, she falls somewhere in between: lonely and ill, yet "taken care of" in a "home for poor consumptives."[28] In order for the hermeneutical process to be an open process, Dilthey underlined that understanding not only returns to the larger context but also goes forward, with the individual parts, in other words, changing the meaning of the larger context or the whole: "a fully sympathetic reliving requires that understanding go forward with the line of the events themselves."[29] This is what Stein spotlights by means of her roaming protagonist. Melanctha has a habit of "wander[ing] widely" and is "too many" for her lover to be able to deal with.[30] She also upturns narrative expectations. At the very end of the story, for example, the narrator's announcement that Melanctha "began to work and to live regular" is abruptly followed by a diagnosis of consumption and imminent death.[31] The narrator is furthermore presented as incapable both of storytelling ("for Melanctha all her life did not know how to tell a story wholly") and of remembering ("Melanctha never could remember right").³² In a sense, Melanctha, as refusing the context of the already known, precedes Djuna Barnes's character Robin Vote in *Nightwood*, who escapes everyone's grasp. Like Barnes's, Stein's protagonist confronts us with the "others" in history whom we cannot fit into existing templates and who ask us to reconfigure the ways in which we think we understand.

Unlike Robin Vote, Melanctha is not silent. Stein's readers are exposed to Melanctha's thoughts and the story comes with long stretches of dialogue. Like the voices of the other two protagonists in *Three Lives*, the Black voices in "Melanctha" have been perceived as imperfect. Jayne L. Walker, for example, argues that Stein confronts us with "characters whose imperfect command of English makes self-expression an arduous labor." This reading starts from an existing standard, or whole, to make sense of individual deviations by "others," which are then understood in terms of "linguistic inadequacy."³³ Stein, however, as we have seen, preferred excess over lack. A rich reading of the dialect in *Three Lives*, Charles Bernstein points out, is one in which the language "*surpasses* the standard language forms."³⁴ Language is always plural, contains many subsystems, such as dialects and codes, and is furthermore always changing. Stein's use of Black English in "Melanctha" can be read in line with Dilthey's forward impulse in understanding. Its deviating from standard English is Stein's attempt to reconfigure the whole, or what counts as the grammar, of that standard English. She asks us to "go forward with the line of the events themselves" and take into account that Black American English is also English, just as, as she explains in "What Is English Literature?" "by English literature I mean American literature too."³⁵ Systems change, Stein points out in writing this story, because history is perpetually in the making.

This is not to say that Stein's use of stylized Black English is not problematic. The following excerpt, in which Dr Jeff Campbell lectures Melanctha about living regularly, shows that Stein cannot be excused from the racism that was part of her early twentieth-century context:

> What I mean Miss Melanctha by what I was just saying to you is, that I don't, no, never, believe in doing things just to get excited. You see Miss Melanctha I mean the way so many of the colored people do it. Instead of just working hard and caring about their working and living regular with their families and saving up all their money, so they will have some to bring up their children better, instead of living regular and doing like that and getting all their new ways from just

decent living, the colored people just keep running around and perhaps drinking and doing everything bad they can ever think of, and not just because they like all those bad things that they are always doing, but only just because they want to get excited. [. . .] No, Miss Melanctha too, I don't mean this except only just the way I say it. I ain't got any other meaning Miss Melanctha, and it's that what I mean when I am saying about being really good.[36]

But Stein does not only replay a racist ideology here. The pivot of the conversation between Jeff and Melanctha is hermeneutics. In her response, Melanctha outs Jeff as a coward with a misguided take on what life and "knowing" amount to:

That certainly does explain to me Dr. Campbell what I been thinking about you this long time. I certainly did wonder how you could be so live, and knowing everything, and everybody, and talking so big always about everything, and everybody always liking you so much, and you always looking as if you was thinking, and yet you really was never knowing about anybody and certainly not being really very understanding. It certainly is all Dr. Campbell because you is so afraid you will be losing being good so easy, and it certainly do seem to me Dr. Campbell that it certainly don't amount to very much that kind of goodness.[37]

Jeff's little speech about colored people and his desire for things not to have "any other meaning" are too simplistic to be "live." The wandering Melanctha, by contrast, embodies the ongoing tension between the known and the strange that a hermeneutics of life implies. Indeed, when she stops wandering and "beg[ins] to work and to live regular," she dies.

The Making of Americans: Understanding all Others

As we have seen, Stein connects *The Making of Americans* and its project of complete description to the time when she was a science student and working with William James. "I was sure," Stein reflects in "The Making of The Making of Americans,"

that in a kind of way the enigma of the universe could in this way be solved. That after all description is explanation, and if I went on and on and on enough I could describe every individual human being that could possibly exist.[38]

Stein's project of covering every "individual human being that could possibly exist" is less bizarre an idea than it sounds. Also, it not only owes something to James's project of a descriptive psychology, but needs to be seen in the context of a larger conversation on the aims and methods of the study of humanity. The two figures that I want to spotlight here enable me to read Stein's ambitions in *The Making of Americans* as more historical and hermeneutical than scientific. They are Josiah Royce and Otto Weininger.

Josiah Royce

When she was a student at Radcliffe in 1896, Stein took a philosophy course with Josiah Royce. Royce is today chiefly remembered as James's lifelong intellectual opponent and the two were engaged in what is called the Battle of the Absolute. Where James stood for a worldly pluralism, Royce proposed an absolute idealism, steeped in German idealism and the debate in hermeneutics. Royce's own theory of interpretation, notably, would lead him to formulate the concept of an infinite community of interpretation in his late work, which is actually less committed to an absolute idealism than to an absolute pragmatism. But even in his earlier work, Royce's understanding of community came with strong historical inflections, as we may expect from a thinker committed to Hegel. In the 1890s, as Stein's teacher, for example, he introduced his students to Dilthey's historicist view on community.

In a famous 1891 address on pedagogy, he draws heavily on Dilthey in formulating a response to the question "Is There a Science of Education?". Because human nature, "as a product of evolution, differs from nation to nation, from century to century," Royce argues, there is no use in formulating a universal a-historical end to education. He echoes Dilthey's critique on the obsolete, eighteenth-century models of state that project a universal, closed form of what a society should be and argues that what we need, in thinking about the future of our communities, is a dynamic, historicist approach. If there is a science of education, it is one that deals in historicist rather than universal truths. At the heart of Royce's rehearsing of Dilthey is a concern for the relationship between individuals and the society in which they function. A complete unity between the two exists only ideally:

> No culture wins to the service of the organism and of the society the united and final co-operation of all human impulses. [. . .] Nor has any form of civilization attained in its completeness the end of

an entire organization of all the original impulses in full and mutual adaptation. Nor yet, again, is an abstractly universal description of just what this unity of human life would be, accessible to us.[39]

Even without a universal or complete end in sight, however, educators, as mediating between individuals and society at large, can organize. Drawing on "the psychological study of the typical forms of human evolution [as it] is pursued in the fashion which the historical and biological investigations of modern times have rendered possible," Royce argues, educators can work with chaotic individual impulses and shape them into "character" and toward a shared goal.[40]

Literature, like pedagogy, mediates between individual and community. Although the typical view on modernist literature is that it invests in hyper-individual truths only, the modernist critique on rhetoric should not be seen as a turn away from collective ideals. Central to Stein's *The Making of Americans* is the desire to come up with a new form for "everyone." Stein considered her big book to be an important piece of modernist literature because, like Joyce's *Ulysses* and Proust's work, it does not tell a story. "A thing you all know," she writes in "Portraits and Repetition," "is that in the three novels written in this generation that are the important things written in this generation, there is, in none of them a story. There is none in Proust in The Making of Americans or in Ulysses."[41] Like Joyce and Proust, who probe a collective identity by reconfiguring literary history or by welding memory to objects and places, Stein goes in search of a new organizational shape to express what communities share. If, in "Melanctha," she addresses the tensions between immigrant individual, or outsider, and community, *The Making of Americans* focuses on America as a community of outsiders. The question of how to conceptualize America as an open whole may count as the book's central issue. In *The Making of Americans* Stein famously claimed to be "writing for myself and strangers," working towards a dynamic unity or a unity-in-the-making.[42] The particular form of that unity, however, changed in the course of writing the book.

Initially, she conceived of the project as a family history. In the opening pages of the book she introduces her readers to two immigrant families, the Dehnings and the Herslands, whose "progress" she intends to unfold across three generations.[43] Stein's allusion to the *Nicomachean Ethics* at the very start of the book signals, however, that her family romance will not offer the traditional moral account of character that we may expect from such a format. In book VII of the *Nicomachean Ethics* Aristotle explains character and makes a distinction between two vices to be mastered: excessive emotion and excessive appetite. The latter is less pardonable than the former, since emotion always also implies reason. "[A]nger and bad temper," Aristotle writes

> are more natural than the appetites for excess, i.e. for unnecessary objects. Take for instance the man who defended himself on the charge of striking his father by saying "yes, but he struck his father, and he struck his, and" (pointing to his child) "this boy will strike me when he is a man; it runs in the family"; of the man who when he was being dragged along by his son bade him stop at the doorway, since he himself had dragged his father only as far as that.[44]

In *The Making of Americans* this becomes the following: "Once an angry man dragged his father along the ground through his own orchard. 'Stop!' cried the groaning old man at last, 'Stop! I did not drag my father beyond this tree.'"[45] In creatively plagiarizing Aristotle at the start of her excessive 925-page book, Stein asks us to rethink the stories and natural structures we use to account for human behavior. She inserts a caesura between the anecdote and the start of her family history, in which it is "the young mothers" who "carried these our fathers and our mothers into the new world inside them."[46] Stein's act of rewriting the typical father–son narrative, Priscilla Wald argues, announces her ambition to break with the machinery of patriarchal narrative.[47]

Including the mothers does not, however, solve Stein's problem of how to write for everyone. The format of the family history, symbolizing the nation, she realizes, cannot accommodate individual difference. "[V]ital singularity," the narrator muses,

> is as yet an unknown product with us, we who in our habits, dress-suit cases, clothes and hats and ways of thinking, walking, making money, talking, having simple lines in decorating, in ways of reforming, all with a metallic clicking like the type-writing which is our only way of thinking, our way of educating, our way of learning, all always the same way of doing, all the way down as far as there is any way down inside to us. We all are the same all through us, we never have it to be free inside to us. No brother singulars, it is sad here for us, there is no place in an adolescent world for anything eccentric like us, machine making does not turn out queer things like us, they can never make a world to let us be free each one inside us.[48]

What comes to replace the framework of a family history is that of a typology; the book shifts to "a history of every kind of men and women and of all the mixtures in them."[49] The stance of the naturalist writer that Stein seems to adopt here may be considered more objective and less moralistic than that of the family chronicler, but still the move is surprising. How can a listing of kinds or types of people further the project of understanding "vital singularity"?

The problem of individuation, and of how individuality relates to type, was a key issue in turn-of-the-century epistemological discussions. It may well have been Royce who introduced Stein to it. In 1896, Stein, as the secretary for the Radcliffe Philosophy Club, had invited Royce to give a paper at one of the Club's meetings. In his response, Royce suggested a paper on "The Principle of Individuation," which dealt with what he described as a "pretty" problem and one "of practical interest to people who desire to call their soul their own."[50] In the paper, Royce tried to configure a way round analytical thinking, which, by his account, leads to types only and thus eclipses individuality. Otto Weininger, by contrast, introduced Stein to typology as theoretical biography, which promises a combination of the abstract or analytical and the historical or individual.

Otto Weininger

Weininger is the author of the widely influential book *Sex and Character* (1903). It is a treatise on sexual types, which presents M as the ideal man and W as the ideal woman, with a continuum of gradations in between. The book's central issue is as much epistemological as it is ethical: how to "identify differences between human beings"?[51] How to know others, in other words, without, on the one hand, reverting to a supra-individual framework, a whole that subsumes individual parts – according to Weininger "[t]here is no such thing" as an empirical general psychology – or, on the other hand, of practicing a psychology without a "soul" where parts supersede the whole?[52]

From Stein's notebooks we know that she read Weininger's book keenly in 1907–8 and that she identified with the category of the male genius that it showcases. The connection between Stein and Weininger has not gone unnoticed and has baffled many, since Weininger's is an outspokenly misogynist and anti-Semitic book. For Barbara Will, for example, the implications of this connection are "potentially enormous," with Stein, a Jewish lesbian woman, reconfiguring Weininger's masculine, racist notion of the genius into "a type that cannot by typed."⁵³ With critics focusing on the effect *Sex and Character*'s categories had on Stein – both kindling her creativity and demanding an ethical reconfiguration – the drawing force of the book's composition for Stein has tended to be overlooked. *Sex and Character* reads as an essayistic search for a framework to make sense of life. The problem of how to tally an empirical, scientific approach with a concern for the larger structures making up human life that is at the heart of life philosophy is also Weininger's central problem.⁵⁴

Sex and Character, Daniel Steuer points out in his introduction, can be read as Weininger's "attempt to navigate his way between 'philosophical irrationalism and modern science.'"⁵⁵ It falls apart, in effect, in two sections: the first is concerned with biology and psychology, and the second is philosophical in scope and centers on logic and ethics. In the second part, Weininger, in echo of Dilthey, criticizes psychology for failing to grasp the fullness of lived experience: "Psychology always tries to deduce the whole from the parts and to present it as being conditional on something else, while any more profound reflection shows that the partial phenomena flow from the whole as their ultimate source."⁵⁶ What Weininger hopes to configure is a framework in which to make sense of the whole of mental life. The name he coins for that framework is theoretical biography:

> The name "theoretical biography" is intended to distinguish its territory from that of *philosophy* and *physiology* better than before, and to *expand* that biological approach which has been one-sidedly paraded and, in part, greatly exaggerated by the most recent school of psychology (Darwin, Spencer, Mach, Avenarius). Such a science would have to account for the mental life as a whole as it progresses from the birth of an individual to his death according to certain laws, just as it does for the coming into being and the passing away, and all the discrete phases in the life of a plant. And it is to be called biography, not biology, because its task is to explore the unchanging laws of the mental development of the individual. So far the history of all species has only known individuals, Bioi. But here the task would be to develop general points of view, to establish types. *Psychology would have to make a start at becoming theoretical biography.* All existing psychology could and would be absorbed in such a science and only then provide a really fruitful foundation for the humanities.⁵⁷

Clive Bush suggests that Stein took this idea very seriously and that *The Making of Americans* amounts to theoretical biography, even if he reads the book as an exercise in satire.⁵⁸ And indeed, Stein's summing up of her intentions resonates with Weininger's formulation. "[S]ometime," she announces, "sometime there will be a history of every man and every woman who ever were or are or will be living and of the kind of nature in them and the way it comes out from them from their beginning to their ending."⁵⁹

The interesting thing about the phrase "theoretical biography" is that it links the concrete or historical, with biography as the prime historical genre, to the theoretical and, as such, potentially universal. The relation of these two directions of thought is where *Sex and Character* starts. "All thinking," Weininger writes in the introduction,

> begins with *intermediate generalizations* and then develops in two different directions, one toward concepts of ever higher abstraction, which encompass ever larger areas of reality by registering properties shared between ever more things, the other toward the intersection of all conceptual lines, the concrete complex unit, the individual, which we can only approach in our thought with the help of an infinite number of qualifications and which we define by adding to the highest generalization, a "thing" or "something," an infinite number of specific distinguishing features.⁶⁰

Thinking, for Weininger, does not lead away from life, as it does for Royce, but can be seen as a vitalist act: a will to power or desire to "bring the world under [. . .] control."⁶¹ The force of Weininger's thinking in *Sex and Character* is that the book reconfigures two of the oldest concepts of humankind: man and woman. Although Weininger introduces them as ideal types, Allan Janik explains that, in Weininger,

> the Ideal Type [. . .] does not refer to a Platonic essence, but to what he termed idealized limiting cases that establish a spectrum along which the significance of empirical data can be evaluated for their cultural significance, that is, to what we would today call "models."⁶²

Models are not natural categories or ideal types but historical constructs. The spectrum of "innumerable gradations" that occur between the ideal types of M and W brings into view a dynamic continuum of culturally inflected gender expressions.⁶³ Stein's complete history as typology, then, can be read as an attempt to map the "innumerable gradations" of Americanness. If Weininger showed that sex could be distinguished from gender and thereby made possible a dynamic sexual identity – even if he notoriously filled the opening he had created by moving away from biological determinism with a new set of stereotypes – then Stein makes it her task to sketch the spectrum of American character.

The notion of character is central to the second part of *Sex and Character*. As a reaction against the fragmented approach of psychology, which he considers all too focused on "changes in the field of the sensations, the motley *world*, while completely neglecting the richness of the self," Weininger concentrates on character "understood as the concept of a constant unified being."[64] Type, for Weininger, is what the kind or "bottom nature" is for Stein. This is how Stein describes her experience of drafting a typology in *The Making of Americans*:

> Sometime each one comes to be a whole one to me. Sometime the bottom nature in each one, the other nature or natures in each one, the mixing or not mixing in them of the natures in them comes to be clear in each one, each one then is a complete one, each one then keeps repeating the whole history of them.[65]

If, for Weininger, "character is not something enthroned behind the thoughts and feelings of the individual, *but something that reveals itself in his every thought and every feeling*," then Stein underlines that "every one always is repeating the whole of them."[66] Character, for both, to put it differently, is what Dilthey calls expression. Like Weininger, Stein approaches the process of observing and describing as a very difficult hermeneutical process in which an empirical overload clouds the typological project or theoretical biography. "The worst thing," for Weininger,

> is that as the interpreter tries to derive general principles, even from successful beginnings, time and again the gravest doubts arise concerning the method for a systematic presentation of any disentangled material, forming a formidable obstacle in particular to the establishment of types.[67]

Stein, in echo, is

> [s]ometimes [. . .] almost despairing. Yes it is very hard, almost impossible I am feeling now in my despairing feeling to have completely a realising of the being in any one, when they are telling it when they are not telling it, it is so very hard to know it completely in one the being in one.[68]

Stein, too, struggles with the relationship between the abstract and the empirical, and the typology is an ambiguous affair from the start. Not only is there little logic to her kinds, which range from, for example, "servant girl being" to "the earthy type," she is also at a loss as to whether and how many "kinds in kinds" there may be, and, most importantly, how she can tally her typological project with her growing fascination for individual lives and expressions.[69]

From genius interpreter to portraitist

For Weininger, it takes a genius to be up to the task of interpreting the scope of human character. In the chapter "Endowment and Genius," Weininger echoes Dilthey's project of seeing typically. At the heart of the chapter is an understanding of a genius as a supreme seer, someone who "understands incomparably more than the average person" and is capable of "liv[ing] in all human beings."[70] Understanding, for Weininger, implies the processes of recreating and appreciating another person's actions without negating one's own experiences. As he sums it up, it "means being **also** that person."[71] Like Dilthey, in other words, he connects the quality of genius to the hermeneutical process of "finding the I in the Thou." The references to his comments on understanding in this chapter, not surprisingly, come with lengthy quotes from Dilthey's essay "Contributions to the Study of Individuality." In that essay Dilthey too teams up reproductive understanding with the quality of genius. "*[I]nterpretation* as the art of reproductive understanding," Weininger quotes Dilthey, "always contains an element of genius, that is, it can achieve a high degree of perfection only through internal affinity and sympathy."[72]

Stein's identification with the Weiningerian concept of genius, I argue, is important not only because it strengthened her beliefs in her own creative abilities, but also because it relates her project to a hermeneutics of life. In connecting the quality of genius with life, she too stresses the converging of experiences. "[T]he essence of genius, of being most intensely alive," for Stein, amounts to

> being one who is at the same time talking and listening [. . .] doing both things, not as if there were one thing, not as if they were two things, but doing them, well if you like, like the motor going inside and the car moving, they are part of the same thing.[73]

Talking and listening, or acting and re-acting, goes to the heart of the double, open-ended hermeneutical process that Dilthey theorized and that Gadamer would later label the hermeneutical conversation. Stein's car metaphor, furthermore, is more than a curious instance of her love of cars. "The car moving" can be read as a comment on Aristotle's moving cause, which consists of a force apart from the thing moving. By extension, Stein's "car moving" functions as a comment on a classic vitalism in which movement is presented as depending on an agent or active principle, rather than as a holistic, interactive process, which is the way in which turn-of-the-century "vitalist" life philosophers tended to view movement.[74]

Bringing Dilthey's "Contributions to the Study of Individuality" into focus helps us understand how *The Making of Americans* shifts from large-scale typology to portraiture. The prompt for Stein's typology as a "complete history" is Weininger's suggestion that it is the genius's prerogative to see the complete picture:

> the more human types together with their opposites an individual unites in [the genius's] personality, the less he will *miss* of what people do and do not do [. . .] the exceptional individual often gets the complete picture of simpler people at the first glance and is often able to characterize them fully at once.[75]

Stein increasingly becomes fascinated by individuals, however, and two-thirds of the way into *The Making of Americans*, she stops investing in a complete panorama of American character and embarks on a lengthy portrait of one individual, David Hersland. As she remembers it in "The Making of The Making of Americans," it was "[w]hile [she] was listening and hearing and feeling the rhythm of each human being" that she became "very consciously obsessed" with the problem of writing down "a whole human being felt at one and the same time, in other words while in the act of feeling that person."[76] Gradually, she opens up the process of writing to the historical dimensions of the hermeneutical process. She positions both herself and the individuals she is portraying in time and tackles the issue of how to relate the moment of knowing (the part) to the whole that is living.

In order not to face the double problem of writing about ongoing experience from the position of ongoing experience, Stein announces the death of her subject. What she will cover, she announces at the start of the David Hersland portrait, is the "living that David Hersland did before he came to be a dead one."[77] That gives her the space to concentrate on her own experience of knowing, which she considered a "terrible trouble."[78] In fact, what she has to say about the "living that David Hersland did" can often be read as a comment on her own changing project. In a sense, the character David Hersland is a figure for Stein's writing of *The Making of Americans*, so when she writes that David did not really feel that life amounts to change until the middle of his life, this reflects on her own revamping of *The Making of Americans*:

> David Hersland was realising all his living that changing is existing in every one and he was not really feeling this thing, really seeing this thing until the middle of the beginning of his middle living and then he was loving this thing and looking at each one and thinking about this thing and living in this thing, and being a little frightened by this thing and being contented by this thing, and being convinced of this thing and telling it to himself about each one he was knowing and being certain that being living was a thing being existing and being then almost completely certain of this thing. He was then one who came to be a dead one at the beginning of the middle of his middle living and he had been one who has been almost completely fully living in changing being existing in every one being living.[79]

David's waking up to life's dynamics in "the middle of the beginning of his middle living," here, more or less coincides with his death, since that is to be situated "at the beginning of the middle of his middle living." Stein's encounter with "being living" as ongoing change, in other words, announces the end of *The Making of Americans'* ambitions to understand everyone. Complete understanding shifts from drawn-out panorama to shorter encounters, with the portraits Stein would start writing around 1909.

In concentrating on her own experience of knowing, the issue that troubled Stein the most was that of "how to make a whole present of something that it had taken a great deal of time to find out."[80] How, in other words, to integrate the process of getting-to-know into the moment of knowing? In "Contributions to the Study of Individuality," Dilthey illuminates the process of understanding by arguing that "all our mental powers are active" in "each fulfilled moment of life." Such a moment, he explains, "is linked to our person like the predicate to the subject" and "always, if ever so dimly, related to the totality of our life and located within it."[81] As in the hermeneutic circle, subject and predicate are bound in an interactive relationship, depending on each other. In "The Making of The

Making of Americans," Stein, too, refers to grammar to clarify her attempts at writing down "a whole present":

> And this brings us to the question of grammar [...] my sentences grew longer and longer, my imaginary dependent clauses were constantly being dropped out, I struggled with relations between they them and then, I began with a relation between tenses that sometimes almost seemed to do it.[82]

Stein's struggles with grammar enable us to see the book as a dynamic network of part–whole relationships. The long paragraphs she experiments with are meant to stress the fact that sentences, or parts, have little meaning on their own and need to be seen as part of a larger structure.

Stein's shift from a panoramic, theoretical biography to a concern for "the living that David Hersland did," and her knowing and writing about that living, shows her moving away from Weininger and into the direction of a Diltheyan hermeneutics of life. If, for Weininger, a genius interpreter is a controlling force who stands outside of time and history, then Dilthey underlines the extent to which the interpreter is affected by the process of interpretation.[83] Interestingly, Dilthey uses portraiture as a metaphor for understanding, or seeing typically. More than in Weininger, Dilthey's seer and seen, or portraitist and portrayed, are engaged in an interactive, contextualized encounter. For Dilthey, the "point of impression," a concept he coins for the point from which the structure of what we are looking at is acquired,

> is ultimately conditioned by the relation of something living to my own life. I find myself inwardly touched in my life-nexus by something productive in another being; from this point of life, I understand the aspects converging there. Thus a type emerges. An individual is the original type; every genuine portrait is a type [...].[84]

Another term that Dilthey uses for one's inner "life-nexus" is "liveliness," which of course underlines the dynamic nature of the constellation of historical and psychological structures that is the nexus. Stein, too, uses liveliness to explain how she experienced the time when she was moving beyond the typological project of *The Making of Americans*. "I was coming to be livelier in relation to myself inside me and in relation to any one inside them," she writes in *Lectures in America*.[85] As a consequence, her writing became livelier as well. The portraits Stein works on while finishing *The Making of Americans* are written in a style similar to that of the paragraphs in which she tries to portray "the whole being" of David Hersland, but her subjects are not dead. She starts writing portraits of the people surrounding her, affecting her: Mabel Dodge, Matisse, Picasso and many others.

Notes

1. Astrid Lorange, *How Reading is Written: A Brief Index to Gertrude Stein* (Middletown, CT: Wesleyan University Press, 2014), 9. Lorange quotes from Shaviro, *Without Criteria*.
2. Natalia Cecire, "Ways of Not Reading Gertrude Stein," *ELH* 82.1 (2015).
3. Tanya E. Clement, "'A thing not beginning and not ending': using digital tools to distant-read Gertrude Stein's *The Making of Americans*," *Literary and Linguistic Computing*, 23.3 (2008).
4. On Stein's network poetics see Sarah Posman and Laura Luise Schultz, "One Who Was Networking," introduction to *Gertrude Stein in Europe: Reconfigurations Across Media, Disciplines and Traditions*, ed. Sarah Posman and Laura Luise Schultz (London: Bloomsbury, 2015).
5. Gertrude Stein, "G.M.P.," in *Matisse, Picasso and Gertrude Stein, with Two Shorter Stories* (Mineola, NY: Dover Publications, 2000), 214.
6. Susan Sontag, *Against Interpretation and Other Essays* (London: Penguin, 2009) 7.
7. Gertrude Stein, *Q.E.D.*, in *Writings: 1903–1932*, ed. Harriet Scott Chessman and Catharine R. Stimpson (New York: Library of America, 1998), 3.
8. Here, the central character, Melanctha, is repeatedly characterized in terms of understanding. We get to know her as, consecutively, someone who "could not learn to understand" / "would try to learn to understand" / "grew stronger in her desire to really understand" / "certainly did begin to really understand" / "began to really understand." She furthermore helps her lover, Jeff, understand her until he is "really understanding" (Gertrude Stein, *Three Lives*, in *Writings: 1903–1932*, ed. Harriet Scott Chessman and Catharine R. Stimpson (New York: Library of America, 1998), 135, 137, 138, 140, 171).
9. Stein, *The Making of Americans*, 294.
10. As Tim Murphy notes, Dilthey occasionally uses the term "Struktur" but he "much prefers the term *der Zusammenhang* to describe this structuring activity of consciousness" (Tim Murphy, *The Politics of Spirit: Phenomenology, Genealogy, Religion* (Albany: State University of New York Press, 2010), 139).
11. Stein, *Q.E.D.*, 63.
12. Ibid., 3–4.

13. Stein, *Three Lives*, 125.
14. F. H. Hitchcock, "Letter to Gertrude Stein, 9 April 1909," in *The Flowers of Friendship: Letters Written to Gertrude Stein*, ed. Donald Gallup (New York: Knopf, 1953), 43.
15. Richard Bridgman, *Gertrude Stein in Pieces* (New York: Oxford University Press, 1970), 46.
16. Stein, *Three Lives*, 66.
17. See Emanuela Gutkowski, "Gertrude Stein and Jules Laforgue: A Comparative Approach," *European Journal of American Culture* 22.1 (2003): 125–38.
18. Charles Altieri, "Reading Bradley after Reading Laforgue: How Eliot Transformed Symbolist Poetics into a Paradigmatic Modernism," *Modern Language Quarterly* 72.2 (2011): 226.
19. Laforgue quoted in Arthur Symons, *The Symbolist Movement in Literature* (London: William Heinemann, 1899), 9, available at: <https://openlibrary.org/books/OL6907922M/The_symbolist_movement_in_literature> (last accessed September 3, 2021).
20. Ibid., 111.
21. Stein, *Three Lives*, 89.
22. On "Melanctha" in relation to Melancthon, see also: John Carlos Rowe, *Afterlives of Modernism: Liberalism, Transnationalism and Political Critique* (Hanover, NH: Dartmouth College Press, 2011), 39.
23. Dilthey, "The Rise of Hermeneutics," 244.
24. On Dilthey and empathy, see, for example, Austin Harrington, "Dilthey, Empathy and Verstehen: A Contemporary Reappraisal." *European Journal of Social Theory* 4.3 (August 2001): 311–29. Available at <https://doi.org/10.1177/13684310122225145> (last accessed September 27, 2021).
25. Dilthey, "The Rise of Hermeneutics," 244.
26. Ibid., 243.
27. Anonymous review of *Three Lives*, originally published in the *Nation* 90 (20 January 1910), 65 and reprinted in Michael J. Hoffman, *Critical Essays on Gertrude Stein* (Boston: G. K. Hall, 1986), 27.
28. Stein, *Three Lives*, 236.
29. Dilthey, *Drafts for a Critique of Historical Reason*, 235.
30. Stein, *Three Lives*, 133, 193.
31. Ibid., 239.
32. Ibid., 163, 136.
33. Jayne L. Walker, *The Making of a Modernist: Gertrude Stein from* Three Lives *to* Tender Buttons (Amherst: University of Massachusetts Press, 1984), 22, 25.
34. Charles Bernstein, *A Poetics* (Cambridge, MA: Harvard University Press, 1992), 147–8.
35. Stein, *Lectures in America*, 195.
36. Stein, *Three Lives*, 151–2.
37. Ibid., 154.
38. Stein, *Lectures in America*, 275.

39. Josiah Royce, "Is There a Science of Education?," *Educational Review* 1.1 (1891), 18, available at: <https://royce-edition.iupui.edu/wp-content/uploads/2018/10/1891-Royce-Is-There-a-Science-of-Education.-I.pdf>.
40. Royce, "Is There a Science of Education?," 19.
41. Stein, *Lectures in America*, 299.
42. Stein, *The Making of Americans*, 289.
43. Ibid., 4.
44. Aristotle, *Nicomachean Ethics*, trans. W. D. Ross, in *The Complete Works of Aristotle*, ed. Jonathan Barnes, vol. 2 (Princeton, NJ: Princeton University Press, 1984), 3897.
45. Stein, *The Making of Americans*, 3.
46. Ibid., 3.
47. Priscilla Wald, *Constituting Americans: Cultural Anxiety and Narrative Form* (Durham, NC: Duke University Press, 1995), 252.
48. Stein, *The Making of Americans*, 47.
49. Ibid., 176.
50. James R. Mellow, *Charmed Circle: Gertrude Stein & Company* (New York: Praeger, 1974), 43.
51. Otto Weininger, *Sex and Character: An Investigation of Fundamental Principles*, trans. Ladislaus Löb, ed. Daniel Steuer with Laura Marcus (Bloomington: Indiana University Press, 2005), 124.
52. Ibid., 135, 175.
53. Barbara Will, *Gertrude Stein, Modernism and the Problem of 'Genius'* (Edinburgh: Edinburgh University Press, 2000), 66.
54. In writing the book, which earned him his doctoral degree, Weininger drew on two earlier academic dissertations he had written, one called *Eros und Psyche*, which deals with love, and the other *Zur Theorie des Lebens*, which presents a theory of individuation.
55. Daniel Steuer, "A Book That Won't Go Away: Otto Weininger's *Sex and Character*," in *Sex and Character: An Investigation of Fundamental Principles*, trans. Ladislaus Löb, ed. Daniel Steuer with Laura Marcus (Bloomington: Indiana University Press, 2005), xxviii.
56. Weininger, *Sex and Character*, 183.
57. Ibid., 114.
58. Clive Bush, *Halfway to Revolution: Investigation and Crisis in the Work of Henry Adams, William James and Gertrude Stein* (New Haven, CT: Yale University Press, 1991), 68.
59. Stein, *The Making of Americans*, 176.
60. Weininger, *Sex and Character*, 9.
61. Ibid., 9.
62. See Allan Janik, *Wittgenstein's Vienna Revisited* (New Brunswick, NJ: Transaction, 2001), 48–9, quoted in Steuer, "A Book That Won't Go Away," xxxix.
63. Weininger, *Sex and Character*, 13; Steuer, "A Book That Won't Go Away," xxxix.
64. Ibid., 72.

65. Stein, *The Making of Americans*, 309.
66. Weininger, *Sex and Character*, 72; Stein, *The Making of Americans*, 294.
67. Weininger, *Sex and Character*, 70.
68. Stein, *The Making of Americans*, 458.
69. Ibid., 172, 359, 344.
70. Weininger, *Sex and Character*, 94, 93.
71. Ibid., 93, emphasis in the original; Ibid., 356. Weininger misunderstands Dilthey ("in this respect I differ from both").
72. Ibid., 355.
73. Stein, *Lectures in America*, 290.
74. See Juliana Chow, "Motion Studies," for more on this quotation in relation to vitalism.
75. Weininger, *Sex and Character*, 97.
76. Stein, *Lectures in America*, 276.
77. Stein, *The Making of Americans*, 724.
78. Stein, *Lectures in America*, 277.
79. Stein, *The Making of Americans*, 844.
80. Stein, *Lectures in America*, 278.
81. Wilhelm Dilthey, *Contributions to the Study of Individuality*, in *Understanding the Human World*, ed. Rudolf A. Makkreel and Frithjof Rodi, Vol. 2 of Dilthey, *Selected Works* (Princeton, NJ: Princeton University Press, 2010), 244.
82. Stein, *Lectures in America*, 278.
83. Weininger, *Sex and Character*, 115, 122.
84. Dilthey, *Contributions to the Study of Individuality*, 249–50.
85. Stein, *Lectures in America*, 280.

PART II

THE CINEMA, OR BEGINNING AGAIN

The portraits Stein started making around 1909, when she was finishing *The Making of Americans*, both continued that project and initiated a new direction.[1] "In the beginning," Stein dramatizes in "Portraits and Repetition," "I continued to do what I was doing in the Making of Americans, I was doing what the cinema was doing, I was making a continuous succession of what that person was until I had not many things but one thing."[2] In tune with *The Making of Americans*, Stein wanted to make a "whole" or "complete" portrait. Yet where she had framed her big book as a history project, she now wants us to look at her texts as cinematic compositions. On the one hand, this is not as odd a step as it may seem. If the pursuit of life itself was central in theoretical discussions on hermeneutics and history, then the cinema of the 1890s and early 1900s, as we will see, was actually considered to capture life itself. The cinema appeared to make it possible to keep the very movements of life in the here and now from fading into the past. Both the tradition of historical reflection that we have been discussing and the cinema, in other words, were seen as ways into life that trumped either older (idealist or positivist) philosophical approaches, or technologies and art forms (photography and painting). On the other hand, Stein's cinema claim is not unproblematic. Where she conceived of all three of the early texts we have discussed as histories, there are few data that actually relate her 1910s texts to the cinema. Even when we take into consideration the two never-produced film scripts she wrote in 1920 and 1929, and the texts she contributed to the film magazine *Close Up* in 1927, there is little that links her work to early twentieth-century cinema.[3] In "Portraits and Repetition," Stein even admits that she "doubt[s] whether at that time [she] had ever seen a cinema." Yet that does not seem to undercut the cinematic quality of her texts. "[A]ny one is of one's period," she explains, "and this our period was undoubtedly the period of the cinema and series production. And each of us in our own way are bound to express what the world in which we are living is doing."[4] While critics have approached Stein's claim that she was doing what the cinema was doing as a prompt to explore the formal analogies between her work and the cinema, they have tended to sidestep the claim's seemingly determinist *Zeitgeist* justification.[5] I argue we need to unpack it. Cinema is key to understanding Stein's thinking post *The Making of Americans*. As a lens that replaced history for grasping "existing," it helps us understand the ways in which she attempted to make sense of her moment.

Stein's shift from history to the cinema, as she presents it in "Portraits and Repetition," hinges on the double problem of how to understand time moving, which is a philosophical issue, and life changing, which straddles the biological and the historical. She starts the lecture by pitting a traditional way of "realizing" the movement of existence against a new mode. If the old way of thinking about movement distorts movement, the new way succeeds in showing it to be "a real thing." By Stein's account, we tend to make sense of lived time through collisions. "But the strange thing about the realization of existence," she writes, "is that like a train moving there is no real realization of it moving if it does not move against something and so that is what a generation does it shows that moving is existing."[6] Time moving, in this train logic, amounts to a sequence of crashes, end points, deaths. By relating such stops to the function of a generation ("that is what a generation does"), she comments on a philosophy of history that cuts up time into different, and clashing, sections. Such a perspective informs the start of *The Making of Americans*, where she rehearses the age-old father–son conflict and has the narrator claim that "[w]e need only realize our parents, remember our grandparents and know ourselves and our history is complete."[7] The book itself, of course, does not follow this through. What actually qualifies her generation, she underlines in "Portraits and Repetition," is a new understanding of movement, in which stops and starts are no longer necessary: "this generation has conceived an intensity of movement so great that it has not to be seen against something else to be known."[8] If this sounds vague, she fills it in a couple of pages into the lecture when she relates the differential movement of life or "existing" to the cinema. Mapping time through habits, calendars or a "coming and going" may lead to a deadening repetition, but:

[e]xisting as a human being [. . .] is never repetition. It is not repetition if it is that which you are actually doing because naturally each time the emphasis is different just as the cinema has each time a slightly different thing to make it all be moving. And each of us has to do that, otherwise there is no existing.[9]

While "Portraits and Repetition" makes it seem evident that a bloodless historical approach to time was replaced by a cinematic understanding of time, "history" and "the cinema" obviously do not amount to clear-cut lenses. In what follows I flesh out the conversations relevant to Stein's grappling with the "intensity of movement" that she associates with her generation. Indeed, the concept of generation is the cue that leads me into an early twentieth-century network of texts probing how to conceive of time moving and of life changing.

Notes

1. There is some discussion on when Stein started writing portraits and which texts should be considered portraits. Wendy Steiner, for example, gives 1908 as the earliest date, whereas Ulla Dydo refers to the 1910 text "Ada" as possibly "the very first portrait Stein wrote" (Wendy Steiner, *Exact Resemblance to Exact Resemblance: The Literary Portraiture of Gertrude Stein* (New Haven, CT, and London: Yale University Press, 1978), 64; Dydo, *Stein Reader*, 100). I think we should follow Stein in working with an open definition of portraiture. She calls *Tender Buttons* (1912) portraits, for example, even though she also makes clear that the text is very different from the people portraits she had been writing in the years before. When we consider Stein's portraits as developing out of *The Making of Americans* I think we can situate the start of her portrait writing around 1909, when she started on "A Long Gay Book," which Steiner situates among Stein's novels.
2. Stein, *Lectures in America*, 294.
3. In June 1927, Kenneth Macpherson, editor of the newly established *Close Up: A Quarterly Devoted to the Art of Films*, solicited work from Stein. In his letter he wrote that he considered her work "exactly the kind of thing that could be translated to the screen" (Kenneth Macpherson, Letter, June 24, 1927, *The Flowers of Friendship: Letters Written to Gertrude Stein*, ed. Donald Gallup (New York: Alfred A. Knopf, 1953), 208). Stein sent in "Mrs Emerson," which was published in the 1927 August *Close-Up* issue, and the longer "Three Sitting Here," which was spread over the September and October issues. On Stein's two film scripts, "A Movie" (1920) and "Film. Deux Soeurs

Qui ne Sont Pas Soeurs" (1929), see Sarah Bay-Cheng, *Mama Dada: Gertrude Stein's Avant-Garde Theater* (New York: Routledge, 2005), and Abigail Lang's "Stein and Cinematic Identity," in *Gertrude Stein in Europe: Reconfigurations Across Media, Disciplines and Traditions*, ed. Sarah Posman and Laura Luise Schultz (London: Bloomsbury, 2015).
4. Stein, *Lectures in America*, 294.
5. See especially Susan McCabe, *Cinematic Modernism: Modernist Poetry and Film* (Cambridge: Cambridge University Press, 2005); Julian Murphet, "Gertrude Stein's Machinery of Perception," in J. Murphet and L. Rainford, eds, *Literature and Visual Technologies* (London: Palgrave Macmillan, 2003); and Heike Schaefer's chapter "'Making a Cinema of It.' Seriality and Presence in Gertrude Stein's Early Portraits," in her *American Literature and Immediacy: Literary Innovation and the Emergence of Photography, Film and Television* (Cambridge: Cambridge University Press, 2020).
6. Stein, *Lectures in America*, 287.
7. Stein, *The Making of Americans*, 3.
8. Stein, *Lectures in America*, 287.
9. Ibid., 295.

Chapter 3

Generation

"Portraits and Repetition" can be considered a sequel to Stein's attempt at a manifesto, "Composition as Explanation." That text, as I have pointed out in the Introduction, is largely concerned with the question of how to make sense of Stein's (artistic) generation. That is not a surprising concern for Stein. The idea of experience as a network or a nexus in relation to history had occupied her since the early 1900s. Yet where, in line with Dilthey's project, her early work had considered such a nexus to provide access to human nature, the work she engages in around 1909 is acutely concerned with the composition of the nexus she feels part of. Composition is one of Stein's central ideas and she uses it to refer both to the constellations in which we live (like that of a generation or a city) and to the way in which we frame knowledge about our shared lives (for instance, by means of a typology or a complete history). "Portraits and Repetition" starts with a reference to "Composition as Explanation," spotlighting the problem of change across generations. "In Composition as Explanation," Stein writes, "I said nothing changes from generation to generation except the composition in which we live and the composition in which we live makes the art which we see and hear."[1] Generation is a key problem in both texts. Tracing the ways in which Stein approaches it enables us to understand how her project intersects with a wider early twentieth-century conversation on the structures and forms we use to make sense of time. I start by focusing on "Composition as Explanation" and work my way towards Stein's claim that her period is "of the cinema" in "Portraits and Repetition."

The first lines of "Composition as Explanation" read as the response to a set of unformulated questions. Stein appears to ask what makes time move and what makes generations different from each other, and then responds:

> There is singularly nothing that makes a difference a difference in beginning and in the middle and in ending except that each generation has something different at which they are all looking. By this I mean so simply that anybody knows it that composition is the difference which makes each and all of them then different from other generations and this is what makes everything different otherwise they are all alike and everybody knows it because everybody says it.

Generations, for Stein, are made by a differential force: composition. When she defines composition as "the difference which makes each and all of them then different from other generations," she opposes the idea that there is some kind of external regulator to the rhythm of history or a mysterious inner rhythm to life. "There is singularly nothing that makes a difference" except composition and what a composition "is" depends on an internal dynamics, something like a *Weltanschauung* or mode of experience. Or, with Stein, "[t]he only thing that is different from one time to another is what is seen and what is seen and what is seen depends on how everybody is doing everything."[2]

The question of whether there is a particular rhythm to the course of history that creates generations has fascinated thinkers since the Enlightenment. Theoretical reflection on the idea of generation as a category for social and cultural–historical research, however, only really started in the beginning of the nineteenth century, in the context of the German Historical School and French sociology.[3] Ranke, for example, conceived of generations as "rows of shining figures who themselves are closely related and in whose antithesis the development of the world continues to progress," and Auguste Comte, in *Cours de philosophie positive* (1830–42), considered the motor of historical change to be the succession of generations, determined by death.[4] After the shared trauma of World War One, the concept of generation once again fueled theoretical reflection. José Ortega y Gasset's *El tema de nuestro tiempo* (1923) and Karl Mannheim's "Das Problem der Generationen" (1928) are the more famous contemporaries of Stein's interest in the concept.[5]

Ortega y Gasset's project at large challenged positivist approaches to history by addressing the connectedness of individual lives and the meaning of history from a phenomenological and existentialist viewpoint. His essay "The Concept of the Generation," however, comes with clear naturalist echoes. "A generation," he writes, "is a variety of the human race in the strict sense given to that term by naturalists. Its members come into the world endowed with certain typical characteristics which lend them a common physiognomy, distinguishing them from the previous generation." Generations, for Ortega y Gasset, are time slots. Change between them is determined by a mysterious "pulse-beat" in the evolution of the human race and there is nothing that can influence the "melody" of those pulse-beats. We should rather "picture each generation by means of the image of a biological projectile launched into space at a definite moment and with pre-determined force and direction."[6] Mannheim, by contrast, critiques the idea that there is a particular rhythm to historical life. He starts his *Essay on the Problem of Generations* by criticizing a quantitative approach to the issue. The idea that we would be able to pinpoint what a generation is by equating it with a particular time span is, by his account, a naïve total answer to the problem of life. The idea of a neat sequence of generations, each typically spanning thirty years, serves a liberal agenda that wants us to think there is a unilinear, dependable course to history. For his own, stratified, account of the concept of generation, Mannheim draws on the qualitative approach of what he refers to as the German "romantic–historical approach," and in particular on the work of Dilthey and the art historian Wilhelm Pinder. Their work, he argues, makes it possible to propose a concept that is less a marker of progress than of lived experience – of how people were seeing and doing things.[7]

In an 1875 essay on the history of human sciences, social science and political science, "Über das Studium der Geschichte der Wisschenschaften vom Menschen, der Gesellschaft und dem Staat," Dilthey had defined the concept of generation as "a signification for a relation of the contemporaneity of individuals."[8] He considered shared (formative) experience to be more important than date of birth. For Dilthey, Mannheim explains, the idea of generation as shared experience offered an "inner" alternative to "external" temporal units such as years or decades. A generation, then, was no longer "a mere chronological datum," but "a state of being." Dilthey thus cleared the way for a phenomenological approach, even if he limited his own research with "happy restraint" to the "genuine" factual historical data.[9] Pinder, but also Martin Heidegger, took up where Dilthey left off, and tried in different ways to grasp the inner workings of a generation. Where Heidegger's *Being and Time* (1927) elaborated on the idea of "fate," as "a distinct set of possibilities determin[ing] the direction of individual destinies in advance," Pinder proposed an inner dynamic or entelechy peculiar to generations.[10]

Key to Pinder's 1926 *Das Problem der Generation in der Kunstgeschichte Europas* (The Problem of Generation in Europe's Art History) is the idea of multiple times. The art historian complicates the notion of contemporaneity by adding "non-contemporaneity" to the discussion, pointing out that there are always different rhythms at play in a particular context: different pasts and futures that qualify time.

> Everyone lives with people of the same and of different ages, with a variety of possibilities of experience facing them all alike. But for each, "the same time," is a different time – that is, it represents a different *period of his self*, which he can only share with people of his own age.[11]

Moments of time, then, become temporal volumes with multiple dimensions, polyphonic in nature. He furthermore considered different generations to have a particular entelechy or Aristotelian actualization process that makes them into qualitative unities. Where, for Dilthey, a generation's "quality" is the result of a passive "imprint" of shared historical factors, Pinder opts for an active dynamic. He sees an "inner aim" or particular worldview at work in generations. That is an idea, Mannheim takes care to indicate, that builds on Alois Riegl's concept of *Kunstwollen*, first proposed in his 1893 volume *Stilfragen* (Questions of Style).[12] The much-debated idea of a *Kunstwollen*, which translates literally as "artistic volition," has had a major impact on modern aesthetics because it asks that we look at art not from the perspective of the intention of the artist but to consider style, or composition, as a formal response to a set of historical circumstances. Pinder translates Riegl's idea of a particular style "willing" or "thinking" to the concept of the generation; a particular generation is not merely "imprinted" by historical circumstance, but has a particular mode of making to it.

Although Mannheim wishes to distinguish his sociology from what he considered Pinder's "excessive" romantic speculative analogies between nature and artistic creativity that ignore the social, and sharply criticizes the art historian's goal to work out a "world-rhythm," he considers both the idea of a non-contemporaneous contemporaneity and the concept of entelechy "a stroke of genius." He even wonders whether he could not use the entelechy concept to come to a better understanding of the creative or generative power of society. "Perhaps," he reflects,

> it would also be fruitful to ask ourselves whether society can produce nothing more than "influences" and "relationships," or whether on the contrary, social factors also possess a certain creative energy, a

formative power, a social entelechy of their own. Is it not perhaps possible that this energy, arising from the interplay of social forces, constitutes the link between the other entelechies of art, style, generation, etc., which would otherwise only accidentally cross paths or come together?[13]

The question of how to understand the dynamics of the relationship between social factors, individual creativity and artistic style is an important motif in Mannheim's essay. With concepts such as influence and relationship failing to do justice to the complexity of what constitutes a particular social or artistic constellation, how to understand its dynamics? Stein tackled that question, too, and, similarly to Mannheim, she paused at the idea of a formative power or entelechy – be it in Steinian terms.

When Stein starts "Composition as Explanation" with the claim that "nothing changes from generation to generation," she can be seen to side with the Dilthey/Pinder/Mannheim line of approach to the concept of generation. For Stein, in contrast to Ortega y Gasset, there is no "rhythm of the ages," no out-of-this-world projectile or historical pendulum. Change cannot be grasped by means of external markers such as periods or generations, typically taken to span a rough thirty years. "One does mean any period of time by a generation," she contends in "Portraits and Repetition." Because, for Stein, a generation may just as well span two years or a whole century, generations are "not important" as temporal categories. They are important, however, as "period[s] of living."[14] Change over time, Stein argues, does not simply happen in life, as if life is a mere container for change. What changes, rather, is the way in which life is made, or, as Stein puts it, "conducted" or composed. "Each period of living differs from any other period of living," she explains, "not in the way life is but in the way life is conducted and that authentically speaking is composition."[15] She considers that process of conducting or composing life to be an active practice, but she does not know how to grasp it. In attempting to describe it, she grants it an autonomous character: "it makes a composition, it confuses, it shows, it is, it looks, it likes it as it is [. . .]."[16] It may not be clear what it is, but in escaping the complete control of the individuals engaged in it, it has a certain power that transcends the individual maker. Like Pinder and Mannheim, furthermore, she is fascinated by the non-contemporaneity of the contemporary. Some of Stein's contemporaries may have been trumpeting that they were ahead of their time, but for Stein that makes no sense. "No one is ahead of his time," she writes, "it is only that the particular variety of creating his time is the one that his contemporaries who also are creating their own time refuse to accept."[17] A generation, then, is a composing of different tendencies, or "a space that is filled with moving," as she puts in it another lecture, which only gradually reveals a particular direction.[18] The ambiguity of the word composition enables Stein to make an analogy between the creation of a composition-as-text, of which she writes that "[n]aturally one does not know how it happened until it is well over beginning happening," and the creation of a composition-as-generation, of which she states that "[a]fter life has been conducted in a certain way everybody knows it but nobody knows it, little by little, nobody knows it as long as nobody knows it."[19] In doing so, she asks us to think about the process of actualization, or entelechy.

Entelechy

Like generation, the concept of entelechy, which was first coined by Aristotle, was part of an early twentieth-century conversation on the question of how life moves, how it originates and changes. Mannheim picks it up in Pinder, but it also occupies a central position in the work of the biologist Hans Driesch, and Henri Bergson's concept of the *élan vital* can be read as a variation on the idea. For early twentieth-century thinkers contemplating life, be it social life as in Mannheim's case, biological life as in the case of Hans Driesch and Bergson, or the life of art as for Stein in "Composition as Explanation," entelechy was a concept that made it possible to think about creation and creativity: life making change rather than life as something in which change occurs. Their interpretations of the idea, furthermore, differ considerably from Aristotle's.

Entelechy is a central concept in Aristotle's theory of movement. One of the works in which he explains it, and with which Stein would have been familiar from her student days, is *De Generatione Animalium* – generation as the process of generating is, of course, part of Stein's interest in the concept of generation. *De Generatione* is one of Aristotle's key texts on biology and central to it is the attempt to explain the process of embryonic development. Aristotle's ideas, as many scholars have noted, are relevant to modern scientific inquiry.[20] One of the most important conclusions he reached is that living beings develop out of matter that has the potential to form them. This formative or generative process needs to be actualized by an impulse. Matter, in other words, has to be triggered in order to generate. The word Aristotle coined for the process in which potentiality becomes actualized is entelechy. Because, in *De Generatione*, entelechy sums up the process by which an embryo grows into an animal, an acorn into an oak or a boy into a man, it is sometimes translated as the process of perfection, as that which carries its "end" or "completion" inside it. The term entelechy, however, is an intricate combination of concepts, and translation is far from straightforward. As Joe Sachs explains, the concept contains "enteles (complete, full-grown) with echein (= hexis, to be a certain way by the continuing effort of holding on to that condition), while at the same time punning on endelecheia (persistence) by inserting telos (completion)." Sachs translates it as "being-at-work-staying-itself," which captures the dynamics of the concept better than perfection.[21]

Aristotle considered the process of entelechy, which he sometimes also refers to as "energeia," more important than the potential to change, or what he called "dunamis." In his *Metaphysics* he grants actuality priority over potentiality for two reasons. The first is that "the actuality is the end."[22] What something is, for Aristotle, is determined by a final causality. Second, actuality trumps potentiality because he considers the actual-as-eternal prior to the potential. Anything with the potential to be can also not be. Only the eternal, as completely actual, is imperishable. This relation between potential and actual is what early twentieth-century vitalist thinkers would reconsider.

Hans Driesch's and Henri Bergson's vitalist projects were landmarks in the early twentieth-century intellectual landscape. Both, in different ways, reconfigured the project of what Frederick Burwick and Paul Douglass have called a "naïve vitalism," which posits an inert substance as life's essence. The modernist "critical vitalism" of Driesch and Bergson tried to conceptualize a dynamic life impulse in the context of an energy-focused ontology.[23] They were not, of course, the first to think of life in terms of force rather than substance. As George Rousseau points out, the most important text to effect that in the context of modern science was a late eighteenth-century essay by Johan Friedrich Blumenbach, *Über den Bildungstrieb und das Zeugungsgeschäfte*, which was translated into English as *Essay on Generation*.[24] As an alternative to the doctrine of preformationism, according to which an organism is "pre-formed" and does not essentially change when it develops (think of the homunculus as the miniature man), Blumenbach posited the idea of formative drive or *Bildungstrieb*. He considered it a universal and constantly active force, in line with Newtonian gravity. More than a century later, Driesch commended Blumenbach's work in biology as the event that made it possible to "move beyond the achievements of Aristotle" because it divorced the actual from the eternal.[25]

Hans Driesch had made a career as a biologist when, early in the twentieth century, he turned to a philosophical vitalism that sought to surpass older vitalist theories about the essence of life. Central to Driesch's vitalism is the question of whether the purposiveness of life can be considered "the result of an autonomy peculiar to the processes [of life]" rather than to any inorganic building blocks.[26] Although he still situates Blumenbach in the tradition of the old vitalism, he shares his interest in the issue of a formative drive. Reflecting on his scientific observations with regard to the process of morphogenesis, which is the process from fertilized egg to grown organism, he notes: "Why then occurs all that folding and bending [...], and all the other processes we have described? There must be something that drives them out, so to say." For that animating and forming mechanism, Driesch used the Aristotelian concept of entelechy, claiming the right to reinterpret the idea. As he explains in *The Science and Philosophy of the Organism*:

> Let us then borrow our terminology from Aristotle, and let that factor in life phenomena which we have shown to be a factor of true autonomy be called Entelechy, though without identifying our doctrine with what Aristotle meant by the word ἐντελέχεια [...] his word is to be a mould which we have filled and shall fill with new contents.[27]

Entelechy, for Driesch, is to be understood as "an intensive manifoldness."[28] Struck by the apparent observation that a complex organism seems to occur out of an undifferentiated egg – which is something he considered impossible – he posited that there must be some kind of underlying manifoldness: not an actual pre-formed "thing," but a potential or intensive manifold. That idea is, to a certain extent, in line with Henri Bergson's notion of the *élan vital*, as he develops it in *Creative Evolution*.

Alongside Driesch's entelechy concept, Bergson proposed the idea of an *élan vital*, or differentiating impulse, to counter mechanist explanations of life, which he criticized for failing to account for the creativity at work in evolution. For Bergson, we cannot find a final cause or plan in nature. "A plan," he explains, "is a term assigned to a labor: it closes the future whose form it indicates." Life, by contrast, "is a creation that goes on for ever in virtue of an initial movement."²⁹ By means of such concepts as "intuition," "qualitative multiplicity" and "the virtual," Bergson too posits forces operative on a level other than that of the actual. Yet where Driesch conceived of the function of life's ongoing movement as working towards and preserving an organic whole, Bergson was more radical in reinterpreting the Aristotelian idea of forms completing themselves. He gave priority to potentiality over actuality. For Bergson, life moves in the direction of proliferating difference, which makes for an odd kind of end at best. Throughout *Creative Evolution* he stresses the open-ended nature of life as movement. "To speak of an end" is impossible because that would imply

> a pre-existing model which has only to be realized. It is to suppose, therefore, that all is given, and that the future can be read in the present [. . .] Life, on the contrary [. . .] is undoubtedly creative, i.e. productive of effects in which it expands and transcends its own being. These effects were therefore not given in it in advance, and so it could not take them for ends.³⁰

If there is anything that the *élan vital* persists in or completes, for Bergson, it is the work of difference.

In *Creative Evolution* Bergson sets his project apart from Aristotle's. He also mentions Driesch, but he is more hesitant in defining his position in relation to his contemporary, noting only that he finds his critique on mechanist theories more interesting than the actual entelechy hypothesis Driesch posits as an alternative.³¹ By Bergson's account, Aristotle's idea of the universe moving towards completion misses the open-ended nature of time or movement, which is at the heart of his own philosophy. Where Aristotle explains the concept of entelechy by giving the examples of an acorn growing into an oak and of a boy becoming a man, Bergson asks us to rethink the boy-becoming-man structure. He writes:

> When we say "the child becomes a man," let us take care not to fathom too deeply the literal meaning of the expression, or we shall find that when we posit the subject "child," the attribute "man" does not yet apply to it, and that when we express the attribute "man," it applies no more to the subject "child." The reality, which is the transition from childhood to manhood, has slipped between our fingers.³²

A better way of grasping what happens to a growing child, Bergson argues, is to say that "[t]here is becoming from the child to the man."³³

In "the child becomes a man," the verb to become, for Bergson, is meaningless since what the phrase gives us is two artificial points of development with an empty space between them. In the phrase "there is becoming from the child to the man," by contrast, the process of becoming comes to the front. And we should think of that becoming not as a fixed route but as an encountering of a myriad of potentialities, of which the constellations are impossible to foresee. Life in itself, Bergson argues, is "an immensity of potentiality, a mutual encroachment of thousands and thousands of tendencies."[34] Becoming, or the process of these tendencies encroaching, intertwining and dissociating, is what Bergson understands by his concept of duration. It is "a stream against which we cannot go. It is the foundation of our being, and as we feel, the very substance of the world in which we live."[35]

Stein does not tell us what she thinks about Aristotle's theory of generation, although Aristotle is a continued presence in her own attempts to grasp movement, from the echo of the *Nicomachean Ethics* in *The Making of Americans*, to the moving cause/car pun and the idea of a composition differentiating in her lectures. The most explicit comment she makes that is relevant to Aristotle's project may well be her criticism of the boy-becomes-man entelechy. "[W]hat is the use," she asks in her mid-1930s *The Geographical History of America or The Relation of Human Nature to the Human Mind*, "of being a little boy if you are going to grow up to be a man?"[36] If the end-point is determined, with man the pinnacle of development, she ridicules, we might as well stop living. For both Stein and Bergson, the "itself" in Sachs's translation of entelechy as "being-at-work-staying-itself" is not determined by the completed form. It rather includes the full differentiating process, of which the end is not to be foreseen. This process is what in "Composition as Explanation" she refers to as making "by being made." There is no plan to it, it is not "a thing prepared." Indeed, to impose such a plan stifles creativity. Stein associates "a thing prepared" with academies, as institutions that police artistic expression, and with war, as the political machinery that claims control over individual lives:

> [W]ar is a thing that decides how it is to be when it is to be done. It is prepared and to that degree it is like all academies it is not a thing made by being made it is a thing prepared. Writing and painting and all that, is like that, for those who occupy themselves with it and don't make it as it is made.

Through the word "occupy" Stein puts the "professionalization" of the arts on a par with war. Those who "occupy" themselves with creativity, for Stein, aggressively curb its becoming. Her championing of creativity does not mean that the artist is a mere receptacle for some mysterious creative force, however. Those few "who make it as it is made," Stein points out, "usually are prepared just as the world around them is preparing."[37] Such a process of preparing does not imply a pre-existing model but the drive to transcend one's own being, which Bergson in *Creative Evolution* calls duration, and which he considers the substance of our world.

While "Composition as Explanation" is concerned with the making of art and art history rather than natural life, Stein conspicuously uses the word "naturally" to describe processes unfolding.[38] Whether she is talking about the development of her own project, the mechanisms of art history or the way in which World War One blasted away the old rhythms and structures, it all seems to happen "naturally" or as "a natural phenomena."[39] The effect of all those natural happenings is that we start thinking about how we tend to frame processes, and about what we take to be evident or normal. How is it natural for artists only to be considered important once they are dead? "Those who are creating the modern composition authentically are naturally only of importance when they are dead because by that time the modern composition having become past is classified and the description of it is classical."[40] And why should we take that mechanism of classification as "a natural phenomena"? Easy analogies between natural development and the workings of (art) history have been suspect since the materialist turns in the philosophy of history and political theory. They smack of the "excessive romanticism" for which Mannheim criticizes Pinder since they gloss over the social conditions that make life and work, obscuring the fact that those can be remade. Bergson's *Creative Evolution*, notably, was criticized by Benjamin and Horkheimer for trapping us in an empty time, in which it is impossible to effect any political change.[41] Stein, while drawn to the vitalist idea of creativity as ever-spreading differentiation, does not try to sell us a philosophy of history modeled on the rhythms of natural life. She does make us see, however, that the way we think about, and live by, the development of historical time is connected to a natural template.

Stein worried about "the quality in a composition that makes it go dead just after it has been made."[42] If lively creativity is essential to making a work of art "as it is made," then that liveliness appears to dissipate once it is a made thing that, via "distribution and equilibration," enters the market and tradition.[43] For Stein, the logic of classification by which art history operates deals in death. In response to the question of how a work of art or writing becomes a classic, she writes:

> Those who are creating the modern composition authentically, are naturally only of importance when they are dead because by that time the modern composition having become past is classified and the description of it is classical. That is the reason why the creator of the new composition in the arts is an outlaw until he is a classic, there is hardly a moment in between and it is really too bad very much too bad naturally for the creator but also very much too bad for the enjoyer, they all really would enjoy the created so much better just after it has been made than when it is already a classic [. . .].[44]

Classification, this quotation makes clear, is an aggressive mechanism that protects those in power from "outlaws" and stands in the way of enjoyment. "The characteristic quality of a classic" may be "that it is beautiful," but beauty in this system means little in terms of affective, or lively, appreciation. Stein wants a work of art to be "irritating annoying stimulating," but if it does that, then typically "all quality of beauty is denied to it."[45]

Classification is a term we tend to associate with the study of nature, as in when, after observation, we arrange species or specimens in groups or classes according to shared characteristics. When Stein uses the term in order to talk about a process in art history, while strewing around "naturallys," she makes us see that the entelechy model, as a key template in the study of nature since Aristotle, has made its way into the study of history. As Clyde Taylor points out, "the literal meaning of entelechy, 'having its end within itself,' describes nicely the posture of entrenched, institutionalized power vis-à-vis the reality of 'Others' whose ends are seen as scattered, undeveloped or otherwise not fully realized." In political terms, entelechy is a process of idealization by which a dominant class is represented as "the generative and normative instance of all other manifestations." Taylor admits to surprise when he looked up the etymology of the word "classic" and saw "that it derived from the Latin word 'classicus,' of the classes of the Roman people, of the first class, of the first rank."[46] Taking that into consideration, Stein's "outlaw" sentence hits the mark. If you are not among the (dead) classics, you do not have a say. And once acceptance has been bestowed, it is easily forgotten what the situation was like before. "[I]t is extremely difficult nothing more so," she adds, "to remember back to [a classic's] not being beautiful once it has become beautiful."[47] Since what matters in the classic entelechy logic is the end, the process is erased. The way in which we tend to think about natural life, Stein knew, is entangled with the politics that shape society. Those structures are not natural in the sense that they cannot be changed. Because we are used to them, however, they may feel "natural": they are grounded in the mesh of practices and views, or depend on "what is seen and what is seen depends upon how everybody is doing everything." Because both are constructions, both are open to change. So, when the question of how biological life develops was reconsidered, as was happening in early twentieth-century vitalism, this was, for Stein, connected to the question of how we make history.

Central to "Composition as Explanation" is the desire to use the "time sense" of becoming or potentiality that goes into the act of creation for historical reflection. In using composition for both art and a historical structure like generation, Stein makes us feel that this should be possible. If we can see the creative process of one composition, then we should also be able to see that of the other. Yet, for the most part, the lecture stresses how the stories of war and classification that dominate the (art) historical moment Stein is part of kill creativity rather than foster it. The last long paragraph of her lecture has been read as a defeatist perspective on her time. This is what Stein writes:

> The time in the composition is a thing that is very troublesome. If the time in the composition is very troublesome it is because there must even if there is no time at all in the composition there must be time in the composition which is in its quality of distribution and equilibration. In the beginning there was the time in the composition that naturally was in the composition but time in the composition comes now and this is what is now troubling every one the time in the composition is now a part of distribution and equilibration. In the beginning there was confusion there was a continuous present and later there was romanticism which was not a confusion but an extrication and now there is either succeeding or failing there must be distribution and equilibration there must be time that is distributed and equilibrated. This is the thing that is at present the most troubling and if there is the time that is at present the most troublesome the time-sense that is at present the most troubling is the thing that makes the present the most troubling. There is at present there is distribution, by this I mean expression and time, and in this way at present composition is time that is the reason that at present the time-sense is troubling that is the reason why at present the time-sense in the composition is the composition that is making what there is in composition.[48]

Luke Carson, for example, argues that Stein here gives us her version of the story of World War One as the historical break that replaced a meaningful order with a market logic. "Now," for Carson, means 1926, in which "'the continuous present' has given way to 'time that is distributed and equilibrated' according to an economy that places the human mind or entity at risk." Stein is troubled, then, because "there is a risk that value will not return."[49] The war, as Carson argues, is important to "Composition as Explanation," but it does not stop Stein from experimenting with, and opening our eyes to, ongoing processes of differentiation.

Composition is the key device by which Stein attempts to put some of that differentiation across; she has it change back and forth from text into context, and from her text and her context into texts/works of art and contexts in general. When she makes a claim about "now" at the end of her lecture, she is referring not only to the post-war climate but also to the moment in her text. "Now" that she is almost done, she is worried that her composition may "go dead."[50] "Now," after talking about how she started writing in the continuous present and then found herself in the romanticism triggered by the war, "now" that she has distributed her composition evenly among her audience, "there is either succeeding or failing," grace or disgrace. "[C]omposition is time" because the composition that is the context uniting Stein and her audience is limited to the duration of her address. That is a "troublesome" insight at the end of a lecture. Stein wanted all of her writing to "go on" – that, too, is what she means by "succeeding," as opposed to the failure of her text "going dead."[51] She asks her audience not to classify, not to forget the "irritating annoying stimulating" intersecting of different stories at work in her text. She also wants them to be confused about how it ends, which is why she denies her lecture a proper conclusion.

The long paragraph, in fact, reads as a satire on the advice you may find in a book on composition: that is, that you should conclude by summing up your argument. Stein may retrace her steps but the temporal markers she uses ("in the beginning," "later," "now") are too wide for the making of her argument and extend the idea of composition to (Stein's) life – which, of course, you never get to sum up. The lecture does not finish on the long paragraph, furthermore. Stein adds two additional one-line paragraphs that each highlight that there is more to come, that the end is not absolute:

And afterwards.
Now that is all.

The "trouble" that Stein packs into her long paragraph is not an instance of nostalgia about a pre-war past in which experience was "continuous." It is an attempt at troubling or activating her audience. She wants them to think of a composition – of a text, a work of art, an event, a generation – not as an eternal substance, but as something that is "different, and always going to be different."[52]

Non-Contemporaneity

When, in "Portraits and Repetition," Stein returns to the problem of generations and artistic creativity, which she now addresses through the idea of portraiture, she introduces the cinema as a way to grasp the ongoing difference that is essential to a composition. She not only claims that, in her portraits, she "was doing what the cinema was doing," but also states that "this our period was undoubtedly the period of the cinema and series production." On one level, Stein's two lectures, written a decade apart, give us two distinct decades. "Composition as Explanation" sketches a 1920s "time sense" in which the war lingers as the contemporary sight and practice to be dealt with, and "Portraits and Repetition" presents the 1930s as a period in which the "seeing and doing" was informed by mass spectacle, of which the cinema serves as prime example, and by the rhythms of industrialization. Yet she also complicates that picture. The main focus of "Portraits and Repetition" is not the 1930s, but Stein's portraits, which she started writing around 1909 and which, by her own account, developed independently of the cinema:

> I of course did not think of it in terms of the cinema in fact I doubt whether at that time I had ever seen a cinema but, and I cannot repeat this too often any one is of one's period and this our period was undoubtedly the period of the cinema and series production. And each of us in our own way are bound to express what the world in which we are living is doing.[53]

How does it make sense for Stein to argue that periods only matter as experience, as "periods of living," if in the 1910s she may not have actually experienced "a cinema"?

The cinema, in Stein, does not really refer to the experience of movie-going. It is a concept that enables her to work against a leveling, uniform understanding of contemporaneity. A uniform contemporaneity, she makes clear in "Composition as Explanation," had been the effect of World War One. The trauma of the war overrode the old hierarchies and united everyone in a new collective experience, but at the same time precluded the generation of new structures of difference. In making "everything alike," it resulted in a "simple," or self-erasing difference: "Everything alike naturally everything was simply different and this is and was romanticism and this is and was war."[54] The cinema, by contrast, makes things anything but "simply" different. Stein's deceptively straightforward claim that "this our period was undoubtedly the period of the cinema and series production" from "Portraits and Repetition" is a clever answer to the question of how to "know" the contemporary composition as a constellation including difference. It enables her to think the non-contemporary as part of the contemporary.

The link between the cinema and series production that she establishes in "Portraits and Repetition" brings the classic entelechy model that lurked in the background of "Composition as Explanation" back into view. If (art) history tends to operate by imposing dominant narratives on a heterogeneous historical reality, then the story about contemporary or modernist art and life, is one of shock. Shock – and, by extension, rupture and death – are how we tend to "classify" modernist expression. In his 1939 essay "On Some Motifs in Baudelaire," Walter Benjamin famously defined the contemporary or modern condition through the specter of shock, which he encountered both in the cinema and in series production. The repetitive sequence of shocks that "determines the rhythm of production on a conveyor belt," for Benjamin, "is the same thing that underlies the rhythm of reception in the film."[55] Stein's portraits have been analyzed as incorporating a Benjaminian "series of shocks and collisions," but collisions, as we have seen, are what she argues her generation has overcome when it conceived "an intensity of movement so great that it has not to be seen against something else to be known."[56] For Stein, what links the cinema to the conveyor belt is not shock per se but ongoing movement. And she can be seen to distinguish between two types of ongoing movement: one made up of deadening repetition and one of lively differentiation. The phrase "this our period was undoubtedly the period of the cinema and series production" should not be read as referring to one period or mode of composition, but to one bifurcating into two: Stein's period is that of series production and of the cinema.

A bifurcating period provides Stein with an escape from a smothering classification logic, from the idea that there is one modern composition. In addition to a story about broken continuity, she indicates in "Portraits and Repetition," there is a story of a new mode of continuity. Shock and rupture are not what Stein associates with the cinema. When she "was doing what the cinema was doing," she explains, she "was making a continuous succession of the statement of what that person was until I had not many things but *one thing*."[57] She wants us to understand that "one thing" as a differentiated and lively sequence rather than as the alienating rhythm of the conveyor belt. At the heart of "Portraits and Repetition" is the contrast between repetitive and differential movement, or what Stein calls insistence. If the latter sums up liveliness, repetition cannot be part of life: "I was [. . .] almost certain then when I began writing portraits that if anything is alive there is no such thing as repetition. I do not know that I have ever changed my mind about that."[58] The examples she gives of movement that is not repetition are all explicitly animate: frogs hopping, birds singing, her "lively little aunts" telling the same stories differently, and "existing as a human being."[59] "It is not repetition," she sums up, "if it is that which you are actually doing because naturally each time the emphasis is different."[60] The point that you should fully or "actually" experience what you are doing to avoid deadening repetition can be read as a critique on series production's repetitive rhythm that was alienating workers from the labor they were doing. Yet Stein's is not a Luddite stance and her understanding of the full experience of differentiated movement does not exclude technology per se. Both the cinema and writing, rather, make such movement possible. Stein finishes the sentence that I have just quoted by comparing lived experience to the cinema: "It is not repetition if it is that which you are actually doing because naturally each time the emphasis is different just as the cinema has each time a slightly different thing to make it all be moving." This is also how she wants us to consider her approach to writing: "I never repeat that is while I am writing."[61] So if "we are bound to express what the world in which we are living is doing," then Stein chose to live in the world of cinematic liveliness rather than that of deadening, repetitive series production.[62]

In *Lectures in America* the cinema functions as a prompt for Stein to critique the idea of a closed development and to create relations of non-contemporaneity. Her claim that, in the 1910s, she did not think of her work "in terms of the cinema" cleverly underscores the non-contemporary quality she attributes to the cinema. It enables her to sketch a generation made up of different modes of experience – lively cinema and deadening series production – and it also helps her circumvent a relationship of influence that would make her work ancillary to the cinema.⁶³ Non-contemporaneity furthermore informs an anecdote that she recounts in the lecture "Pictures," about a cinematic experience she had a good decade before the cinema came into being. Somewhere in the 1880s, or when she "was about eight years old," she went to see a Waterloo panorama painting:

> and it was very exciting, it was exciting seeing the panorama of the battle of Waterloo. There was a man there who told all about the battle, I knew a good deal about it already because I always read historical novels and history and I knew about the sunken road where the french cavalry were caught but though all that was exciting the thing that was exciting me was the oil painting. It was an oil painting a continuous oil painting, one was surrounded by an oil painting and I who lived continuously out of doors and felt air and sunshine and things to see felt that this was all different and very exciting. There it all was the things to see but there was no air it just was an oil painting. I remember standing on the little platform in the center and almost consciously knowing that there was no air. There was no air, there was no feeling of air, it just was an oil painting and it had a life of its own [. . .].⁶⁴

The terms Stein uses to describe this experience hint at the cinema. An "excited" feeling of immersion or "being surrounded," many film historians have pointed out, is what drew audiences to the cinema.⁶⁵ Continuous movement defined the medium, and because of its ability to keep movement from disappearing after it had happened, the cinema was attributed life-giving potential. The paradox of cold technology "creating" life characterizes the early reception of film. Late nineteenth- and early twentieth-century names of cameras and projectors such as vitascope, vitagraph, bioscope and biograph, for example, alluded to the cinema's task to create life.⁶⁶ As Leigh Wilson points out, film was often considered in magical terms because it "produces life, movement and action from light, making it seem organic (as light produces life and growth in the natural world), but also uncanny (the creation of life and movement from nothing)."⁶⁷ In Stein's anecdote, this paradox takes the form of an opposition between life and death. The phrase "[t]here was no air," making clear that the panorama spectators were inside looking at a picture of an outside, is in dialogue with the claim that the oil painting "had a life of its own." Without air there can be no life and yet the airtight painting, for Stein, was alive.

In remembering the 1880s panorama painting cinematically, Stein invites us to think carefully about the history of the cinema. That history, Tom Gunning has argued, should not be written solely from the standpoint of the feature film. Doing so results in a teleological exercise that makes the cinema's first decade, from the mid-1890s until 1906–7, into a mere primitive stage. Early cinema, rather, should be seen as part of a developing nineteenth-century culture of visual spectacle and entertainment in which attraction was the main element.[68] Gunning's work on the continuities between a nineteenth-century visual culture and the emergence of the cinema asks that we take into consideration different and interlocking temporalities and structures of development. Yes, the cinema baffled audiences with its novelty, but that novelty was also anticipated. As early as 1877, the journal *Scientific American*, for example, published an article, "The Talking Phonograph," in which the author foresees the effect of "real presence" that the actual cinema would have:

> It is already possible by ingenious optical contrivances to throw stereoscopic photographs of people on screens in full view of an audience. Add the talking phonograph to counterfeit their voices and it would be difficult to carry the illusion of real presence much further.[69]

The panorama installation, now, was one of the nineteenth-century spectacles that prefigured such a cinematic sense of presence. It was a huge painted canvas, often depicting a historical event like a battle, mounted in a circular building with a viewing platform in the middle. Some panoramas rotated, with the paintings moving round the viewers. As the first visual mass medium, it was a very popular form of educational entertainment from the late nineteenth century onwards, when a man called Robert Barker invented it, up until World War One. Gunning takes the panorama to be a vital part of the history of cinema because it anticipated a cinematic perception: "the panorama could never be seen entirely from a single viewpoint – or in a single moment."[70] For an early cinema audience, film's continuity would have been related to that of the panorama. Stein's memory of her childhood visit to the Waterloo panorama makes us see that a cinematic experience is not necessarily neatly contemporaneous with the cinema.

Yet where Gunning argues that a panorama installation was different from a picture gallery because it demanded a more visceral response from a more eclectic audience, Stein stresses that the panorama "was just an oil painting." Identification processes in Stein, however, are rarely straightforward, and especially the experiences she labels "exciting" tend to harbor complex dynamics. The phrase "an oil painting a continuous oil painting" asks us to think about medium specificity. The landmark essay on that topic is Gotthold Ephraim Lessing's *Laocoon* (1766), which pits painting and poetry against each other. While both art forms, according to the treatise, are equally successful in representing "absent things," they are constrained by their respective mediums. "[P]ainting employs [...] forms and colors in space." Poetry, by contrast, "articulate[s] sounds in time."[71] All good art, for Lessing, has to adhere to its medium-specific restrictions; painting has to limit itself to the description of objects existing side by side in space, and poetry to the unfolding of actions in time. Lessing's guidelines were an important trigger for modernist artists and writers eager to subvert aesthetic traditions.[72] Stein's "continuous oil painting" connects what is typical for poetry to the medium of painting. Tellingly, she does not write that it was the panorama that created a sense of continuity, but an oil painting, highlighting the painterly medium. This response to Lessing not only is an instance of Stein's modernist drive to make it new, but also fits in with her take on the structure of development. In line with Bergson's understanding of a radically open development, Stein has painting "transcend its own being." In framing the panorama painting in cinematic terms, she locates the virtual presence of the new art of the cinema in it.

An additional layer of non-contemporaneity opens up if we delve into early twentieth-century reflection on the cinema. For Walter Benjamin, as we will see, the cinema both separated us from tradition, isolating us in a new time, and opened up a hidden zone of experience, revealing a time within time. Bergson, however, initially refuted the cinema's time sense and thought it contradicted a time worth living. Reading Stein in dialogue with Benjamin and Bergson, two of modernism's most famous theorists of life and cinema commentators, results in a complex web of relations that reveals not only the extent to which early twentieth-century cinema was entangled with a life-centered discourse, but also how the cinema changed the way in which we think about time changing. That makes us see, finally, how the cinema, for Stein, came to replace history as guiding concept. The relations central to the following chapter, furthermore, are themselves characterized by interlacing non-contemporaneities. In one way or another Stein, Benjamin, Bergson and the cinema were refusing each other's contemporariness. Stein "was doing what the cinema was doing," but on her own terms and without any references to films or film theory; despite his apparently naïve appreciation of the cinema, Bergson was considered a cinematic thinker by his contemporaries; and Benjamin critiqued Bergson's project for failing to historicize the modern experience that it was a product of, while at the same time borrowing from it. For all their refusals, these three thinkers envisaged a new mode of thinking about collective experience to which the cinema offered a gateway.

Notes

1. Stein, *Lectures in America*, 287.
2. Stein, "Composition as Explanation," 520.
3. For a history of the concept of generation, see Hans Jaeger, "Generations in History: Reflections on a Controversial Concept," *History and Theory* 23.3 (1985). For a more recent overview, see Jennie Bristow, *The Sociology of Generations: New Directions and Challenges* (London: Palgrave MacMillan, 2016).
4. Leopold von Ranke quoted in Jaeger, "Generations in History," 274.
5. Gasset's *El tema de nuestro tiempo* was published in English as *The Modern Theme* in 1931, translated by James Cleugh (London: C. W. Daniel). Mannheim's essay "Das Problem der Generationen" was published in *Kölner Vierteljahrshefte für Soziologie* 7.2–3 (1928–9), 157–85 and 309–30. It was published in English as "The Problem of Generations," in *Essays on the Sociology of Knowledge*, ed. Paul Kecskemeti (London: Routledge and Kegan Paul, 1952). Better known than "Composition as Explanation" is, of course, Ernest Hemingway's anecdote about Stein labeling the World War One veterans a "lost generation," which he recalls in *A Moveable Feast*. Overhearing a garage owner scolding a young mechanic with the words "You're all a '*génération perdue*," Stein told Hemingway in the 1920s "That's what you are. That's what you all are [. . .] all of you young people who served in the war. You are a lost generation." See Ernest Hemingway, *A Moveable Feast* (Harmondsworth: Penguin, 1966), 27–8, available at: <https://openlibrary.org/books/OL24214522M/A_Moveable_feast> (last accessed September 3, 2021).
6. Gasset, *The Modern Theme*, 15, 16.
7. Mannheim, "The Problem of Generations," 276, 281.
8. Wilhelm Dilthey quoted in Owensby, *Dilthey and the Narrative of History*, 131.
9. Ibid.
10. Mannheim, "The Problem of Generations," 282.
11. Wilhelm Pinder quoted in Mannheim, "The Problem of Generations," 283.
12. Ibid., 283.
13. Ibid., 285.
14. Stein, *Lectures in America*, 287.
15. Stein, "Composition as Explanation," 523.

16. Ibid., 520.
17. Ibid., 521.
18. Stein, *Lectures in America*, 286.
19. Stein, "Composition as Explanation," 521, 523.
20. See, for example, William M. R. Simpson, Robert C. Koons and Nicholas J. Teh, eds, *Neo-Aristotelian Perspectives on Contemporary Science* (New York: Routledge, 2018).
21. Joe Sachs, *Aristotle's Physics: A Guided Study* (New Brunswick, NJ, and London: Rutgers University Press, 1998), 245.
22. Aristotle, *Metaphysics*, in *The Complete Works of Aristotle*, trans. W. D. Ross, ed. Jonathan Barnes, vol. 2, Bollingen Series LXXI.2 (Princeton, NJ: Princeton University Press, 1984), book IX, chapter 8, 3565.
23. Frederick Burwick and Paul Douglass, introduction to *The Crisis in Modernism: Bergson and the Vitalist Controversy*, ed. Frederick Burwick and Paul Douglass (Cambridge: Cambridge University Press, 1992), 1.
24. George Rousseau, "The Perpetual Crisis of Modernism and the Traditions of Enlightenment Vitalism: with a Note on Mikhail Bakhtin," in *The Crisis in Modernism: Bergson and the Vitalist Controversy*, ed. Frederick Burwick and Paul Douglass (Cambridge: Cambridge University Press, 1992), 37.
25. Driesch, *The History and Theory of Vitalism*, 65.
26. Ibid., 1.
27. Hans Driesch, *The Science and the Philosophy of the Organism: The Gifford Lectures 1907*, vol. 1 (London: Adam and Charles Black, 1908), 50, 144, available at: <https://openlibrary.org/books/OL23410462M/The_science_and_philosophy_of_the_organism> (last accessed September 3, 2021).
28. Ibid., 144.
29. Bergson, *Creative Evolution*, 104, 105.
30. Ibid., 52.
31. Ibid., 42.
32. Ibid., 312–13.
33. Ibid., 313.
34. Ibid., 272.
35. Ibid., 41.
36. Stein, *The Geographical History of America or The Relation of Human Nature to the Human Mind*, 371.
37. Stein, "Composition as Explanation," 520.
38. For more on Stein's understanding of nature, and her use of the term "naturally," see Chapter 6.
39. She writes, for example: "It is a natural phenomena a rather extraordinary natural phenomena that a thing accepted becomes a classic" ("Composition as Explanation," 522).
40. Ibid., 521.

41. See Walter Benjamin, "On Some Motifs in Baudelaire," in *Selected Writings: 1938–1940*, vol. 4, ed. Howard Eiland and Michael W. Jennings (Cambridge, MA: Belknap Press of Harvard University Press, 2006), and Max Horkheimer, "On Bergson's Metaphysics of Time," trans. Peter Thomas and Stuart Martin, *Radical Philosophy* 131 (2005 [1934]): 9–19.
42. Stein, "Composition as Explanation," 529.
43. Ibid., 528. William Vesterman points out that the phrase "distribution and equilibration" hints at the post-war discourse in which "a new political 'distribution' had created new national and international balances of power or 'equilibrations' through the destruction of the old multinational empires." See William Vesterman, *Dramatizing Time in Twentieth-Century Fiction* (New York: Routledge, 2014), 42.
44. Stein, "Composition as Explanation," 521.
45. Ibid., 522.
46. Clyde Taylor, *The Mask of Art: Breaking the Aesthetic Contract – Film and Literature* (Bloomington and Indianapolis: Indiana University Press, 1998), 58–9.
47. Stein, "Composition as Explanation," 522.
48. Ibid., 529.
49. Luke Carson, *Consumption and Depression in Gertrude Stein, Louis Zukofsky and Ezra Pound* (Basingstoke: Macmillan, 1999), 61.
50. Stein, "Composition as Explanation," 529.
51. In "Poetry and Grammar" Stein explains that she has always wanted writing to "go on": "When I first began writing, I felt that writing should go on, I still do feel that it should go on" (*Lectures in America*, 318).
52. Stein, "Composition as Explanation," 523.
53. Stein, *Lectures in America*, 294.
54. Stein, "Composition as Explanation," 527.
55. Benjamin, "On Some Motifs in Baudelaire," 328.
56. Stein, *Lectures in America*, 287. Susan McCabe argues that "[t]he 'period of the cinema' [. . .] became for Stein the period of the volatile fragment, of the reflexive body that does not quite hold together or congeal" (McCabe, *Cinematic Modernism*, 60). I will come back to McCabe's reading of Stein later in this chapter.
57. Stein, *Lectures in America*, 294.
58. Ibid., 292.
59. Ibid., 288, 289, 295.
60. Ibid., 295.
61. Ibid., 295.
62. As McCabe points out, Stein "alludes [. . .] to the potentially numbing effects of mechanical repetition in *The Making of Americans*" (*Cinematic Modernism*, 59). McCabe quotes the following section from *The Making of Americans*: "If they get deadened by the steady pounding

of repeating they will not learn from each one even though each one always is repeating the whole of them they will not learn the completed history of them, they will not know the being really in them" (*The Making of Americans*, 294).
63. It is pretty doubtful that Stein would not have "seen a cinema" in the 1910s. As Tom Gunning, Bernice Rose and Jennifer Wild have shown, the Parisian avant-garde set – who met regularly in Stein's salon before the war – was an enthusiastic cinema audience. See *Picasso, Braque and Early Film in Cubism*, ed. Bernice Rose (New York: Pace Wildenstein, 2007).
64. Stein, *Lectures in America*, 227.
65. On cinematic immersion, see Alison Griffiths, *Shivers Down Your Spine: Cinema, Museums and the Immersive View* (New York: Columbia University Press, 2008).
66. In *Theory of Film* Siegfried Kracauer refers to Georges Sadoul's *Histoire générale du cinema: L'Invention du cinéma* (1946), in which the French film historian "sagaciously observes that the names given the archaic film cameras offer clues to the then prevailing aspirations. Such names as vitascope, vitagraph, bioscope, and biograph were undoubtedly intended to convey the camera's affinity for 'life,' while terms like kinetoscope, kinetograph and cinematograph testified to the concern with movement" (Siegfried Kracauer, *Theory of Film: The Redemption of Physical Reality* (Princeton, NJ: Princeton University Press, 1997), 28)). See also: Louis-Georges Schwartz, "Cinema and the ~~Meaning~~ of Life," *Discourse* 28.2/3 (2006). Schwartz (25n7) remarks that there is an error in Kracauer's pagination when he refers to Sadoul's *L'Invention du cinéma* (Paris: Denoël, 1950).
67. Leigh Wilson, *Modernism and Magic: Experiments with Spiritualism, Theosophy and the Occult* (Edinburgh: Edinburgh University Press, 2015), 103.
68. Attraction, for Gunning, is an appealing force that solicits your attention and immerses you in an alternative reality. See Tom Gunning, "The Cinema of Attraction: Early Film, Its Spectator and the Avant-Garde," in *Early Cinema: Space Frame Narrative*, ed. Thomas Elsaesser (London: BFI, 1990).
69. "The Talking Phonograph," *Scientific American* 37.25 (December 22, 1877), 384–5, 385. The article was later reprinted in *Nature*, 17.427 (January 3, 1878), 190–2. I take the quotation from Jan Holmberg, "Ideals of Immersion in Early Cinema," *Cinémas: revue d'études cinématographiques / Cinemas: Journal of Film Studies* 14.1 (2003). For cinema "beyond film," see also the volume *Cinema Beyond Film: Media Epistemology in the Modern Era*, ed. François Albéra and Maria Tortajada (Amsterdam: Amsterdam University Press, 2010).
70. Tom Gunning, "The Art of Succession: Reading, Writing, and Watching Comics," *Critical Inquiry* 40.3 (2014): 38. On the panorama, see Stephan

Oettermann, *The Panorama: History of a Mass Medium*, trans. Deborah Lucas Schneider (New York: Zone Books, 1997). On Stein in relation to the genre of the panorama, see Jane Palatini Bowers, "The Composition that All the World Can See," in *Land/Scape/Theater*, ed. Elinor Fuchs and Una Chaudhuri (Ann Arbor: University of Michigan Press, 2002).
71. Gotthold Ephraim Lessing, *Laocoon: An Essay upon the Limits of Painting and Poetry*, trans. Ellen Frothingham (New York: Dover, 2005), unabridged reprint of the 1898 edition published by Little, Brown and Company (Boston), 91.
72. See Murray Krieger, *Ekphrasis: The Illusion of the Natural Sign* (Baltimore and London: Johns Hopkins University Press, 1992).

Chapter 4

Tradition

Walter Benjamin's comparison between the cinema and the conveyor belt in "On Some Motifs in Baudelaire" encompasses more than a comment on the accelerated and automatized rhythm of modern life. At the core of the essay is the issue of the structure of experience, which Benjamin considers to have changed under modernity. He distinguishes between experience integrated in tradition, or what he refers to as *Erfahrung*, and experience in isolation, for which he uses the term *Erlebnis*, and claims that the former has become inaccessible. Modern life, with its industrialization processes, expanding cities and loss of rituals, subjects us to a series of perceptive shocks, which challenge our traditional structures for making sense of the world. Since we fail to insert these shocks in our collective memory, we tend to process them as fragmented impressions:

> The greater the shock factor in particular impressions, the more vigilant consciousness has to be in screening stimuli; the more efficiently it does so, the less these impressions enter long experience [*Erfahrung*] and the more they correspond to the concept of isolated experience [*Erlebnis*].[1]

Modern individuals, in other words, have developed a coping mechanism, or "shock defense," to deal with the overload of new stimuli, which, Benjamin argued, the cinema and conveyor belt epitomized.

For Susan McCabe, a Benjaminian "shock defense" is exactly what is at work in Stein's portraits. "Like Benjamin's cinematic 'conveyer belt' with its mechanical repetition," she argues, "Stein's writing reproduces a shocked body." Shock after shock, the body is asked to process what is happening; attention goes in overdrive, memory is compromised and with each resuscitative jolt occurs a new instant. Stein's writing, then, "forgets itself as it perambulates" and continuity is torn to shreds.[2] Yet such a reading sits uneasily with how Stein frames her portraits in "Portraits and Repetition." Rather than having fragments express a disintegrated modern experience, she wanted to make "a whole portrait."[3] What she finds in the cinema is the cue to make "not many things but one thing."[4] Turning to the early portraits themselves, furthermore, readers might find the a-narrative quality of the texts shocking, but the bodies Stein portrays are less in shock than engaged in an ongoing living.

In the 1911 "Matisse" and "Picasso" portraits, for example, Stein embeds various threads of activity – the painter ruminating, the painter working, the painter as the topic of ongoing conversation – in the larger composition of her subject's life. This is how "Matisse" starts:

> One was quite certain that for a long part of his being one being living he had been trying to be certain that he was wrong in doing what he was doing and then when he could not come to be certain that he had been wrong in doing what he had been doing, when he had completely convinced himself that he would not come to be certain that he had been wrong in doing what he had been doing he was really certain then that he was a great one and he certainly was a great one. Certainly every one could be certain of this thing that this one is a great one.[5]

And these are the first paragraphs of "Picasso":

> One whom some were certainly following was one who was completely charming. One whom some were certainly following was one who was charming. One whom some were following was one who was completely charming. One whom some were following was one who was certainly completely charming.
>
> Some were certainly following and were certain that the one they were then following was one working and was one bringing out of himself then something. Some were certainly following and were certain that the one they were then following was one bringing out of himself then something that was coming to be a heavy thing, a solid thing and a complete thing.
>
> One whom some were certainly following was one working and certainly was one bringing something out of himself then and was one who had been all his living had been one having something coming out of him.[6]

Matisse's artistic self-doubt takes place in the context of a continuous life ("his being one being living") and Picasso's captivating productivity is, likewise, part of a larger whole ("all his living"). Matisse, furthermore, is presented as "one telling about being living," even if, most of the time, "very many [. . .] were not listening."

The relation between telling and living is a marked presence in Stein's early portraits, written in late 1910 and 1911, and is an obvious outgrowth of *The Making of Americans*, in which she considered herself to be "not doing anything but telling about sense in living, sense from living, sense of living, sense for living, sense about living in men and in women."[7] Yet where *The Making of Americans* has Stein suffer under the weight of her task – telling a complete history – the portraits reveal a very different relation between telling and living. The 1910 text "Ada," for example, which Dydo considers Stein's "very first portrait," connects a feminine mode of storytelling to a happy living.[8] Ada, modeled on Toklas, had loved living with her mother because they "had always told very pretty stories to each other." When her mother dies, she finds herself taking care of her male relatives and in desperate need of "charming stories and happy telling of them." This she finds again when she moves away from her father to be with "one being loving" (Stein), who "was then telling stories having a beginning and a middle and an ending."[9] The stories Stein tells as a portraitist are different from those she tells as a comforting lover, but they too want to "make" a life.

Stein's emphasis on storytelling, and on the connection between "working" and "living" in "Picasso," brings to mind Benjamin's figure of the storyteller. For Benjamin, the storyteller embodies artisanal creativity and safeguards our "ability to share experiences."[10] Reading Benjamin's 1936 essay "The Storyteller" and its counterpart, "The Work of Art in the Age of Technological Reproducibility," in dialogue with Stein enables me to nuance our understanding of Stein's portraits, which have tended to be read as tributes to a modern sense of discontinuity rather than as attempts to reconfigure a sense of continuity.[11] Central to both Benjamin essays is a concern with the marred access to collective memory, as a key aspect of modern life. In both, the cinema functions as a product of that modern situation and as a possible way out.

Storytelling

For Benjamin, "telling about being living," as Stein puts it, had become a modern impossibility in the sense that there is no longer any framework in which modern experience can be integrated. As he phrases it, "the storyteller in his living efficacy is by no means a force today." Stories used to make it possible for an event to be shared with others as part of a meaningful *Erfahrung*: a living open to and understandable for many "ones." The story, Benjamin argues, "submerges the thing into the life of the storyteller, in order to bring it out of him again. Thus, traces of the storyteller cling to a story the way the handprints of the potter cling to a clay vessel."[12] In modern life, however, artisanal creativity gets replaced by a mode of production that has as its model the newspaper. This, he explains in "On Some Motifs in Baudelaire," thrives on "newness, brevity, clarity, and, above all, lack of connection between the individual news items."[13] What is produced is not a story but shreds of information.

This new mode of creating, for Benjamin, triggered new ways of making sense of art, or, in the first place, demolished old ways of looking at art. In "The Work of Art in the Age of Technological Reproducibility," also published in 1936, Benjamin explains that technological reproducibility alters the way in which we experience and find meaning in art. It used to be the case that an artwork had power over an audience. That power, which Benjamin labels aura, derived from the artwork's status as a unique object. As an object, it existed in a particular location at a particular time, and from this unique existence unfolded its "life" or duration in a tradition; it invited different responses as the historical circumstances changed. "The uniqueness of the work of art," Benjamin writes, "is identical to its embeddedness in the context of tradition. Of course, this tradition itself is thoroughly alive and extremely changeable."[14] In looking at a work of art, for Benjamin, an audience was engaging with a tradition, whose authority they recognized. He presents this process of recognition as a dialogic encounter, in which the audience's gaze is reciprocated by the artwork. "Experience of the aura," he points out in "On Some Motifs in Baudelaire,"

> thus arises from the fact that a response characteristic of human relationships is transposed to the relationship between humans and inanimate or natural objects. The person we look at, or who feels he is being looked at, looks at us in turn. To experience the aura of an object we look at means to invest it with the ability to look back at us.[15]

Photography and film, as modes of technological reproducibility, however, lift the object from the domain of tradition. They undercut its singular position in time and space (we can look at a photograph everywhere we want to) and complicate the relationship between original and copy (a photograph may show us things we failed to notice in the original). Furthermore, a camera does not return our gaze. Benjamin refers to the daguerreotype, a technique that preceded photography and film, as an "inhuman" and "deadly" process because it asked for a prolonged staring into the camera without the subject's gaze being met in any meaningful way.[16]

Benjamin does not merely critique modernity, however. The end of traditional storytelling does not mean the end of storytelling per se, and the camera's cold stare opens up new possibilities. In "On Some Motifs in Baudelaire," he elaborates on two of his literary heroes, for whom the fall from *Erfahrung*-as-we-know-it counts as the motor of their work. Both Baudelaire and Proust experimented with new forms for experience, rooted in chance rather than ritual, with ritual as the long-established gateway to *Erfahrung*. Where *Les Fleurs du mal* wrests "genuine historical experience" out of the lost "*correspondances*," or meaningful rituals that constituted a former life, for Benjamin, *A la recherche du temps perdu* channels access to a meaningful past through what Proust called a "*mémoire involontaire*."[17] Where conscious recollection fails in that it only yields information about the past without any actual "trace" of the past, a chance encounter with a madeleine cake may plunge you into the sensuous immediacy of the past.[18]

Stein compared herself to Proust in her *Lectures*. "A thing you all know," she writes in "Portraits and Repetition,"

> is that in the three novels written in this generation that are the important things written in this generation, there is, in none of them a story. There is none in Proust in The Making of Americans or in Ulysses.[19]

Stein is not claiming that she was influenced by Proust or Joyce. She rather wants us to see that all three of them lived up to the challenge of reinventing storytelling – since that is what their generation had to do – in their own way.

Proust reconfigures the storyteller's function from that of the craftsman molding the clay of tradition to that of the gambler taking his chances on meaningful experience or *Erfahrung*. In doing so, he concentrates on his own childhood, without, however, referring to rituals or festivals that would make it a childhood like all others. That, Benjamin points out in "On Some Motifs in Baudelaire," is "a fundamental problem," since it complicates the storyteller's function to unite individuals in a shared experience – and the fact that

Proust does not succumb to the problem is a credit to his genius.[20] Stein avoids the eddies of personal experience and makes the idea of embedding that is central to *Erfahrung* into a formal operation; she creates "moving" paragraphs.[21]

Stein's paragraphs move not by appealing to an audience's feelings but by tracing a sentence changing shape, transcending itself. If we look at the Picasso portrait, for example, we can read the first paragraph as consisting of one sentence refusing to settle into a singular form. By shifting around the words "certainly" and "completely" Stein has the sentence fluctuate. This goes to the heart of a discovery Stein associates with *How to Write*, which is a collection of essays that, as Sharon Kirsch points out, was written between 1927 and 1931 but "elaborates [...] many of Stein's primary concerns from the previous three decades."[22] In *How to Write*, Stein tells us in *Lectures in America*, she discovered "that sentences are not emotional and that paragraphs are," and she emphasizes that "this difference was not a contradiction but a combination."[23] Punning on the etymology of the word emotion, consisting of the Latin elements *ex* (from or away) and *movere* (to move), she wants us to think about a sentence moving outside itself. Such an operation can happen only on the level of the paragraph; Stein needs a couple of sentences to show how the process of a sentence moving outside itself works. Sentence and paragraph are not in contradiction, however, since she is working only with one sentence that needs the length of the paragraph to unsettle. Read thus, Stein's portraits are not collections of isolated sentences. The emphasis, rather, is on the sentences creating their own larger context. The fact that the Matisse and Picasso portraits are also about artists whose work is part of a larger "living" underscores Stein's concern for rethinking the relationship between individual element and larger, meaningful whole. The make-up, or indeed composition, of that larger context is no longer given, as it was in the age of storytelling. It is renegotiated in the modern work of art: in Proust's *madeleine* memories, in Matisse's painterly "telling about being living," in Picasso's "charming" work ethos that inspires a host of followers like storytellers used to, and in Stein's sentences combining into paragraphs.

The moving paragraph is not Stein's catch-all solution to the problem of her generation's relationship to experience. She did not tackle that problem on a formal level only. In "Portraits and Repetition" she relates the intense movement she considered characteristic of her generation to the issue of remembering. "[W]e in this period," she writes, "have not lived in remembering, we have living in moving being necessarily so intense that existing is indeed something, is indeed that thing that we are doing."²⁴ "[L]iving in moving," here, takes the place of living in remembering. The fact that Stein keeps the structure of the phrase more or less intact, exchanging moving for remembering, signals differential continuity rather than a break: living goes on. Unlike McCabe, I do not think that Stein dismisses memory and has her portraits enact a modern amnesia. Such an interpretation sidesteps the fact that quite a few of Stein's early portraits spotlight acts of remembering. "[L]iving in moving," I argue, amounts to a different mode of engaging with the collective experience or tradition that makes up *Erfahrung* rather than its erasure.

Memory

In "On Some Motifs in Baudelaire" Benjamin explains the concept of *Erfahrung* by referring to Bergson's "monumental book" *Matter and Memory* (1896).[25] Given the fact that, for Benjamin, time was, first and foremost, historical time, punctured by rupture and death, whereas Bergson considered time in ahistorical terms as a creative flow of which the "tremendous push" may ultimately prove able to overcome death, this is a surprising connection.[26] Benjamin, indeed, distances himself from Bergson's vitalism, yet the congruence between their respective projects deserves more scrutiny. As Claire Blencowe has shown, Benjamin "extends a Bergsonian conception of creativity," which centers on the renewal of *Erfahrung*.[27] His understanding of *Erfahrung*, Benjamin himself indicates in "On Some Motifs in Baudelaire," is in line with Bergson's take on true experience as he explains it in *Matter and Memory*. He values the collective nature of Bergson's memory concept and its unconscious dynamics. "Experience," Benjamin writes, reflecting on Bergson's book, "is indeed a matter of tradition, in collective existence as well as private life. It is the product less of facts firmly anchored in memory [*Erinnerung*] than of accumulated and frequently unconscious data that flow together in memory [*Gedächtnis*]."[28] Tradition is not a concept that Bergson uses, but in *Matter and Memory* he highlights the continuous flow of experience by which memory keeps changing. Memory should not be pictured as some kind of individual storage where we can deposit and retrieve memories, but rather as a series of dynamic layers or planes of experience informing the present. That is what Bergson's famous cone image symbolizes: how we actually experience the present (the cone's tip) depends on which virtual memory layers (the cone's body) we activate. "The interest of a living being,"

Bergson sums up, "lies in discovering in the present situation that which resembles a former situation, and then in placing alongside of that present situation what preceded and followed the previous one, in order to profit by past experience."[29] Our individual memories, furthermore, are always part of a larger, collective memory, which extends as far as the level of the species and even the cosmos.

So, to a certain extent, what *Erfahrung* is for Benjamin – meaningful experience rooted in tradition – memory is for Bergson. The Proustian distinction between *mémoire involontaire* and *mémoire volontaire* that Benjamin finds so productive, second, can be seen to correspond with Bergson's distinction between the virtual and the actual. Although Benjamin argues that Proust corrects Bergson's theory, we can think of Bergson's concept of the actual as the readily accessible but bland experience of Proust's voluntary memory, which Benjamin associates with *Erlebnis*. Like Proust, for whom the *mémoire volontaire* is "as vapid as an exhibition of photographs," as opposed to the rich sensual perception accompanying the *mémoire involontaire*, Bergson presents the difference between virtual and actual in terms of that between a mere picture and the full thing "encased in its surroundings."[30] Benjamin's figure of the storyteller as the one who makes it possible to exchange experiences and who passes on wisdom, third, is reminiscent of Bergson's figure of the mystic, which he introduces in his 1932 book *The Two Sources of Morality and Religion*. For Benjamin, Nikolai Leskov, a Russian author whom he takes to embody the figure of the storyteller, "approach[es] the mystical."[31] Bergson's *The Two Sources of Morality and Religion* stages the mystic as the savior of what he calls "closed societies," and by which he targets his war-stricken generation, in the grip of the ideas of progress and efficiency and with little possibility of delving into the depths of memory. If Benjamin mourns the disappearance of the figures of the sage and teacher, who as storytellers advised us on how to live, Bergson refers to "the saints of Christianity, [. . .] the sages of Greece, the prophets of Israel, the Arahants of Buddhism" as exemplary men.[32] Of course, there are also significant differences. Benjamin sharply criticizes vitalism for sidestepping the historical conditions of life (individuals living in a society) and for allying itself with fascism:

> Their [the vitalists'] point of departure, understandably enough, has not been the individual's life in society. Instead they have invoked poetry, or preferably nature – most recently, the age of myths. Dilthey's book *Das Erlebnis und die Dichtung* represents one of the earliest of these efforts, which culminate with Klages and Jung, who made common cause with fascism.[33]

He furthermore argues that Bergson is misguided in "lead[ing] us to believe that turning to the contemplative realization of the stream of life is a matter of free choice."[34]

Bergson, while hardly unconcerned with social life, approached the idea of society from a transhistorical, sociobiological stance. By his account, we are biologically wired to live together in a certain way, which is that of an efficient or closed society. The obstacles we face in gaining access to memory, and through memory to a better, open society, are not historically conditioned. Bergson rather stages a conflict between two mental faculties: the intellect, which works towards closure, and intuition, via which we can enter into a creative relation with the past and work towards an open society. Both faculties come with universal dimensions. For Benjamin, by contrast, experience comes in a particular form, relevant to a historical context. For a long time, *Erfahrung* took shape in rituals and stories. Modernity, however, means that we no longer live rituals and stories. Rather, consumption and information, as forms of short-lived *Erlebnis*, have become the dominant modes of experience. Because Bergson fails to ground the flow of time in history, Benjamin considers duration an empty concept: "[i]t is the quintessence of an isolated experience [*Erlebnis*] that struts about in the borrowed garb of long experience [*Erfahrung*]."[35]

The question of how to think *Erfahrung* situated in modernity is one that Benjamin returned to again and again. In reflecting on the relation between experience and modern technology, he often refers to the cinema and earlier photographic techniques. As modes of mechanical reproduction, film and photography destroyed the aura of the work of art. But this loss of aura, in Benjamin, is a complex phenomenon. On the one hand, it breaks the authoritative spell; we are no longer answerable to tradition, or, as Diarmuid Costello puts it, we experience a "salutary purge of atavistic residues." On the other hand, the crumbling of aura also implies the crumbling of meaning. Aura-less objects stop the dialogue, or reciprocal looking, we were used to engage in. And that, Costello sums up, is a barbaric condition.[36] This ambiguity seeps through in Benjamin's comments on film and photography. In his "Little History of Photography," for example, he writes that most modern photography simply fails to "grasp a single one of the human connections in which it exists." Because it lacks aura, it lacks meaning. There are exceptions, however. Atget's photographs of Paris, for example, "emancipate" the object from its aura and make us see that we can work towards new forms of meaning. Atget, Benjamin writes, captures the city looking "like a lodging that has not yet found a new tenant."³⁷ Analogously, Benjamin considers cinema both the seat of modern "*chockförmige Wahrnemung*" (perception conditioned by shock), or isolated *Erlebnis* that fails to sink into memory, and a privileged access point to memory.³⁸

In a short text on Proust that he wrote in 1932, Benjamin relates Proust's *mémoire involontaire*, by which the writer reinvents storytelling, to the cinema.

> Concerning the *mémoire involontaire*: not only do its images appear without being called up; rather, they are images we have never seen before we remember them. This is most clearly the case in those images in which – as in some dreams – we see ourselves. We stand in front of ourselves, the way we might have stood somewhere in a prehistoric past, but never before our waking gaze. Yet these images, developed in the darkroom of the lived moment, are the most important we shall ever see. One might say that our most profound moments have been equipped – like those cigarette packs – with a little image, a photograph of ourselves. And that "whole life" that, as they say, passes through the minds of people who are dying or confronting life-threatening danger is composed of such little images. They flash by in as rapid a sequence as the booklets of our childhood, precursors of the cinematograph, in which we admired a boxer, a swimmer or a tennis player.³⁹

The cinema, here, is not situated on the level of *Erlebnis* but on that of *Erfahrung*. The experience of one's "whole life" is like that of the flipbooks Benjamin remembers from his childhood, and which he considers cinematic in nature. The confrontation with these memory flashes is not a second-hand experience; rather than take us back to something we already know, the images present us with something we have never seen before ("they are images we have never seen before we remember them"). Like Bergson's virtual memory, Benjamin's cinematic Proustian *mémoire involontaire* reconfigured the way in which think about memory. For both, to remember is to experience the past in its living, moving immediacy. And that was exactly what the cinema made possible.

The Cinema's Living Images

Early cinema was in various ways caught up in the late nineteenth- and early twentieth-century discourse on life that I am tracing in this book. As Louis-Georges Schwartz points out, using an interesting entelechial turn of phrase, "[e]ven before the cinema had become itself," experiments with "moving pictures" were connected to the need to produce knowledge about life and living beings.[40] The experiments with proto-cinematic devices that Jules-Etienne Marey conducted, for example, were part of his scientific ambitions to unravel the secret of life. In 1886 Marey published *Du mouvement dans les fonctions de la vie*, in which he argued it was high time for scientists to go beyond the form and structure of living beings and take into consideration "what matters most about them: [. . .] life."[41] And life, for Marey, was synonymous with movement in time.

A famous example that indicates the extent to which the development of early cinematic technologies served the study of movement is the attempt to settle the question of whether a horse's four feet left the ground or not in gallop. In his study *Animal Mechanisms* (*La Machine animale: Locomotion terrestre et aérienne*, 1873), Marey had documented his experiments with graphic inscription and recording techniques to analyze the movement of animals. The British cinema pioneer Eadweard Muybridge impressed Marey with his photographs of a horse on a racetrack. Prompted by his French colleague, Muybridge strung together the shots on a rotating glass disk to recreate the gallop. This device, based on a toy called the zoetrope, caused a stir when Muybridge presented it in Paris in the 1880s. According to Marey, it was the first time that anyone had succeeded in synthesizing motion. He was furthermore convinced that these moving photographs would trigger an artistic "revolution" because they "could furnish [artists] with true attitudes of movement," and thus of life.[42]

When, in the 1890s, the Lumière brothers started commercializing cinematography – an invention in which Marey played a central if also tragic role – early audiences were amazed by film's ability to isolate life.[43] Schwartz refers to a collection of quotations, assembled by the French film historian Georges Sadoul in a small volume on Louis Lumière, which expresses early film critics' amazement at the cinema's capacity to retain the liveliness that used to be swallowed up by time. In an article published in *Le Monde illustré* of January 25, 1896, for example, "the cinematograph" is taken to "produc[e] a portrait that is, at last, living, instead of the cold and languishing images that are never resemblances when they pretend to represent the mobile graces of certain beings."[44] For another critic, speculating about the future of cinematography in the March 1895 issue of *Le Magasin pittoresque*, the production of life itself in all its colorful and aural nuance was imminent:

> When we'll finally be able to photograph colors and to join color cinematography with the phonograph, then and there we'll have simultaneously harvested, simultaneously recorded and then simultaneously reproduced with rigorous exactitude, movement and speech, that is to say life.[45]

The idea that these portraits reproduce life, and, in doing so, circumvent death, is made explicit in an article published in *Le Radical* in September 1895. Commenting on the memorializing potential of film, the critic writes that "we will be able to see those close to us act again, long after we have lost them." "Death," for another author still, "will cease to be absolute."[46] As Schwartz points out, film changes the function of portraits as memorials. The quotations make it clear that film was taken not to fix an image, like the popular nineteenth-century photographs of the dead, but to "creat[e] life beyond life."[47]

The sense that film created a life somehow independent from the life we are actually living is made explicit by Benjamin in "The Work of Art in the Age of Technological Reproducibility." Referring to early cinema, which often centered on movement for the sake of movement, Benjamin wants us to think about a person walking and points out that it is thanks to the camera that we can grasp that process:

> Whereas it is a commonplace that, for example, we have some idea what is involved in the act of walking (if only in general terms), we have no idea at all what happens during the split second when a person actually takes a step. [. . .] This is where the camera comes into play, with all its resources for swooping and rising, disrupting and isolating, stretching or compressing a sequence, enlarging or reducing an object. It is through the camera that we first discover the optical unconscious [. . .].[48]

The important point that Benjamin makes is not so much that film shows us movement in more accurate detail, but that it opens up for us "entirely unknown" qualities of movement. "Clearly," he writes, "it is another nature which speaks to the camera as compared to the eye." The camera enables a move from a "space informed by human consciousness" to one where the unconscious is the determining factor.[49] The camera, in other words, reveals a different mode of life.

By Benjamin's account, the camera does for perception what psychoanalysis does for our drives and impulses. This is relevant to his thinking on memory since, in "On Some Motifs in Baudelaire," he compares Proust's *mémoire involontaire* to Freud's thinking on the unconscious. Freud's "fundamental thought" in *Beyond the Pleasure Principle*, for Benjamin, is that "emerging consciousness takes the place of a memory trace." Translated to Proustian terms, he explains, "this means that only what has not been experienced explicitly and consciously, what has not happened to the subject as an isolated experience [*Erlebnis*], can become a component of *mémoire involontaire*."[50] In a similar sense, yet without reference to psychoanalysis, Bergson, too, considered the intellect (as conscious experience) qualitatively different from intuitive experience (in which the riches of virtual experience could be tapped). Although I do not want to overemphasize the way in which Bergson's and Benjamin's theories intersect, an important question they shared was that of how to mediate between two realms of experience. For both Benjamin and Bergson, the cinema made it possible for isolated and continuous experience to meet. In granting the cinema the potential to reveal "another nature" and make available for conscious perception what normally sinks into the depths of the *mémoire involontaire*, Benjamin grants the cinema the role of mediator between intellect and intuition. Bergson famously refuted the cinema as a technological device catering to the needs of the intellect in *Creative Evolution*, but modified his stance in an interview several years later, coming to view the cinema as an aid to memory.

In his early works, *Time and Free Will* and *Matter and Memory*, Bergson pits his intuitive understanding of movement against Marey's chronophotographs, which broke down movement in photographs "taken at very short and equal intervals of time."[51] In *Creative Evolution* (1906) he draws on the cinema to explain what is wrong with the classic boy-becomes-man entelechy that I have touched on in the previous section:

> It [the entelechy] behaves in much the same way as the movement, always the same, of the cinematographical film, a movement hidden in the apparatus and whose function it is to superpose the successive pictures on one another in order to imitate the movement of the real object.

The cinema, Bergson believes, merely repeats the old error, made famous by Zeno's paradox, of reconstituting movement through immobile sections or positions in space. It serves the intellect and leads away from intuition. In order to be able to think something like "there is becoming," he argues, we have to find a way to "escape from the cinematographical mechanism of thought."[52] In a 1914 article, however, he surprisingly turns to the cinema as a potentially helpful tool for philosophers.

Interviewed for *Le Journal* in 1914 on the occasion of his election to the Académie française, Bergson expands on what the cinema may do:

> Obviously, this invention, a complement to instant photography, can suggest new ideas to a philosopher. It could be an aid to the synthesis of memory, or even of thought. If the circumference [of a circle] is composed of a series of points, memory is, like cinema, a series of images. Immobile, it is in a neutral state; in movement, it is life itself.[53]

Although he does not recant the stance he took with *Creative Evolution*, he no longer considers the cinema's moving images a "contrivance," but something that can help us attain "the synthesis of memory, or even of thought." Such a synthesis, in Bergson, refers to the integration of a virtual memory plane (the cone's body) with perception in the present (the cone's tip), which he outlines in *Matter and Memory*. We need both levels to work together since both a pure memory and a pure perception would lock us up in a state in which we are only half alive. If we ignore what is in front of us, we lead the life of the dreamer. Conversely, if we block memory, we are little more than "a conscious automaton." Where the dreamer would "see wherein [each image] differs from others and not how it resembles them," the automaton "would only distinguish in any situation that aspect in which it practically resembles former situations."[54] The living images of a synthetic memory, which Bergson compares to the cinema, make it possible for our intellect to engage with what normally remains hidden.

Stein's account of memory in relation to her portraits should be read in this context of reflection on a cinematic, living memory, which intersected with theories of perception. Like Bergson, she wanted to liberate remembering from the constraints of an overbearing system. Remembering is a "bother," Stein remarks in "Portraits and Repetition," because it leads to "two things and not one." She connects remembering to scientific observation or "looking" ("looking [. . .] forced remembering"), which is a method she opposed to her ongoing "talking and listening," and to the tracing of resemblances between people, which had been a central aspect of her early typological efforts ("one can notice this thing notice this resemblance and in doing so they have to remember some one and this is a different thing from listening and talking").⁵⁵ Remembering, in other words, is closely related to systems for efficiently processing information, which is how Bergson understands the intellect. It leads to "two things and not one" because it adds the requirements of the system to the thing or person one is looking at. Observation and typology, Stein well knew, are ways of constructing something for a particular purpose. By contrast, the cinema, and especially the early cinema in which the actualities registered what was happening for no other reason than that it could be registered, was considered to capture duration itself.⁵⁶ In creating a "continuously moving picture," it did not limit what a person or a thing was to the constraints of a particular system. Filming duration itself implies that the layers of virtual becoming were kept intact. "Funnily enough," Stein writes,

> the cinema has offered a solution of this thing. By a continuously moving picture of any one there is no memory of any other thing and there is that thing existing, it is in a way if you like one portrait of anything not a number of them.⁵⁷

In constituting "one portrait of anything not a number of them" the cinema, like Bergson's memory cone, contains a myriad of virtual potentialities. There is "no memory of any *other* thing" because it does not ask you to mold what you are seeing to a set of conventions, as in typology or portrait painting, or, indeed, "looking."

Stein's claim that "looking [...] forced remembering" can be read as a reference to an influential late nineteenth-century account of perception, formulated by the nineteenth-century German physiologist and physicist Hermann von Helmholtz. In his *Treatise on Physiological Optics* (*Handbuch der Physiologischen Optik*), Helmholtz proposes a radically subjectivist take on perception: what we experience is not the world, but symbols of the world, lodged in our memory and acquired through a process of "unconscious inference."⁵⁸ Looking, in the Helmholtzian scheme, chains us to a stored collection of stock responses to stimuli. Helmholtz's theory of the relation between memory and perception, Jonathan Crary argues, is the "unacknowledged target" in Bergson's *Matter and Memory*.⁵⁹ Bergson's theory, too, relates perception to memory but, like Proust and Benjamin, he differentiates between different memory modes: one practical and one virtual. For Helmholtz, memory is practical only. "In my opinion," he writes, "there can be no possible sense in speaking of any other truth of our own ideas except as a *practical* truth."⁶⁰

Helmholtz's and Bergson's different accounts of the function of memory in relation to perception imply a different attitude towards history. Bergson may not be a historical thinker in that he seems unaware of the fact that lived experience is largely "made" by material conditions; he is concerned with the question of how we can best draw on the past to create a better future. By his account, an intuitive engagement with memory amounts to a method for liberating ourselves from the structures and systems of an oppressive present order serving the liberal ideal of progress. Helmholtz's project, by contrast, serves such an order. Where Bergson wants us *not* to be enslaved by the systems, institutions and technologies by which the intellect has installed an imperialist modernity, Helmholtz "was committed to expanding and optimizing the productive functioning of a socio-economic world (in particular that of imperial Germany)."[61] His understanding of an "ordered" universe served a conservative socio-political agenda. In an 1878 lecture on the facts of perception, for example, he establishes a link between "political freedom," which he considers an unfortunate development, and the political unrest in Germany. For Bergson, freedom was the ultimate aim and it is a constant in his work, from the early *Time and Free Will*, in which it is a personal project, to *The Two Sources of Morality and Religion*, in which it comes with the political plea to work towards an open society.

According to Dydo, there is no doubt that Stein knew about and was influenced by Helmholtz's work.[62] Stein's negative appreciation of looking via remembering includes a critique on the aggressive agenda that informs Helmholtz's project. Let us look at the full sentence from "Portraits and Repetition" in which she relates "looking" to "forced remembering":

> The trouble with including looking, as I have already told you, was that in regard to human beings looking inevitably carried in its train realizing movements and expression and as such forced me into recognizing resemblances, and so forced remembering and in forcing remembering caused confusion of present with past and future time.[63]

Stein's choice of words is revealing; she semantically embeds perception in an aggressive modernity through the words "train" (as a symbol of global industrialization), "realizing" (which suggests that the "movements and expression" that make up human life have to be brought to an end), and the verb to force, which is repeated three times. Looking "forces" Stein into a logic of identification ("recognizing resemblances") and "forces" remembering – Benjamin's auratic gaze is not far off here. Both Stein and memory, in other words, suffer the violation of a system that stresses resemblance over difference. This act of aggression, furthermore, leads the present to be ruined by "past and future time." Helmholtz's conservative scheme tried to keep the present from changing; what we see are stored recollections and there is no reason to want it otherwise since the route to progress seamlessly connects past to future. For Stein, as for Bergson, however, the present is where the past can change and the future hold the promise of the genuinely new.

History via Cinema

In order to understand how the cinema acted as a prompt for an understanding of history centered on an open present, we need to make a brief detour via Siegfried Kracauer, for whom film and photography held the potential to do what history should be doing. In echo of his friend Walter Benjamin, Kracauer considered film to reveal the invisible. "Film," he wrote, "renders visible what we did not, or perhaps even could not, see before its advent." Film helps us to "redeem [the physical] world from its dormant state, its state of virtual non-existence, by endeavoring to experience it through the camera."[64] Although he articulated this in his 1960 book *Theory of Film*, Kracauer's late work, which also includes *History: The Last Things Before the Last*, shows the critic returning to his 1920s work on photography. As he puts it himself in the introduction to *History*: "Lately I came across my piece on 'Photography' and was completely amazed that I had compared historicism with photography already in this article of the twenties."[65] For Kracauer, the historian should strive to uncover a hidden dimension of reality, in analogy to what photography and film were doing. Like Benjamin, he refers to Proust and specifically to a moment in *Le Côté de Guermantes* in which Marcel experiences an alienating perception of his grandmother, as if he were a photographer. For Proust, Kracauer argues, the photographer is "the witness, the observer, the stranger."[66] His point is emphatically not that the historian's gaze in analogy to the camera succeeds in capturing the world "as it really is." Although he used the concept of *Lebenswelt* to refer to historical reality, he made it clear that it denotes an atypical totality, one "full of intrinsic contingencies which obstruct its calculability, its subsumption under the deterministic principle."⁶⁷ The camera and the historian are capable of bringing to light some of the forces operative in the *Lebenswelt* precisely because they operate on a level below or "before" a totalizing system like, for Kracauer, (idealist) philosophy or art. As he sums it up in his last book:

> One may define the area of historical reality, like that of photographic reality, as an anteroom area. Both realities are of a kind which does not lend itself to being dealt within a definite way. The peculiar material in these areas eludes the grasp of systematic thought; nor can it be shaped in the form of a work of art. Like the statements we make about physical reality with the aid of the camera, those which result from our preoccupation with historical reality may certainly attain to a level above mere opinion; but they do not convey, or reach out for ultimate truths, as do philosophy and art proper. They share their inherently provisional character with the material they record, explore and penetrate.⁶⁸

Although Kracauer is perhaps the least political of those thinkers associated with the Frankfurt School, he reads an anarchic promise in the provisional, contingent dimensions of (filmed) historical reality. "True," he writes, "things may change under a unified global management of human affairs but then the question arises to what extent can the living forces which produce the contingencies be subjected to world-wide control without either revolting or withering." "[O]rder," for Kracauer, "tends to beget anarchy."⁶⁹

The work that Stein produced in the period between 1909 and 1912 shows her exploring the "provisional character" of historical reality that, by Kracauer's account, the cinema made explicit. As Stein remembers it in "Portraits and Repetition," she "[came] to the conclusion that what is inside every one is not all there is of any one" and decided to "describ[e] what any one feels acts and does in relation to any other one."⁷⁰ This led to the texts "A Long Gay Book," "Many Many Women," "G. M. P." and a series of portraits. The texts do not, however, amount to an altogether different project from *The Making of Americans*. Stein wants us to consider her new work as developing out of her big book, which, as I have argued, is to a large extent a history project. As she puts it in "The Gradual Making of the Making of Americans":

> At any rate what happened is this and every one reading these things, A Long Gay Book, Many Many Women and G.M.P. will see, that it [*The Making of Americans*] changed, it kept on changing, until

at last it led to something entirely different something very short and lively to the Portrait of Mabel Dodge and the little book called Tender Buttons [. . .].[71]

Although she had planned for "A Long Gay Book" to be "even longer than The Making of Americans," it in fact "did not go on." For Stein, length and scope are connected to liveliness. "Does one," she asks in "Portraits and Repetition," "if one is really lively and I was really very lively then does one go on."[72] Liveliness is no longer connected to her ambitions to document human character – Dilthey's nexus at its widest – but to short and seemingly random encounters – just the sort of things the cinema was creating.

The cinema, as Mary Anne Doane points out, came into being at a time when the interaction of two temporalities was speeding up modernity: a heightened rationalization and systematization of time on the one hand and a celebration of chance and contingency on the other. "The significance of the cinema, in this context," she argues,

> lies in its apparent capacity to perfectly represent the contingent, to provide the pure record of time. And this effort is particularly legible in the most dominant genre of the early cinema – the actuality, which appeared to capture a moment, to register and repeat "that which happens."[73]

Famous Lumière actualities, such as *Sortie d'usine* (*Workers Leaving the Lumière Factory*, 1895) or *Arrivée d'un train en gare à La Ciotat* (*Arrival of a train in La Ciotat station*, 1895), for example, show random moments in which people do little more than move about. The workers emerge from the factory talking to each other, bumping into each other and exiting to the left or to the right. On the station platform, people get off the train while others wait to get in. Some are talking, some are helping each other, others rush by. Such short films, in which display is more important than the creation of a fictional world and in which a raw temporality trumps narrative development, Tom Gunning argues, dominated the first decade of the cinema, from the mid 1890s until 1906–7, and were still a marked presence "until World War I and the rise of the classical [narrative] paradigm."[74] Without claiming any direct influence of the genre of the actuality on the texts that Stein wrote in the period 1909–12, I think that we can make sense of those texts by aligning them with the actualities' investment in the contingent. Actualities embodied the drive to look beyond a system or a framework so as to discover life itself that is such an important theme in the work of Dilthey and Bergson. The contingency they celebrated signaled a resistance to systematizing forces.

I want to focus on "Many Many Women," a text Stein wrote in 1910 and of which she stresses the provisional nature when she remembers she wrote it as an "illustration" to *A Long Gay Book*.[75] The text was published in 1933 in the volume *Matisse Picasso and Gertrude Stein*, which also contains "A Long Gay Book" and "G. M. P."[76] Of the three texts, "A Long Gay Book" has received the most attention – it is also the text that Stein tends to spotlight – because it is the most obvious one to change. As Jennifer Ashton argues, its radical shift in style and subject matter, from repetitive sentences to a playful vocabulary and from a focus on people to things, announces *Tender Buttons*.[77] "Many Many Women," however, is interesting for my purposes because it shows Stein tackling the intertwined issues of remembering and telling.

In *The Making of Americans*, the David Hersland chapter announces a change in both remembering and telling. Early on in the book, remembering amounts to collecting resemblances and reconstructing. With reference to the grandparents of the Hersland family, for example, Stein writes:

> They never however any of them, the three Hersland children came to any realisation of them until later they remembered them and reconstructed them and realised them and then reconstructed and realised the foreign parents from a reconstruction from their reconstructed children.[78]

Remembering, here, is more or less a mechanical operation; parents and children can be reconstructed from each other. It is such a second-hand "realizing" that Stein, as we have seen, rejects when she reflects on her portraits in "Portraits and Repetition." The David Hersland portrait reveals a very different mode of remembering.

With Proustian overtones, Stein here connects memory to a sensuous chance encounter:

> Some are smelling something and then they are remembering something. Some are smelling something and are then completely remembering something. David Hersland was sometimes smelling something and then remembering something, he was interested enough in this thing.[79]

Right before she starts the lengthy portrait, she also announces a new mode of telling, stating that "[t]his is the ending of just this way of going on telling about being being in some men and in some women."⁸⁰ If, in *The Making of Americans*' concluding chapter, Stein's focus is on seeing (and hence remembering and telling) beyond a typology by engaging with one individual life, then "Many Many Women" shows her zooming in on an anonymous collective existence. It is important, furthermore, that this collective life is female.

The two short opening sentences of "Many Many Women," "Any one is having been that one. Any one is such a one," make clear that a past condition ("having been that one") continues in the present ("Anyone is having been that one"). Memory is what keeps the past alive in the present. "Any one having been that one," the text continues, "is one remembering something of such a thing, is one remembering having been that one."⁸¹ In repeating the word "one," Stein not only refuses a concrete identity – she is writing about "any one" here – she also stresses a differentiated unity. In sentences such as "Each one is one," "Each one has been one" or "Each one being one," the word "one" both refers to itself (thus creating a sense of unity) and to an unspecified past state or condition (adding difference). She soon narrows her scope, however, and identifies "one" as "she." This "she," furthermore, is involved in a curious game of remembering and forgetting:

> One who is one is remembering that she is one forgetting anything. One who is one is remembering that she is forgetting everything again and again. She is remembering this thing. She is not interested in this thing. She is remembering this thing and she is remembering that this is a quite necessary thing, it is quite a necessary thing that she is remembering that she is forgetting anything.⁸²

Stein's anonymous female protagonist is a "lonesome" modern individual.⁸³ In tune with Benjamin's understanding of a fragmented and fleeting modern experience, "she is forgetting everything again and again." At the same time, however, she is not. She fulfills the "necessary" role of "remembering that she is forgetting anything." In other words, she insists on a connection between a fragmented modern experience, as a mode of forgetting, and an underlying remembering – bridging the unbridgeable, like the cinema.

The contrast between remembering and forgetting that Stein toys with in the opening pages of "Many Many Women" goes beyond her love of paradox. In having her remembering protagonist refuse to accept an undifferentiated remembering that cancels out forgetting – "[s]he is one objecting to any one being one remembering that they are not forgetting anything" – she works with the intersecting of memory and oblivion that is key to modern experience and the representation of it.[84] The remembering/forgetting that she engages in brings to light the dynamics of the *Lebenswelt*. As Kracauer puts it, the many activities people engage in – their "doing everything," to refer back to "Composition as Explanation" – constitute the materials out of which the *Lebenswelt* is built. "Many of these materials, such as customs, rites, certain institutions, ever-recurrent routine activities, and the like," he writes, "coincide in forming the background of our social existence." What characterizes them is that they "largely fall into that zone of inertia in which the mind resides absent-mindedly."[85] It is this zone that Stein enters with her portrait. Her focus on many, many women creates a parallel between the background of social life and the lives of women. In a long series of paragraphs, she sketches a female *Lebenswelt* in which an anonymous woman engages in activities that are typically overlooked by institutionalized history channels. Those include marrying, having children, mentioning, feeling, feeding, seeing, sitting, loving children, helping, waiting, asking and giving, continuing, curing, not taking everything, and thanking. Stein keeps these activities vague; there is no narrative development to her paragraphs, no character development, no markers of time or place. "She" could be anyone. Stein spotlights this background, but also keeps intact its peculiar quality. In refusing to make the activities she records into concrete little situations, she denies them the status of *Erlebnis* or an experience that is processed and forgotten. It is the flow of *Erfahrung* that resounds in her paragraphs.

What adds to the sense of *Erfahrung* is the marked emphasis on both "continuing," or its alternative "going on," and "telling," which are repeated hundreds of times. On page 139, for example, Stein strings together "going on being living" and "telling," enjoying the rhyme between telling and smelling, and the hidden link between smelling and remembering:

> One going on being living, and she was going on being living, one going on being living was one telling quite telling, clearly telling that some who are ones being living are ones smelling and being living and smelling they are needing being ones using anything and being ones not having everything are ones taking what they are needing and being ones taking everything are ones smelling.[86]

Erfahrung is ongoing life, which used to be made accessible in and passed on by storytelling. Stein well realized that, for her generation, the form of the story could no longer accommodate everyone's experience. In having her mode of telling approach that of the early, non-narrative cinema, she makes it clear that telling became liberated from an authoritative tradition. In effect, the following paragraph can be read as a comment on that situation:

> There are many who are telling anything in some way. Every one is one telling something in some way. One was one telling anything in one way. That one was one being that one. That one had been one loving in that way, loving in a way and telling something in a way, and telling anything in a way. The way she was telling anything was a way that was a way she was realising anything could be something. She was realising anything was something and the way she was telling about anything was the way she was one being surprised by the thing that was anything. She was surprised by anything being something. She was realising anything was something. She was telling about anything telling about it in the way anything surprised her by being something. She had been loving. She had not been surprised by everything of that thing. She had been surprised by something of that thing. She was telling everything in the way she had been surprised by something. She was telling anything in a way. She was telling everything in a way.[87]

Stein's early portraits are often also portraits of herself and here, in connecting "loving in a way" to "telling something in a way," she can be seen to situate both her sexuality and her work outside of tradition, or "away" from it. Of the two activities, telling is more invested in the new than loving. If the latter amounts to a modified source of wonder, the discovery that her way of telling can make anything "be something," is a repeated surprise. This not only sketches a portrait of the artist as one discovering her own creative potential; the stress on "anything" also reflects on the cinema's celebration of contingency.

As Deleuze puts it in his Bergsonist account of the cinema, cinematic movement is defined by "any-instants-whatever" rather than by "privileged instants." While film, of course, often creates suspense by accentuating certain moments over others, that does not detract from the fact that all instants on film are no longer "the moments of actualization of a transcendent form" but immanent to movement. Movement, in other words, takes over from a set of hierarchical moments (or "there is becoming" replaces the moments "boy" and "man," to refer back to our entelechy example). The importance of this changing status of movement, from set of fixed positions to "the accumulation of banalities," lies in a changed artistic configuration of time.[88] In tune with the cinema, Deleuze writes, modern painting, dance, ballet and mime were abandoning figures and poses

> to release values which were not posed, not measured, which related movement to the any-instant-whatever. In this way, art, ballet and mime became actions capable of responding to accidents of the environment; that is, to the distribution of the points of a space, or of the moments of an event. All this served the same end as the cinema.[89]

Cinematic art, in other words, is art that is fully awake to the present in all its contingency. The present is then no longer a station in a sequence. In the present, rather, anything can happen or, with Stein, "anything can be made into something."

In "Many Many Women" the emphasis on continuity does not cancel out change. Continuity is key to existing, a paragraph like the following makes clear:

> She in living continued being living and this being what was happening she was continuing being that one. In continuing being that one she, doing everything, was continuing and in continuing she was one being one steadying that continuing is existing. Continuing is existing, she was being one and being one, continuing not being existing, she would not be one. She was one and she would be one if she was one. If she was one and she was one, if she was one she was one continuing. She was one. She was continuing.[90]

But such continuity does not mean that the routines and activities Stein brings to light enslave her anonymous protagonist. As "the realm of contingencies," in Kracauer's formulation, historical reality necessarily harbors new beginnings.[91] And that works on a collective as well as an individual level. Because Stein keeps the identity of "she" nondescript, it is possible to read an individual life into it, with "she" as one individual character who sometimes seems to coincide with Stein herself, but it is equally possible to take "she" to refer to a collective female identity, encompassing the lives of many, many women. So, when Stein writes the following reflection on development and change, we can read it both as a comment on womanhood and as an assertion of individuality:

> She was telling that in developing she had not been changing and this was something that was a curious thing as she was coming to be one deciding to choose to be changing enough to be telling that which she was going on telling.[92]

With the present unhinged from a historical pattern and positions, including subject positions, freeing themselves from prescribed roles, it was possible for many women to choose to change their lives. This kind of change is not change in the old sense of moving to a different developmental stage. It should be understood, rather, as bound up with Stein's way of telling and the movement peculiar to it.

Notes

1. Benjamin, "On Some Motifs in Baudelaire," 319.
2. McCabe, *Cinematic Modernism*, 59, 60.
3. For McCabe, Stein's fascination with "the whole thing" should be read as an assembled, fragmented whole (*Cinematic Modernism*, 60).
4. Stein, *Lectures in America*, 294.
5. Gertrude Stein, "Matisse," in *Writings: 1903–1932*, ed. Harriet Scott Chessman and Catharine R. Stimpson (New York: Library of America, 1998), 278.
6. Gertrude Stein, "Picasso," in *Writings: 1903–1932*, ed. Harriet Scott Chessman and Catharine R. Stimpson (New York: Library of America, 1998), 282.
7. Stein, *The Making of Americans*, 674.
8. See Dydo's introduction to "Ada" in her *Stein Reader* (100): "Storytelling, or talking, which leads to writing, is the central theme of *Ada*. It is an early way for mother and daughter and then for women to relate. Men like to hear Ada talking, but for her, talking with men and listening to their stories is uncomfortable and turns into something 'not nice.'"
9. Gertrude Stein, "Ada," in *Geography and Plays* (Mineola, NY: Dover Publications, 1999), 14–16.
10. Walter Benjamin, "The Storyteller: Observations on the Works of Nikolai Leskov," in *Selected Writings: 1935–1938*, vol. 3, ed. Howard Eiland and Michael W. Jennings (Cambridge, MA: Belknap Press of Harvard University Press, 2002), 143.
11. Linda Voris, for example, argues that 'Stein's method emphasizes discontinuity.' See Linda Voris, *The Composition of Sense in Gertrude Stein's Landscape Writing* (New York: Palgrave Macmillan for Springer Nature, 2016), 87.
12. Benjamin, "The Storyteller," 143, 149.
13. Benjamin, "On Some Motifs in Baudelaire," 316.
14. Walter Benjamin, "The Work of Art in the Age of Its Technological Reproducibility, Second Version," in *Selected Writings: 1935–1938*, vol. 3, ed. Howard Eiland and Michael W. Jennings (Cambridge, MA: Belknap Press of Harvard University Press, 2002), 105).

15. Benjamin, "On Some Motifs in Baudelaire," 338.
16. Ibid., 338.
17. Ibid., 336, 333, 315.
18. Ibid., 315.
19. Stein, *Lectures in America*, 298–9.
20. Benjamin, "On Some Motifs in Baudelaire," 316.
21. See also Murphet, "Gertrude Stein's Machinery of Perception," 78.
22. Sharon J. Kirsch, "How to Read *How to Write*," in *Primary Stein: Returning to the Writing of Gertrude Stein*, ed. Janet Boyd and Sharon J. Kirsch (Lanham, MD: Lexington Books, 2014), 110.
23. Stein, *Lectures in America*, 244. The text "Sentences and Paragraphs" in *How to Write* has as its motto the sentence "A Sentence is not emotional a paragraph is" (Stein, *How to Write*, 23).
24. Stein, *Lectures in America*, 297.
25. Benjamin, "On Some Motifs in Baudelaire," 314.
26. Bergson, *Creative Evolution*, 271.
27. Claire Blencowe, "Destroying Duration: The Critical Situation of Bergsonism in Benjamin's Analysis of Modern Experience," *Theory, Culture & Society* 25.4 (2008): 139.
28. Benjamin, "On Some Motifs in Baudelaire," 314.
29. Henri Bergson, *Matter and Memory*, trans. N. M. Paul and W. S. Palmer (New York and London: Zone Books and MIT Press, 1988), 242.
30. Benjamin, "On Some Motifs in Baudelaire," 338; Bergson, *Matter and Memory*, 36.
31. Benjamin, "The Storyteller," 160.
32. Bergson, *Two Sources of Morality and Religion*, 34.
33. Benjamin, "On Some Motifs in Baudelaire," 314.
34. Ibid., 315.
35. Ibid., 336.
36. Diarmuid Costello, "Aura, Face, Photography: Re-Reading Benjamin Today," in *Walter Benjamin and Art*, ed. Andrew Benjamin (London and New York: Continuum, 2005), 182.
37. Walter Benjamin, "Little History of Photography," in *Selected Writings: 1913–1934*, vol. 2, ed. Howard Eiland, Michael W. Jennings and Gary Smith (Cambridge, MA: Belknap Press of Harvard University Press, 2005), 519.
38. Benjamin, "On Some Motifs in Baudelaire," 328.
39. Walter Benjamin, "Short Speech on Proust" [1932], quoted in Miriam Bratu Hansen, *Cinema and Experience: Siegfried Kracauer, Walter Benjamin and Theodor Adorno* (Berkeley and Los Angeles: University of California Press, 2002), 111–12. Hansen takes the quotation from Benjamin's *Gesammelte Schriften*, vol. 2, ed. Rolf Tiedemann, Hermann Schweppenhäuser, et al. (Frankfurt: Suhrkamp, 1972–89), 1064.
40. Schwartz, "Cinema and the ~~Meaning~~ of Life," 9.

41. Etienne-Jules Marey, *Du mouvement dans les fonctions de la vie* (Paris: Germer Baillière, 1868), 8. My translation.
42. Etienne-Jules Marey quoted by Anson Rabinbach, *The Human Motor: Energy, Fatigue and the Origins of Modernity* (Berkeley and Los Angeles: University of California Press, 1992), 101.
43. In the 1890s Marey's own experiments with a moveable film ribbon would lead to the development of cinematography. As Rabinbach points out, "The story of Marey's role in the history of the development of 'synthetic motion' (or the motion picture camera/projector) is full of drama, tragedy and betrayal, deserving of a more detailed treatment. Briefly, Marey and Demeny [Marey's assistant] each developed several motion picture cameras and projectors in the early 1890s but the devices were ultimately denied a patent according to a law prohibiting the patenting of inventions published in scientific journals. In 1890, Demeny did, however, obtain a patent for an apparatus which synthesized eighteen chronophotographic images on a rotating disc, the phonoscope. A commercial failure, Demeny eventually sold his patent to the far more successful Lumière brothers in 1895 after a long and painful public schism with Marey" (*The Human Motor*, 333 n141).
44. Schwartz, "Cinema and the Meaning of 'Life,'" 11, and Georges Sadoul, *Louis Lumière* (Paris: Seghers, 1964), 120.
45. Schwartz, "Cinema and the Meaning of 'Life,'" 10, and Sadoul, *Louis Lumière*, 120.
46. Schwartz "Cinema and the Meaning of 'Life,'" 11, and Sadoul, *Louis Lumière*, 119.
47. Schwartz "Cinema and the Meaning of 'Life,'" 12.
48. Benjamin, "The Work of Art in the Age of Its Technological Reproducibility," 117.
49. Ibid., 117.
50. Benjamin, "On Some Motifs in Baudelaire," 317.
51. Marey, "The History of Chronophotography," quoted in Rabinbach, *The Human Motor*, 107. On Bergson and Marey, who worked together at the Collège de France, see Rabinbach, *The Human Motor*, 110.
52. Bergson, *Creative Evolution*, 313.
53. Michel Georges-Michel, "Henri Bergson Talks to Us About Cinema," originally published in *Le Journal* (February 20, 1914), translated by Louis-Georges Schwartz, *Cinema Journal* 50.3 (2011): 81.
54. Bergson, *Matter and Memory*, 155.
55. Stein, *Lectures in America*, 293, 301.
56. Mary Ann Doane writes that "[f]ilm was perceived as the imprint of time itself" (*The Emergence of Cinematic Time: Modernity, Contingency, the Archive* (Cambridge, MA, and London: Harvard University Press, 2002), 22).
57. Stein, *Lectures in America*, 293–4.

58. The term used by Helmholtz is *"unbewusster Schluss"*; see Hermann von Helmholtz, *Handbuch der physiologischen Optik* (Leipzig: Leopold Voss, 1867), 430. The translation "unconscious inference" occurs in Edwin G. Boring, *A History of Experimental Psychology* (New York and London: D. Appleton Century Company, 1929), 300–4.
59. Jonathan Crary, *Suspensions of Perception: Attention, Spectacle and Modern Culture* (Cambridge, MA: MIT, 2001), 319.
60. Hermann von Helmhotz quoted in Crary, *Suspensions of Perception*, 320. The quotation is taken from Chapter 26 of Helmholtz's *Handbuch der physiologischen Optik*.
61. Crary, *Suspensions of Perception*, 321. While, at some instances, Bergson's project comes with a nostalgic slant, Claire Colebrook has shown that Bergsonism can also be seen to work for a techno-future; see Colebrook, *Deleuze and the Meaning of Life*.
62. Dydo, *The Language that Rises*, 266.
63. Stein, *Lectures in America*, 301.
64. Kracauer, *Theory of Film*, 300.
65. Siegfried Kracauer and Paul Oskar Kristeller, *History: The Last Things before the Last* (Princeton, NJ: Marcus Wiener, 1995), 4. For work on the relation between Kracauer's early and late work, see D. N. Rodowick, "The Last Things before the Last: Kracauer and History," *New German Critique* 41 (Spring/Summer 1987): 109–39; Inka Mülder-Bach and Gail Finney "History as Autobiography: The Last Things before the Last," *New German Critique* 54 (Autumn 1991): 139–157.
66. Kracauer, *Theory of Film*, 14 and Kracauer, *History*, 50.
67. Kracauer, *History*, 45.
68. Ibid., 191. See also Rodowick, "The Last Things before the Last: Kracauer and History," 132.
69. Kracauer, *History*, 45.
70. Stein, *Lectures in America*, 280.
71. Ibid., 280.
72. Ibid., 278, 280.
73. Doane, *The Emergence of Cinematic Time*, 22.
74. Tom Gunning, "Attractions: How They Came into the World," in *The Cinema of Attractions Reloaded*, ed. Wanda Strauven (Amsterdam: Amsterdam University Press, 2006), 36.
75. Stein, *Lectures in America*, 278.
76. *Matisse, Picasso and Gertrude Stein* constitutes the fifth and final volume in Stein's and Toklas's Plain Edition imprint.
77. Jennifer Ashton, "Introduction" to Gertrude Stein, *Matisse, Picasso and Gertrude Stein with Two Shorter Stories* (Mineola, NY: Dover Publications, 2000), 3.
78. Stein, *The Making of Americans*, 261.
79. Ibid., 850.
80. Ibid., 719.

81. Stein, "Many Many Women," 119.
82. Ibid., 119.
83. Ibid., 121.
84. Ibid., 120. There is a curious analogy here between Stein's emphasis on the intersecting of remembering and forgetting and Adorno's response to Benjamin's Baudelaire essay: "Is it not the case that the real task here is to bring the entire opposition between *Erlebnis* and *Erfahrung* into relation with a dialectical theory of forgetting? Or one could equally say, into relation with a theory of reification. For all reification is a forgetting: objects become purely thing-like the moment they are retained for us without the continued presence of their other aspects: when something of them has been forgotten" (Walter Benjamin and Theodor Adorno, *The Complete Correspondence 1928–1940*, ed. Henri Lonitz and trans. Nicholas Walker (Cambridge, MA: Harvard University Press, 1999), 321).
85. Kracauer, *History*, 22–5.
86. Stein, "Many Many Women," 139.
87. Ibid., 133.
88. Gilles Deleuze, *Cinema 1: The Movement Image*, trans. Hugh Tomlinson and Barbara Habberjam (London: Continuum, 2005), 6.
89. Ibid., 7.
90. Stein, "Many Many Women," 158 .
91. Kracauer, *History*, 31.
92. Stein, "Many Many Women," 167.

Chapter 5

Cinematic Collectivities

If "Many Many Women," like *The Making of Americans*, invests in a collective history, then the portraits of individuals that Stein starts writing by late 1910 appear to have a very different scope.[1] Yet the fact that these texts are about individuals does not mean that Stein gives up on the issue of how to understand a modern collective experience. Quite to the contrary: in the period between 1910 and 1913, Stein is intensely focused on the issue of a collective being, which she explores in dialogue with the cinema. She makes, for example, a series of group portraits about the figure of the crowd, that most modern of protagonists. In a number of those portraits, she moves the crowd from its habitat, the streets, to the famous Bon Marché department store in Paris. Here, again, Stein adds counterweight to the typically masculine symbols of modern city life: "the public sphere, the man of the crowd, the stranger, the dandy, the flâneur."[2] Department stores, as Lauren Rabinovitz indicates, were intertwined with a cinematic culture in that they were the subjects of early films, which tended to mock the consumerist frenzy. Like the panorama, furthermore, they were part of the nineteenth-century culture of spectacle out of which the cinema emerged. Or, as Rabinovitz puts it,

> [a]s one of the chief urban spaces in which women freely circulated in the late 19th century, they prepared women for the cinema by providing exemplary spectacles both inside the store and within the framed window displays set into the stores' facades along the street.[3]

Another way in which Stein tackles the issue of a modern collectivity is through plays. Plays, Stein herself points out, share the cinema's "impulse to solve the problem of time in relation to emotion and the relation of the scene to the emotion of the audience."[4]

What she means by this is that both art forms manage to create one experience made up of diverging temporalities, which she considered the fundamental problem of her generation. As we will see, the plays that Stein writes seek to locate a cinematic collective experience within the text. First, however, I want to show how her individual-centered portraits intersect with the cinema in creating new formations for a shared life, beyond the grasp of tradition. My focus is on "Orta Or One Dancing."

Family Living

"Orta Or One Dancing" may well be considered Stein's most cinematic portrait. Its protagonist, Orta Davray, is modeled on the American dancer Isadora Duncan, as an earlier title of the piece suggests.[5] Dance, Kracauer argues in his *Theory of Film*, is one of the three quintessential cinematic movements, the others being the chase, which Stein experiments with in her 1920 film script "Film," and nascent motion.[6] Dance, for Kracauer, epitomizes the "cinematic nature of movements which grow out of life itself" and, in doing so, opens up dimensions of life that are normally overwritten by habit or custom. In the case of several people dancing, film reveals social designs "as delicate as lacework" that are normally hidden from view. When the camera acts as a voyeur and zooms in on an individual dancer,

> [h]is self-forgetting rapture may show in queer gestures and distorted facial expressions which are not intended to be watched, save by those who cannot watch them because they themselves participate in the dancing. Looking at such secret displays is like spying; you feel ashamed for entering a forbidden realm where things are going on which must be experienced, not witnessed.[7]

Although Kracauer's examples are to be situated later than 1911 – he refers to René Clair and Fred Astaire, among others – his point about the cinematic nature of dance can be extended to the early cinema and its relation to the dance culture of which the subject of Stein's portrait, Isadora Duncan, was part.[8]

Dancers are prominent among the subjects of Marey's and Muybridge's photographic experiments and by the mid-1890s a central feature of early cinema was the so-called serpentine dance, made famous by the American expat dancer Loïe Fuller. Fuller's highly popular 1890s performances, in which the dancer's body, fabric and light merged into something of a vortex, led to scores of short dance films in which she, or other dancers imitating her, worked themselves in and out of meters of flowing cloth. For the French filmmaker Germaine Dulac, twenty years younger than Fuller, the link between her cinematic work and Fuller's dance performances was obvious:

> Loïe Fuller created her first harmonies of light at the same moment that the Lumière Brothers gave us the cinema. Strange coincidence at the dawn of an era which will be that of visual music; the work of Loïe Fuller borders on ours and that is why cinéastes render her a profound and ultimate homage.[9]

In echo of Dulac, Tom Gunning points out that Fuller "invented the cinema" because she performed on stage what early films would bring to the screen: pure movement, galvanized by an intricate usage of light technology.[10] Fuller's dance, moreover, exemplifies the Deleuzean–Bergsonist argument about the changing nature of movement, from transcendental forms to cinematic duration. If a set of forms, or positions, is central to traditional ballet, then "Fuller's dance, as the art of motion, seemed to offer forms dissolved by cinema."[11]

Isadora Duncan started her European dance career as a protégée of Fuller. Duncan – whose life parallels that of Stein in that both had grown up in Oakland, California, and then spent some time on the East coast of the USA before moving first to London and later to Paris – was invited by Fuller to join her company on a tour to Germany and Austria in 1902. Her career took off from there, and soon she enjoyed a reputation equal to that of Fuller. The two dancers were often compared to each other, which sparked something of a competition between them over the question of whose methods were the most natural. A 1911 critic, for example, found it "curious" that "[Fuller's] students all dance like Isadora Duncan."[12] On the issue of naturalness, Duncan provocatively scored better points. She stripped Fuller's dreamlike female figures and showed audiences what a real, almost naked, female body in motion looks like.[13] Rather than evoking the movements of a snake or butterfly, like Fuller, she focused on the movements of the human body itself.[14] Although, unlike Fuller, Duncan did not have a career in film, her performances were at the center of an aesthetics of women in motion, which cinematic dance was popularizing in the early twentieth century.[15]

If Fuller symbolized a clichéd feminine sensuousness – mysterious and fragile like the butterfly she conjured up – then Stein's portrait of Isadora Duncan corrects that representation of the female dancer. "Orta Or One Dancing," Dydo remarks, was written "while [Stein] was grappling with the nature of the creative personality in *Two*, a long double portrait of her brother Leo and her sister-in-law Sarah Stein."[16] *Two* is an unflattering portrait of two separate poles, with Leo representing the typically masculine intellect, out of touch with sensuous experience, and Sarah as his opposite. "Orta Or One Dancing," by contrast, unites thinking and dancing in the performance of the dancer:

> She was dancing then. She certainly was thinking then. She had been thinking some. She was meaning everything then. She was completely then meaning everything then and thinking then thinking that meaning is existing and she was dancing then, quite dancing then. She was dancing then, she was meaning that thing, meaning dancing, she was dancing then, she was meaning thinking then, she was thinking then, she was meaning everything, she was dancing.[17]

Stein's emphasis ("certainly") on the combination of sensuous bodily and cerebral activity brings to mind Bergson's method of intuition, which asks the intellect and instinct to work together. As we have seen, such a meaningful synthesis of the intellect and instinct, or conscious and unconscious activity, was theorized as the cinema's feat in early film theory. The combination of sensuous immediacy and reflection was taken to make possible a new kind of shared experience, outside of the grasp of tradition – it made for an uncanny "taking part in," in Kracauer's terms, and for *Erfahrung* rather than *Erlebnis* in Benjamin's.

Stein cleverly inscribes the possibility of a new collective experience in her portrait. On one level she tells an individual life story – in the sparsest of terms – about a woman living a new kind of life, one in which she can independently work and raise a family:

> She was one beginning being living and there were then others who were ones doing that thing, being living. Her mother was being living and was living then with four children. The mother was one having been married to some one and she was one then not needing that thing enough not needing that thing so that the one to whom she had been married could then marry another one.
>
> She was living then with four children and all of them all the four children were being living then, were quite commencing then being ones being living [. . .].[18]

This excerpt spotlights a dimension of the early twentieth-century aesthetics of women in motion that the symbolists ignored in their portraits of dancers. Stein's Orta is not an animal-like sexual creature, existing for the male imagination, but a woman making a living and setting an example for her children and others. On another level, Stein makes her portrait about more than just Orta/Duncan, or even Orta/Duncan as the new woman.

After having been part of an Isadora Duncan performance, one spectator observed how "[i]n this [. . .] free, simple, happy, expressive, rhythmic movement was focussed all I and a hundred others had been dreaming."[19] In analogy to that comment, Stein emphasizes the extent to which Orta needs others to make her "one being dancing." No dance performance is complete without an audience. Stein makes us see how Orta is both the one in complete charge of her family and at the same time completely dependent on others:

> She was one beginning being living and then she was one being that one being dancing. She was beginning then being on being existing. She was then being one and every one in her family living was needing then needing being completing that thing, completing her being one being dancing. She was then beginning being living. She was then one being like some and she was then one being existing, being one who was a young one and family living was being existing and she was then one completing that thing completing family living in being one being dancing and being the one each one was then completing as being one being dancing. She was being then quite like some. She was then feeling anything in any one being one completing her being one being dancing. She was then being one feeling anything in being one completing the family living in being one being dancing. She was then being one feeling anything in being one needing being that one, the one she was then.[20]

"[E]very one in her family living was needing" Orta's dance career to work out, for her to complete her ambitions. At the same time, she is in touch with those who are "completing her being one being dancing." When, in the next paragraph, she is described as "creating family living being existing," it is unclear whether we should understand that as Orta successfully providing for her children or generating a new kind of family living by making spectators feel connected to her and to each other. This deliberate ambiguity is added to by the key verbs in the two consecutive paragraphs, which are "exceeding" and "contradicting." In dancing, Orta exceeds and contradicts life as tradition has shaped it. While the "meaning" that dancing brings into being may not be that of tradition, dancing does not amount to a break with memory. To the contrary, the "feeling in thinking in meaning being existing" that dancing amounts to makes for a valid and unrestricted mode of remembering. Stein asserts that "[r]emembering being dancing is something" and describes Orta as "remember[ing] everything of being one who could be dancing."[21]

As portraitist, furthermore, Stein takes on the role of rememberer. What early film did for Loïe Fuller, she does for Isadora Duncan; her record of a Duncan dance performance grants it a life after it has happened. She does not write about Duncan's dancing, but makes the new sense of motion that both the early cinema and Duncan's modern dance were exploring – what Stein calls "believing in moving in any direction" – integral to her portrait. A quotation from Bergson on the movement of thought makes this particularly clear. For Stein and Bergson alike, meaning was to be found in how things move rather than in the things themselves. "[M]eaning," Bergson explains in a 1911 lecture, "is less a thing thought than the movement of thought, less a movement than a direction."[22] Thoughts, for Bergson, are processes "spread[ing] out more and more over the successive planes of the mind" until they find an expression in language. Once a thought reaches the plane of speech, Bergson argues,

> it expresses itself by means of a sentence, that is by a group of pre-existing elements; but it can almost arbitrarily choose the first elements of the group provided that the others are complementary to them; the same thought is translated just as well into diverse sentences composed of entirely different words, provided these words have the same connection between them.[23]

The idea of thought developing is an apposite analogy for Stein's portraiture. The words Stein chooses are hardly arbitrary – indeed, her emphatic use of the terms "being," "existing," "living," "developing" and "changing" aligns her with the life-focused discourses that are the subject of this book – but the combination of a restricted, abstract vocabulary with grammatically patterned sentences foregrounds the ways in which the words relate to each other. These changing relations or connections, the push and pull of denial and affirmation or the shifting affirmations of being, are more important than the sentences' individual statements. "Orta Or One Dancing" is not the first portrait in which Stein experiments with dynamic sentences or "moving paragraphs," but it is in Duncan's dancing-as-thinking that she found the apt figure for her own practice. As Dydo points out, there is one phrase in the manuscript that makes explicit Stein's identification with Duncan, which Stein deleted in a later typescript: "She was then resembling some one, one who was not dancing, *one who was writing*, she was then resembling some all of whom were ones believing in thinking [. . .]."[24]

Crowds

Stein was not only interested in the ability of individual artists like Isadora Duncan and Picasso to unite people in an aesthetic family living, whether as an audience completing the performance or as a host of followers, she was also fascinated by the ways in which people assemble in different kinds of groups. By her own account, the goal of the book she started working on after *The Making of Americans* – *A Long Gay Book* – "was to describe [. . .] every possible kind of pairs of human beings and every possible threes and fours and fives of human beings and every possible kind of crowds of human beings."[25] That project was never accomplished but quite a few of Stein's portraits written in the early 1910s show her exploring different group constellations. In "Many Many Women," as we have seen, she sketches a large female counter-tradition, but she also often writes about smaller groups to work on the question of how people connect. This can be through a character trait (as in "Four Dishonest Ones"), kinship ties (as in "A Family of Perhaps Three"), artistic ambitions ("G. M. P.") or, as in the texts I want to focus on here, a shared setting.

In four texts written in 1911–12 Stein zooms in on the figure of the crowd, as the anonymous, consuming protagonist of the early twentieth-century Parisian metropolis. "Flirting at the Bon Marche," "Bon Marche Weather," "Rue de Rennes" and "Galeries Lafayette" by their titles refer to places where people shop, and show "a very great many" engaged in ongoing, aimless shopping.[26] The crowds that are the subject of these portraits are modern in an almost comically clichéd sense. If such films as *Bargain Day* (1903) or *Bargain Fiend, or Shopping à la Mode* (1907) poke fun at female shoppers going crazy during the sales, Stein leaves the gender of the crowd undetermined. Yet, like early films set in department stores, she concentrates on an element of dehumanization, be it not by animating mannequins, which is what happens in films such as *Shocking Stockings* (1904) or *Four Beautiful Pairs* (1904). In Stein's texts it is the crowd that turns into something of an automaton since it

148   *Vital Stein*

lacks the ability to change and meaningfully express itself that is central to Orta's "being one being living." In "Flirting at the Bon Marche" Stein's shoppers try to suppress *ennui* with the thrill of consumption:

> Some are coming to know very well that they are living in a very dreary way of living. Some are coming to know very well that they are living in a very sad way of living. Some are coming to know very well that they are living in a very tedious way of living. Some are coming to know very well that they are living in a very dull way of living.
>
> These go shopping. They go shopping and it always was a thing they were rightly doing. Now everything is changing. Certainly everything is changing. They go shopping, they are being in a different way of living. Everything is changing.[27]

Everything, of course, does not change and the tedium continues. Stein does not rule out the possibility that the shoppers may actually change their lives beyond the lure of shopping, however, and ends the portrait by divorcing "changing" from buying and selling. In contrast to the dull refrain of commercial interaction, the portrait concludes, actual change comes in different modes: "sometimes in some quite some changing, in some quite completely changing, in some some changing, in some not very much changing."[28]

In a similar vein, "Galeries Lafayette" underlines the conformity and stasis that shopping implies. Here the crowd is a big group ("there are many of them") in which "[e]ach one of them is one." Unlike Orta's being one, which implied "moving in every direction," the individuals that make up the crowd are presented as stuck in their roles as customers (which the repetition of the phrase "accustomed to it" hints at). "One" in this portrait is not the open "any one" that Stein often makes central to her texts, but a hollow and constricting group identity. The role of customer has become a habit, something "each one is accustomed to" and "used to."[29] Stein mocks the commercial rhetoric that targets everyone in their uniqueness. The fact that "[e]ach one is one and is that one and is especially that one [. . .] and is certainly very well accustomed to be especially that one" blocks the difference and change that make individuals unique. In "Bon Marche Weather" this commercial erasure of individuality is showcased by interchangeable pronouns. "We," "I," "everybody" and "you" all share the same bland experiences that make up the meaningless conversations we engage in with fellow customers or shop attendants:

Very pleasant weather we are having. Very pleasant weather I am having. Very nice weather everybody is having. Very nice weather you are having.

Very nice eating every body is having. Very nice eating I am having. Very nice eating they are having. Very nice eating you are having.[30]

If, in "Bon Marche Weather," there is a comic element to the experiences the shoppers are exchanging as if they were possessions – they are "having" weather, eating, travelling and "a very bad season" – then "Rue de Rennes" makes explicit how scary an encounter with this homogeneous crowd can be. The portrait is different from the other three in that it is not concerned with shopping per se but with the hold of money on the crowd's life. The "frightening thing" at the center of the portrait is the regularity of the crowd's existence, which is determined by making money and paying for life:

This thing that is such a thing, this thing that is existing, that is a frightening thing to one, is a way of living of very many being living, a way of living of some who are being ones steadily working, who are ones steadily saving, who are ones paying what they are always needing to be paying that is enough to be ones going on being living, who are doing what every one who is of them is needing so that each one of them can be one going on in being living [. . .].

The one "telling it again and again" how much this situation terrifies her is not alone in her negative stance. There are the snobs who think such a life is "ugly," "common" or "simple," and those for whom it is a "pleasant" or "charming" thing – which only adds to the portrait's ominous tone. And sadly, there are also those for whom it is the only possible reality ("the only complete thing").[31]

For Benjamin, the artistic representation of the crowd was an important task for nineteenth-century artists and writers. In "On Some Motifs in Baudelaire," for example, he lauds Edgar Allan Poe's story "The Man of the Crowd" for detailing hidden social dynamics.[32] Yet Stein, working in the early twentieth century, soon lost interest in her position of crowd-watcher. What she saw, looking at the Bon Marché customers, conforms to what Benjamin, in "The Work of Art in the Age of its Technological Reproducibility," calls the "compact mass" of the petty bourgeoisie, that "impenetrable, compact entity" that has been the subject of mass psychology.[33] By 1912 Stein was done with the psychologist's stance. She wanted to find a way to penetrate her generation and describe its workings from within. To that end she approaches the idea of the group differently, and with new energy. The style of her work changes radically; texts such as *Tender Buttons* and "What Happened. A Five Act Play" are no longer clustered around a limited vocabulary and repetitive gerund constructions but charm readers with sensuous nouns, puns and playful associations.[34] What best sums up her new approach to the crowd is the following quotation, taken from the lecture "Plays," in which she explains how she wanted to get at the hidden stories and forces making up collective life, as an insider: "So naturally what I wanted to do in my play was what everybody did not always know nor always tell. By everybody I do of course include myself by always I do of course include myself."[35] That act of including herself is most obvious in *Tender Buttons*, Stein's playful self-portrait that, as we will see below, triggered her play writing.

Odd Familiarities

A constant in Stein's reflections on *Tender Buttons*, the poetry collection on which she started work in 1912, is, perhaps surprisingly, a concern for visual perception. In *The Autobiography of Alice B. Toklas*, for example, she relates the book to her desire to express "the rhythm of the visible world," and in "Portraits and Repetition" she states that "the excitement in me was then that I was to more and more include looking to make it a part of listening and talking."[36] Where, as we have seen, she initially sought to avoid looking because of the entanglements between a theory of observation and a conservative understanding of memory, she now admits that "looking could not entirely be left out."[37] The looking Stein engages in from *Tender Buttons* onwards has little to do with perception as theorized by Helmholtz. It is, rather, a mode of perception that keeps track with the cinema in that it makes strange the ordinary and the familiar.

For Benjamin, the cinema played a key part in a changed, modern perception. "Film," he writes in a note to the third version of "The Work of Art in the Age of Its Technological Reproducibility," "corresponds to profound changes in the apparatus of apperception – changes that are experienced on the scale of private existence by each passerby in big-city traffic, and on a historical scale by every present-day citizen." These changes first and foremost amount to a "deepening of apperception."[38] In the second version of the essay Benjamin uses the image of the surgeon entering the patient's body with his hands to get across the work of the camera. The surgeon is to the magician what the cinematographer is to the painter. The second of each pair maintain a "natural distance" between themselves and the subject they are treating or painting. The first of each pair, by contrast, "penetrat[e] deeply" into the tissue before them. Where the work of the magician/painter is invested in an authoritative tradition – in that the community accepts the magician's power to heal and the painter's power to create – the surgeon/cinematographer makes visible a composition alien to tradition's scope. The surgeon "abstains at the decisive moment from confronting his patient person to person." What he or she looks at, and touches, are organs. Similarly, the cinematographer's image is not the "total image" of the painter, but a "piecemeal" composition, "its manifold parts being assembled according to a new law."[39]

This "new law" governing a modern composition is that of what Benjamin calls "the second technology," which he associates particularly with film. If the first technology is one of seriousness and rigor, in which humans seek to master nature, the second is rooted in play, devoted to the exploration of "the interplay between nature and humanity." From ancient modes of making rooted in ritual to the machine age, technology sought to establish results that are "valid once and for all." The second technology, by contrast, establishes results that are "wholly provisional" as "it operates by means of experiments and endlessly varied test procedures." Most importantly, for Benjamin, the second technology holds a liberating potential. Indeed, in a note he posits that "this technology aims at liberating human beings from drudgery."[40] Its reconfiguration of the relation between the elements involved in its system expands our scope for play and brings into view utopian goals. Film is Benjamin's prime example because it creates a different world, one we could not *see* before the invention of cinematic technology. As we have seen, film not only reveals movements hitherto invisible to the human eye, but it also establishes new kinds of subject positions. If, on the stage, actors embody their role in front of an audience, film actors find themselves freed from the spectator's – and tradition's – gaze. They act in front of an apparatus, not a living audience. Their performance, furthermore, is not bound to the here and now of the play but is shot over the course of several days or weeks, and then edited into a sequence that was never acted out as such. Film, in other words, places a human being "in a position where he must operate with his whole living person, while foregoing its aura."[41]

In addition, the audience is no longer confined to a purely receptive position. The masses that used to be silenced by tradition can now take part in their own representation. News reels make it clear that "*[a]ny person today can lay claim to being filmed*," and in the fact that in Russian cinema, for example, workers are asked to "portray themselves" Benjamin sees new social opportunities.[42]

Dynamic Lifes

With *Tender Buttons* Stein penetrates the skin of her domestic life. In explaining the project in *The Autobiography of Alice B. Toklas*, she too sets up a contrast between her mode of looking and that of the painter. For Stein, "tormented by the problem of the external and the internal," painters essentially fail in representing the internal life of human beings. Where it is up to writers to peer into souls and minds, the world of the painter is that of the visible, of surface and texture. That divide is what "sends the painter to painting still lifes" – and by "still lifes" Stein wants us to understand not only paintings of motionless objects but also stilled lives, or deathly portraits. She herself, of course, wanted to rethink that divide and *Tender Buttons* is the most radical result of her "struggle" to create dynamic lifes, or living portraits.[43]

Reading *Tender Buttons* as a collection of dynamic life portraits is somewhat out of step with Stein criticism. Wendy Steiner's hallmark study of Stein's portraits set the tone in 1978 by excluding *Tender Buttons* from its scope because the volume deals with objects, food and rooms rather than human beings.[44] To be sure, the volume has been met with lots of outstanding scholarly work, but critics tend to read it as an exception to Stein's fascination with people.[45] I nevertheless think that when Stein states that she "made her chief study people and therefore the never ending series of portraits," *Tender Buttons* fits into that never-ending series because it amounts to a long self-portrait.[46] With the volume, Stein cleverly twists the issue of how to represent the "internal" that is the writer's domain. Like Benjamin's surgeon, she avoids the form of the person in order to be able to touch the fragments on the inside of the space in which she lives and into which she invites her readers – trading body for home.

Tender Buttons functions as a portrait without a protagonist; "[a]ct so that there is no use in a center" is the programmatic opening sentence of the "Rooms" section.[47] It is hardly an empty text, however. Indeed, if the book can be said to be about something, it is about contents. Many of the titles in the "Objects" section refer to containers of some kind, including "A Carafe, that is a blind glass," "A substance in a cushion," "A box" (in different versions), "A long dress," "A purse," "Shoes" and "Book." If readers are observing these "holders" in the first section, they are confronted with their own bodies as containers in the second section. Food, after all, is what we take in. With the third section the perspective shifts again, since we now find ourselves contained by spacious rooms in which looking and eating take place. The absence of the owner of the objects, or the tenant of the rooms, enables Stein to give the elements making up her life free rein. On a micro-level, the associative logic that steers the descriptions, as she calls them, makes the contents of the vignettes impossible to be held by their containers. A carafe, as we have seen, is not only "a blind glass," but also

> A kind in glass and a cousin, a spectacle and nothing strange a single hurt color and an arrangement in a system to pointing. All this and not ordinary, not unordered in not resembling. The difference is spreading.[48]

In other words, a carafe is not a looking glass, even it is a kind of glass or a member of the glass family *and* something ordinary to look at *and* something that frames a color *and* a word serving an indexical function ("a system to pointing"). It is "all this" because, different from ordinary life, the poem orders it not to resemble, not to fall in line. Doing so, it enables the difference to spread. On the level of the collection, the volume refuses to pin down its contents. The contents list to the "Food" section on page 34 functions as an odd poem in its own right, mildly disrupting the hierarchy of text and paratext. In addition, it is incomplete; it does not indicate that many of the poems have different versions ("Orange," for example, comes in four variants) and it leaves unmentioned the "Chain-boats" poem. With masterful wit, this text signals that even the contents cannot contain the contents. The deletion of a protagonist–owner makes room for the things by which she organizes her life to take on a life of their own. Stein translates her hope for paintings – she "passionately hoped that some picture would remain out of its frame [. . .] that the painting will move, that it will live outside its frame" – to a poetic act of deframing, or decentralizing, the contents of her life. *Tender Buttons*, then, is the whole of Stein's being, stripped of its aura.[49]

Tender Buttons' "dynamic lifes" move in the sense that one thing constantly turns into another thing – carafe, glass, spectacle, color, word, poem – but they also dynamize life. In tune with the cinema's living portraits, which, as we have seen, triggered a revaluation of the concepts of life and death, Stein's tender vignettes divorce life from the living individual. Parallel to the early cinema's ability to reproduce the life of deceased people again and again runs a fascination with the animation of dead matter. Long before Jean Epstein's famous essay "De quelques conditions de la photogénie" (1923), which calls the cinema "animistic," early filmmakers had been experimenting with object animation, in both avant-garde and popular cinema.[50] Often these experiments center on domestic contexts; the spaces in which we live and the objects in them magically come alive and escape our control. In Georges Méliès's *The Bewitched Inn* (1897), for example, someone undresses, only to see that his clothes start living, and in J. Stuart Blackton's *The Haunted Hotel* (1907) objects with a will of their own inhabit a hotel. Vachel Lindsay's *The Art of the Moving Picture* (1915) refers to a French Pathé film in which, on moving day, household objects relocate themselves.[51] The best part, for Lindsay, is the family's shoes "walking down the boulevard" with a "masterful air of their own as though they were the most important part of a human being."[52] *Tender Buttons* does not cast objects in character roles, but it makes clear that, in its domestic world devoid of human beings, "there is breath," "plenty of breathing" and also breeding ("breed, breed that").[53]

In tune with such films about living household objects, moreover, *Tender Buttons* serves its audience a homely alienation. It asks them to enter a world they do not know that is nevertheless stuffed with everyday elements. For Benjamin, it was the cinema's feat that it could empower people through such a peculiarly familiar yet, at the same time, new experience. To make his point he asks us to think about what he calls "*[r]eception in distraction.*" Such a distracted reception "*finds in film its true training ground*" but actually captures a relationship to art that is as old as architecture. For buildings, Benjamin points out, are received not only optically but also through use and touch:

> Such reception cannot be understood in terms of the concentrated attention of a traveler before a famous building. On the tactile side, there is no counterpart to what contemplation is on the optical side. Tactile reception comes about not so much by way of attention as by way of habit.[54]

Touch brings back to mind the image of the surgeon handling organs. As opposed to contemplation, or the situation in which spectator or traveler keeps a respectful distance faced with the aura of a work of art or a famous building, touch enables an entering. The distraction that Benjamin spotlights (and that is, of course, where the surgeon analogy dissipates) adds to the open quality of the process; a cinema audience, like tenants in a building, assume their position without questioning whether they have the right to be there or feeling excluded by the artwork's elitism. They do not need to focus their way in, but "absorb the work of art into themselves. Their waves lap around it; they encompass it with their tide." Distraction or habit, almost as the refrain of inhabiting, is not, for Benjamin, the obstruction to change that it was for many other modernists. The distracted mass audience of the cinema accepts the cinema as part of its world, and thus not only is open to the change it may project, but also feels enabled to criticize. Everyone is a user, a "quasi-expert."[55]

As an experimental poetry collection written by an unknown author and published by the little-known press Claire Marie in a print run of only 1,000 copies, *Tender Buttons* did not appeal to a mass audience – although it did manage to create quite some commotion.[56] Yet its domestic vantage and outspoken emphasis on sensuous touch and multifarious use place it in line with what the cinema was doing, according to Benjamin. The book may have been fueled by Stein's "desire to express the rhythm of the visible world," but it also immediately makes clear that the visible is not solely to be looked at. Touch, as Rebecca Scherr has argued, is key to Stein's aesthetics from *Tender Buttons* onwards.[57] Texture, from wood over wool, lace and leather, is a key dimension of the poems in the Objects section. The visual title "Red roses," for example, unfolds into a description in which touch precedes sight, with a hand making an explicit appearance: "A cool red rose and a pink cut pink, a collapse and a sold hole, a little less hot."[58] The food too is described in ways that imply tactile perception, from "pale hot" salad, "cold coffee" for lunch, to "lovely snipe and tender turn" accompanying roast beef and "carved" beef. The reader is also explicitly asked to hold the contents of *Tender Buttons*; "Hold the pine, hold the dark, hold in the rush, make the bottom" goes one sequence of imperatives. Touching and holding, moreover, are intertwined with using: "what is used as it is held by holding."[59]

While *Tender Buttons* relates habit to tyrannical authoritative structures, use and care are celebrated.[60] In the space Stein creates with the volume, use does not serve a closed functionalist scheme in which, as in Benjamin's first technology, "man" seeks to master his surroundings, but implies living with and caring for the things you have collected – "care" is, according to the volume's final sentence, what makes food ("a magnificent asparagus") and objects ("and also a fountain").[61] And living with/caring for is a distracted process; you often forget where exactly you placed an object ("Book was there, it was there. Book was there"), to whom you have lent it or given it away ("and perhaps if borrowing is not natural there is some use in giving"), or how long you have had it for or which color it used to have, as in "A Purse":

> A purse was not green, it was not straw color, it was hardly seen and it had a use a long use and the chain, the chain was never missing, it was not misplaced, it showed that it was open, that is all that it showed.[62]

The stuff we live with also tends to change. Through heavy ("long") use it can change color, or as Stein puts it in "A substance in a cushion": "The change of color is likely and a difference a very little difference is prepared." Objects may break (punning on chinaware she writes: "There can be breakages in Japanese, or they may be put to unexpected usages"). In "A shawl," for instance, "A shawl is a hat" before it is "a wedding." The objects we acquire may also have a history, to which our use will add. Say you bought a "glazed and glittering" bowl at the flea market yesterday and wondered about the purposes it has served. You may note that "It was chosen yesterday, that showed spitting and perhaps washing and polishing."[63] Use, in sum, creates a dynamic constellation; elements do not occupy a fixed position, and dead and animated, and human and non-human, are not in strict opposition. As such, finally, the rooms and their cluttered contents become a figure for Stein's generation.

Reading *Tender Buttons* as both a twist on a self-portrait and, in an abstract sense, a portrait of her generation, or, better, a portrait of the concept of a generation, is not as contradictory as it may seem. *Tender Buttons*, Stein tells us in "Poetry and Grammar," was poetry.[64] Stein's understanding of poetry in the lecture is, surprisingly, openly romantic. We may be used to her spotlighting the extent to which she worked according to her own criteria, but "Poetry and Grammar" shows her engaging with the traditions of romantic poetry. She introduces, for instance, an anecdote about a "very much older brother," whose passionate gaze turned "any little square of grass" into a vibrant world "filled with birds and bees and butterflies" – the name Walt Whitman is mentioned on the next page. And the way in which she sings the fluidity of nouns as names, and the poet's task to "refuse them by using them," brings to mind Keats's epitaph "Here lies one whose name is writ in water."[65] Romantic poetry's agenda to let the individual speak for the collective – with, most famously, Whitman's "I contain multitudes" – is often taken as clashing with modernism's hyper-individual stance. Yet, as Joel Nickels has argued, modernist poetry also often set in motion an erasure of the self in order to bring back into view a collectivity.[66]

In "Poetry and Grammar" Stein emphatically relates poetry to the collective. After mentioning Whitman she writes:

> We that is any human being living has inevitably to feel the thing anything being existing, but the name of that thing of that anything is no longer anything to thrill any one except children. So as everybody has to be a poet, what was there to do.[67]

For Stein, focused on the issue of naming, the poetry of *Tender Buttons* offered a solution to that question. Many other modernist artists and critics, however, sought a new complete experience, where individual and collective meet, in the cinema. Yet, curiously, early cinema was considered a form of poetry. As R. Bruce Elder points out, in the early twentieth century, "[c]inema had a status analogous to that of 'Transcendental Poetry' in the work of Friedrich von Schlegel" and "many artists and thinkers of the early twentieth century believed that cinema was [Transcendental Poetry's] closest approximation."[68] *Tender Buttons* as poetry, then, does not contradict Stein's "doing what the cinema was doing" – not even when we consider it as the starting point of Stein's playwriting.

Almost Strangers in Real Scenes

If the cinema's synthetic force appeared to be a non-contemporary response to the ambitions of romantic poetry, the cinema was also, and perhaps in a more obvious sense, the new theater. As Laura Marcus shows, "[c]inema was seen variously as a threat to theatre, or as its salvation from massification."[69] For Hugo Münsterberg, under whose supervision Stein had done laboratory work at Radcliffe College, the cinema surpassed the theater in galvanizing the dramatic representation of life. In his 1916 study *The Photoplay*, Münsterberg lauds the many lifelike connections that film makes possible:

> Life does not move forward on one single pathway. The whole manifoldness of parallel currents with their endless interconnections is the true substance of our understanding. It may be the task of a particular

art to force all into one steady development between the walls of one room, but every letter and every telephone call to the room remind us even then that other developments with other settings are proceeding in the same instant. The soul longs for this whole interplay, and the richer it is in contrasts, the more satisfaction may be drawn from our simultaneous presence in many quarters. The photoplay alone gives us our chance for such omnipresence.[70]

The cinema is true to life, for Münsterberg, because the "endless interconnections" of parallel currents it knows how to capture are in tune with how we tend to think about things happening in real life.

In 1913, in between the writing of *Tender Buttons* and its publication, Stein started working on plays. Reflecting on those texts in her lecture "Plays," she denies a direct influence between her work and any dramatic performances she may have seen in Paris. She digresses about going to the theater and the opera as a child, loving "the circus that is the general movement and light and air which any theatre has," but wants us to know that she has "practically never been inside of any kind of a theatre" since she started writing plays.[71] In analogy with the way in which she frames her relationship to the cinema in that lecture – the statement "I myself never go to the cinema or hardly ever practically never and the cinema has never read my work or hardly ever"[72] – she turns herself into a near stranger of contemporary theater. The veracity of this claim is doubtful. We know, for example, that Stein and Toklas attended the June 2 performance of the infamous production *Le Sacre du printemps* in 1913.[73] But anecdotal truth, or the spotlighting of Stein's original genius, is not the point. What matters is that Stein and the theater/cinema relate to each other as relative strangers. That type of relation, being-almost-a-stranger, is precisely what she explores with her plays. In terms of genre experiment, she basically continues to do what she had been doing. She extends her project from portraits to plays in order to further open up writing to a dimension traditionally considered alien to it. Where her written portraits seek to parallel the cinema's ability to create "living portraits," her plays seek a way of including the excitement of the unique event included in writing. In terms of aesthetic project, she comes to see that the "excitement" of relating to each other as strangers, which she attributes to "a real scene," is the prism through which she can look at her generation.

Throughout "Plays," Stein conspicuously blurs the boundaries between theater and life by using "scene" for both theatrical element and actual situation, and "actors" to refer to the people involved in the situation. The excitement of a real-life situation, for Stein, lies in the fact that the unexpected or strange tends to occur as part of the familiar. Or, as she puts it:

> In a real scene, naturally in a real scene, you either have already very well known all the actors in the real scene of which you are one, or you have not. More generally you have than you have not, but and this is the element of excitement in an exciting scene, it quite of course is the element of excitement in an exciting scene that is in a real scene, all that you have known of the persons including yourself who are taking part in the exciting scene, although you have most probably known them very well, what makes it exciting is that insofar as the scene is exciting they the actors in the scene including yourself might just as well have been strangers because they all act talk and feel differently from the way you have expected them to act feel or talk.[74]

The theater has a hard job in rivaling that situation since there is no process of acquaintance that occurs between audience and actors: "when the actors are there they are there and they are there right away."[75] Yet, as the long quotation with its playful mixing up of life and theater indicates, Stein did not think it impossible. Indeed, she ends "Plays" on a cautious self-congratulatory note, claiming that her landscape plays, which I will elaborate on in the next chapter, "almost [did] what [she] wanted." A landscape, after all, "does not have to make acquaintance. You may have to make acquaintance with it, but it does not with you."[76]

Stein may consider her landscape plays her most successful solution to the problem of strange familiarity in relation to plays, but the first play she wrote, "What Happened. A Five Act Play," is a pretty smart attempt too.[77] Centered on a dinner party, the text in a sense gives us *Tender Buttons* with people in it; clustered around the "perfect central table" of the dining room, there are elements of a meal ("lemons oranges apples pears and potatoes"), belongings ("a rapt and surrounded overcoat securely arranged with spots") and, most importantly, voices.[78] As Dydo explains, the numbers heading the paragraphs indicate constellations of voices rather than "proper" characters. The first act, for example, starts with "One," followed by "Five," "Two," "Two" and "Three," while the second act consists of "Three," "The same three" and "The same three" again. The fact that there is no indication about *which* "one" or "five" or "same three" are supposed to play the scenes makes possible many different versions of the play. Stein, in other words, opens her play to contingency; the elements are known (or familiar) but how exactly they will combine when the play is played is not (enter the unexpected).

Stein's penchant for contingency has been linked to the neo-avant-garde compositional practice of John Cage. For Joan Retallack, for example,

> [b]oth Gertrude Stein and John Cage ask implicitly in their art, and explicitly in their writing about it, How does one develop a contemporary aesthetic, a way of being an artist who connects with the unprecedented character of one's times?[79]

But the contingency that fascinated Stein is closely connected to the newness of the cinema. Indeed, when she states that "[t]he business of Art [. . .] is to live in the actual present, that is the complete actual present, and to completely express that complete actual present," she makes sure the cinema is on our mind. When she makes the statement in "Plays," she has just, in a characteristically Steinian move, established and dismantled a connection between her (take on) plays and the cinema. The cinema comes in when she explains that she does not like to think about the theater through a theatrical lens, preferring "the standpoint of sight and sound and its relation to emotion and time, rather than in relation to story and action." If story and action are traditional dramatic elements, sight, sound, emotion and time suggest the cinema. And sure enough, the lecture continues with Stein's claim that her particular fascination for the theater "is the same [. . .] general form of conception as the inevitable experiments made by the cinema." Yet as soon as she has stated this, she asserts that their methods "[have] naturally nothing to do with [each] other."[80] With the cinema's "inevitable experiments" in the background, then, "the actual present" that is "the business of Art" not only adds to the lecture's vanguard ambition of conflating life and art, it also hints at the actuality, as a widespread phenomenon of the early cinema "business."

The actuality, as we have seen, symbolized the early cinema's capacity to portray contingency. As "the most dominant genre of the early cinema," it delighted audiences with its apparently immediate representation of "that which happens."[81] "What Happened," Rob King points out, was actually a popular title for early films, such as *What Happened When a Hot Picture Was Taken* (American Mutoscope & Biograph, 1898) or *What Happened to a Camera Fiend* (Paley and Steiner, 1904).[82] I have already traced an analogy between the actuality's sense of immediacy, which brought with it a perceived escape from oppressive structures and systems, and Stein's portraits. "What Happened. A Five Act Play" is a more direct allusion to the "inevitable" cinema and shows Stein tackling the paradox of the actuality, which is its tendency to erase the aspect of contingency it sought to hold on to. As Doane remarks, "the goal of pure inscription or recording was, from the first, self-defeating. The act of filming transforms the contingent into an event characterized by its very filmability, reducing its contingency."[83] A single-shot film, such as *What Happened on Twenty-third Street* (Edison, 1901), showed not purely "what happened," but the all in all predictable event of a gush of wind lifting a woman's skirt. The film, in other words, is both record and performance. By the early 1900s, after the public's fascination with the promise of pure registration had quieted down, film producers quickly steered the genre of the actuality into the direction of narrative comedy, emphasizing narrative development over pure time, and performance over record. Stein, too, spotlights the theatrical quality of "What Happened"; her text is, emphatically, "A Five Act Play." Yet instead of editing out the contingency factor, she makes it a central constraint. As such, "What Happened. A Five Act Play" accentuates the unique character of each potential performance while holding on to a cinematic mode of looking. Differently put, Stein's play combines the irreproducibility that is specific to the theater, in the sense that no performance is ever the same, with the cinema's capacity to erase the aura and look beyond the familiar. To a large extent, the play continues *Tender Buttons*' project of making strange a domestic setting by zooming in on details ("a cake is a powder") or by making unexpected combinations, involving the surface of indefinite or deleted things and their setting ("A simple melancholy clearly precious and on the surface and surrounded and mixed strangely").[84] Yet where *Tender Buttons*' synthetic force "made poetry," she pits her plays against literary tradition. Central to the making of "What Happened. A Play in Five Acts" and her other early plays, Stein tells us, is her attempt "to tell what happened without telling stories."[85] The plays, in other words, make possible a new mode of shared experience, beyond the form of the story.

In the light of Benjamin's work on modern experience, storytelling and the cinema, Stein's playwriting as a mode of telling without telling stories can be seen as a response to the question of how to make sense of a collective modern experience – in other words, to the problem of one's generation. As we have seen, for Stein, "a real scene" asks for people you know, including yourself, to act like strangers:

> this that they feel act and talk including yourself differently from the way you would have thought that they would act feel and talk makes the scene an exciting scene and makes the climax of this scene which is a real scene a climax of completion and not a climax of relief.[86]

Processes run their course but there is no relief in the drama that is modern life. There can be no cathartic conclusion since the rhythms that are up and running do not keep track with each other. The combination of different processes is the idea Stein returns to again and again in "Plays," and she addresses it through such supposedly theatrical elements as familiarity and alienation, sight and sound, lived time and story time. Those are not, of course, limited to the theater. The problem, she sums up, "is in short the inevitable problem of anybody living in the composition of the present time, that is living as we are now living as we have it and now do live it."[87]

Notes

1. In December 1910 Stein wrote "Ada." Her 1911 portraits of individuals include "Matisse," "Picasso," "Orta Or One Dancing" and "Nadelman." She probably also started "Portrait of Constance Fletcher" in 1911, and then added a second and third part to it in 1912; see Dydo, *Stein Reader*, 260.
2. Rita Felski, *The Gender of Modernity* (Cambridge, MA: Harvard University Press, 1995), 16. On women and the modern city, see also Lisa Rado, *Modernism, Gender and Culture: A Cultural Studies Approach* (New York: Routledge, 1997); Anke Gleber, *The Art of Taking a Walk: Flanerie, Literature and Film in Weimar Culture* (Princeton, NJ: Princeton University Press, 1999); Deborah L. Parsons, *Streetwalking the Metropolis: Women, the City and Modernity* (Oxford: Oxford University Press, 2000).
3. Lauren Rabinovitz, "Department Stores," in *Encyclopedia of Early Cinema*, ed. Richard Abel (London and New York: Routledge, 2005), 177.
4. Stein, *Lectures in America*, 251.
5. Richard Bridgman points out that "[a]lternate titles for this were 'Orta Davray,' 'Alma Davray,' and 'Isadora Dora Do.' The last suggests that the portrait had some connection with Isadora Duncan – whom the

Steins knew well" (*Gertrude Stein in Pieces* (New York: Oxford University Press, 1970), 96).
6. On the film script, see Lang, "Stein and Cinematic Identity."
7. Kracauer, *Theory of Film*, 43–4.
8. "Orta Or One Dancing," like "Ada," "Matisse" and "Picasso," portrays an individual Stein to whom felt close. Isadora Duncan and Gertrude Stein shared a similar background; both had grown up together in Oakland, and they had each escaped a stifling American context (the New York dance scene for Duncan, the university for Stein) to pursue their creative work, first in London and then in Paris.
9. Germaine Dulac, *Écrits sur le cinéma: 1919–1937*, quoted in Tom Gunning, "Light, Motion, Cinema!: The Heritage of Loïe Fuller and Germaine Dulac," *Framework* 46.1 (2005): 107.
10. Tom Gunning, "Light, Motion, Cinema!," 107.
11. Tom Gunning, "The Birth of Film Out of the Spirit of Modernity," in *Masterpieces of Modernist Cinema*, ed. Ted Perry (Bloomington and Indianapolis: Indiana University Press, 2006), 34. See also Erin Brannigan, *Dancefilm: Choreography and the Moving Image* (New York and Oxford: Oxford University Press, 2011), 26.
12. Nozière, "L'École de la Loïe Fuller," *Matinale* (June 22, 1911), quoted in Rhonda K. Garelick, *Electric Salome: Loie Fuller's Performance of Modernism* (Princeton, NJ, and Oxford: Princeton University Press, 2007), 174.
13. Duncan shocked Fuller and the Vienna audience when she performed in a see-through dress during Fuller's tour in 1902. For an account of the anecdote, see Garelick, *Electric Salome*, 159.
14. On Isadora Duncan, see Carrie J. Preston, "The Motor in the Soul: Isadora Duncan and Modernist Performance," *Modernism/Modernity* 12.2 (2005).
15. There is one surviving film clip of Duncan, the 2008 documentary *Je n'ai fait que danser ma vie* by Elisabeth Kapnist. Duncan's work, moreover, counted as an important inspiration for filmmakers.
16. Dydo, *Stein Reader*, 120.
17. Gertrude Stein, "Orta Or One Dancing," in *Writings: 1903–1932*, ed. Harriet Scott Chessman and Catharine R. Stimpson (New York: Library of America, 1998), 293.
18. Stein, "Orta," 289.
19. Quotation taken from Ann Daly, *Done into Dance: Isadora Duncan in America* (Middletown, CT: Wesleyan University Press, 1995), 120. Daly's source is W. R. Titterton, "Classical Dancing in England," *T. P.'s Magazine* [May 1911], Isadora Duncan Clippings, DC.
20. Stein, "Orta," 291–2.
21. Ibid., 296–7.
22. Bergson delivered the text "Philosophical Intuition" as an address to the Philosophical Congress in Bologna in 1911.

23. Bergson, *The Creative Mind*, 121.
24. Dydo remarks that "[i]n the typescript that Stein retained but not in the manuscript and not in a typescript she sent to Carl Van Vechten, she lined out the phrase about herself in a revision that shows her care with the single focus of the portrait" (*Stein Reader*, 120). The phrase does not appear in the version of "Orta Or One Dancing" that is included in *Gertrude Stein: Selected Writings 1903–1932*.
25. Stein, *Lectures in America*, 278.
26. Le Bon Marché and Galeries Lafayette are famous Parisian department stores and Rue de Rennes is a commercial street. On the texts: "Flirting at the Bon Marche" can be found in Catharine Stimpson's and Harriet Chessman's *Gertrude Stein: Writings 1903–1932*. "Bon Marche Weather" can be found in Dydo's *Stein Reader*, "Galeries Lafayette" in Stein's *Portraits and Prayers* and "Rue de Rennes" in Gertrude Stein, *Two: Gertrude Stein and her Brother and Other Early Portraits, 1908–1912* (New Haven, CT: Yale University Press, 1951). The phrase 'a very great many' is taken from "Bon Marche Weather," in *Stein Reader*, 150.
27. Gertrude Stein, "Flirting at the Bon Marche," in *Writings: 1903–1932*, 304.
28. Stein, "Flirting at the Bon Marche," 306.
29. Gertrude Stein, "Galeries Lafayette," in *Portraits and Prayers* (New York: Random House, 1934), 169.
30. Gertrude Stein, "Bon Marche Weather," in *Stein Reader*, 149.
31. Gertrude Stein, "Rue de Rennes," in *Two: Gertrude Stein and her Brother and Other Early Portraits*, 349–50.
32. Benjamin, "On Some Motifs in Baudelaire," 324. Poe's 1840s story, interestingly, has a cinematic setting to it, with the protagonist seated in front of a window and becoming absorbed in the spectacle of the London street scene as if it were a film unreeling in front of his eyes.
33. Benjamin, "The Work of Art in the Age of Its Technological Reproducibility," 129 n24.
34. Ulla Dydo sees this style change originating in Stein's portrait of Constance Fletcher. See Dydo, *Stein Reader*, 260.
35. Stein, *Lectures in America*, 260.
36. Stein, *The Autobiography of Alice B. Toklas*, 781; Stein, *Lectures in America*, 303.
37. Stein, *Lectures in America*, 301.
38. Benjamin, "The Work of Art in the Age of Its Technological Reproducibility," 281n42, 265. On this deepening of apperception, see Rodolphe Gasché, "The Deepening of Apperception: On Walter Benjamin's Theory of Film," *Mosaic* 41.4 (2008).
39. Benjamin, "The Work of Art in the Age of Its Technological Reproducibility," 115, 116.
40. Ibid., 107, 124n10.

41. Ibid., 112.
42. Ibid., 114.
43. Stein, *The Autobiography of Alice B. Toklas*, 781, 782.
44. Steiner, *Exact Resemblance to Exact Resemblance*, 64.
45. See, for example, Ulla Haselstein, "*Tender Buttons*: Stein et ses portraits des choses," in *Carrefour Stieglitz*, ed. Jay Bochner and Jean-Pierre Montier (Rennes: Presses Universitaires de Rennes, 2012).
46. Stein, *The Autobiography of Alice B. Toklas*, 782.
47. Stein, *Tender Buttons*, 63.
48. Ibid., 11.
49. Stein, *Lectures in America*, 241.
50. Jean Epstein, "On Certain Characteristics of *Photogénie*," in *French Film Theory and Criticism: A History/Anthology*, vol. 1 1907–1929, ed. Richard Abel (Princeton, NJ: Princeton University Press, 1988), 316.
51. The film Lindsay refers to could be *Le Garde-meubles automatique* (Pathé-Comica, 1912). See Keith Williams, *H. G. Wells, Modernity and the Movies* (Liverpool: Liverpool University Press, 2007), 59. My examples here are taken from Williams.
52. Vachel Lindsay, *The Art of the Moving Picture* (New York: Random House, 2000 [1915]), 86–7. Lindsay's is a particularly interesting account of the cinematic life of things because it struggles with the question of how objects should live on the screen. On the one hand, he criticizes *Moving Day* for being "too crassly material," urging filmmakers to pursue a more anthropomorphic object-oriented cinema: "Let the stick be the outstanding hero, the D'Artagnan of the group." On the other hand, he finds himself caught up in the non-human lure of objects and their "arousing" alienating effects on the audience, as is the case when he discusses "the jewelled strangeness" of the slipper in a Cinderella film (88, 160). Linsday's account is almost textbook fetishistic. For an account of the way in which Stein "escapes the obsessive singularity of the male fetishist" in her poem "Shoes," see Elisabeth Frost, *The Feminist Avant-Garde in American Poetry* (Iowa City: University of Iowa Press, 2003), 26.
53. Stein, *Tender Buttons*, 11, 76, 30. There is a lot of human activity going on in *Tender Buttons* but almost no recognizable human figures. Readers familiar with Stein's biography may read the sentence "I hope she has her cow" as an erotic message that Stein addresses to Toklas, but the text does not relate the "I" and "she" to human characters. Quite to the contrary, it erases them. The title of the poem in which the line occurs is "A little called Pauline," which we can read as "A little ~~girl~~ called Pauline" (27). As can be expected of a trickster like Stein, she has fun playing with the human/non-human boundaries. The "Mutton" poem, for example, mentions students: "Student, students are merciful and recognised they chew something," making us see the students in the Parisian streets as sheep (40). "Suppose an eyes" mentions a soldier,

which can refer to a private but also to a strip of bread or a tin soldier. That poem also has "little sales ladies" transform into "little saddles of mutton": "Little sales ladies little sales ladies little saddles of mutton" (29). On breath in *Tender Buttons*, see also Sarah Posman, "Breed That," Twenty-two on "Tender Buttons," *Jacket2* (March 2015). Available at <https://jacket2.org/reviews/breed> (last accessed September 3, 2021).
54. Benjamin, "The Work of Art in the Age of Its Technological Reproducibility," 120.
55. Ibid., 119, 114. On Benjamin's understanding of distraction, see Carolin Duttlinger, "Between Contemplation and Distraction: Configurations of Attention in Walter Benjamin," *German Studies Review* 30.1 (2007).
56. On the making of *Tender Buttons*, see, for example, Joshua Schuster, "The Making of 'Tender Buttons': Gertrude Stein's Subjects, Objects and the Illegible," *Jacket2* (April 21, 2011. Available at <https://jacket2.org/article/making-tender-buttons> (last accessed September 3, 2021). On *Tender Buttons*' reception, see, for example, Leonard Diepeveen, *Modernist Fraud: Hoax, Parody, Deception* (Oxford: Oxford University Press, 2019), 33–5.
57. Rebecca Scherr, "Tactile Erotics: Gertrude Stein and the Aesthetics of Touch," *Lit: Literature Interpretation Theory* 18.3 (2007).
58. Stein, *Tender Buttons*, 26.
59. Ibid., 59, 50, 37, 39, 24, 66–7.
60. The poem "A time to eat" in the Objects section describes the habit of eating meals at fixed times as follows: "A pleasant simple habitual and tyrannical and authorised and educated and resumed and articulate separation. This is not tardy" (*Tender Buttons*, 25). Liesl Olson has argued that "[w]hat we see in *Tender Buttons* – a refusal of the ways in which we habitually associate things together – emerges, in her later writings, as an appreciation of the power of habits in ordinary lives" ("Gertrude Stein, William James and Habit in the Shadow of War," *Twentieth-Century Literature* 49.3 (2003): 338) and for Lisi Schoenbach Stein's understanding of habit comes with an institutional dimension (see the chapter "'Peaceful and Exciting': Stein's Dialectic of Habit," in Schoenbach's *Pragmatic Modernism* (Oxford and New York: Oxford University Press, 2012)). Omri Moses reads Stein's approach to habit as a creative character-shaping force in line with Darwin and Bergson. His sketch of the dominant modernist approach to habit, however, misses nuance as he sums up Benjamin's view on habit as a "regularizing" response to modern life rather than a dynamic and a productive one (see Omri Moses, "Gertrude Stein's Lively Habits," *Twentieth-Century Literature* 55.4 (2009): 446).
61. Stein, *Tender Buttons*, 76.
62. Ibid., 30, 11, 21.
63. Ibid., 11, 29.

64. Stein, *Lectures in America*, 330.
65. Ibid., 330, 325.
66. Nickels, *Poetry of the Possible*.
67. Ibid., 331.
68. R. Bruce Elder, *Harmony + Dissent: Film and Avant-Garde Art Movements in the Early Twentieth Century* (Waterloo, Ontario: Wilfrid Laurier University Press, 2010), xxii and xxiv.
69. Laura Marcus, *The Tenth Muse: Writing about Cinema in the Modernist Period* (Oxford: Oxford University Press, 2007), 12.
70. Hugo Münsterberg, *The Photoplay: A Psychological Study* (New York and London: D. Appleton and Company, 1916), 103–4.
71. Stein, *Lectures in America*, 256.
72. Ibid., 251.
73. See Appendix A to *The Letters of Gertrude Stein and Carl Van Vechten*, ed. Edward Burns, 2 vols (New York: Columbia University Press, 1986), for the story of Stein's attending the performance.
74. Stein, *Lectures in America*, 252.
75. Ibid., 254.
76. Ibid., 269, 263.
77. In "Plays" Stein refers to "What Happened. A Five Act Play" as "the first" play she wrote (*Lectures in America*, 260). As always, it is difficult to check. The text "Play," for example, predates "What Happened. A Five Act Play." Dydo situates it in 1911 but the 1934 edition of *Portraits and Prayers* gives 1909 as the date of composition. It does not, however, share the division into acts that characterizes "What Happened" and, as Dydo points out, the manuscript has the word "Story" written at the top of the first leaf, in Stein's handwriting (*Stein Reader*, 147).
78. Stein, "What Happened. A Five Act Play," in *Geography and Plays* (Mineola, NY: Dover, 1999), 207, 205.
79. Joan Retallack, *The Poethical Wager* (Berkeley and Los Angeles: University of California Press, 2003), 18.
80. Stein, *Lectures in America*, 251. The following sentence, not surprisingly, again spotlights "the same impulse" that Stein's take on theater shares with the cinema. "The fact remains that there is the same impulse to solve the problem of time in relation to emotion and the relation of the scene to the emotion of the audience in the one case as in the other."
81. Doane, *The Emergence of Cinematic Time*, 22.
82. *What Happened to a Fresh Johnnie* (American Mutoscope & Biograph, 1900), *What Happened on Twenty-third Street, New York City* (Edison, 1901), *What Happened to the Inquisitive Janitor* (Pathé Frères, 1902), *What Happened in the Tunnel* (Edison, 1903), *What Happened to the Milkman* (Lubin, 1903). See Rob King, "Laughter in an Ungoverned Sphere: Actuality Humor in Early Cinema and Web 2.0," in *New Silent Film*, ed. Paul Flaig and Katherine Groo (New York: Routledge, 2016), 302.

83. Doane, *The Emergence of Cinematic Time*, 23.
84. Stein, "What Happened," 205.
85. Stein, *Lectures in America*, 262.
86. Ibid., 252.
87. Ibid., 251.

PART III

AND AGAIN, NATURALLY

At some point in the 1920s, Stein remarks towards the end of "Portraits and Repetition," she "began to feel movement to be a different thing than [she] had felt it to be." Movement became "a less detailed thing and at the same time a thing that existed so completely inside in it." If spreading difference constituted the baseline of *Tender Buttons*, then an artisanal sense of containment appears to be what lies at the heart of her 1920s texts. Stein prompts us to "think of how you fold things or make a boat or anything else out of paper or getting anything to be inside anything, the hole in the doughnut or the apple in the dumpling" to help us understand what she was doing in the 1920s. Of course, since many of the *Tender Buttons* poems are also containers of some kind – from the "carafe that is a blind glass" to the rooms to which she devotes a whole section – the newness of Stein's understanding of movement constitutes not so much a break with her 1910s writings, as it does a shift in emphasis. After all, as Stein rephrases her take on repetition towards the end of the lecture, there is little that actually changes, apart from "our emphasis and the moment in which we live."[1]

The moment in which Stein lived in the 1920s was a happy one. She may have been "leading a very complicated and perhaps too exciting every day living," but there was also a sense of tranquility that enabled her to truly focus on her work and steer her writing into new directions.[2] The post-war atmosphere brought with it a positive appreciation of her writing: she made new friends, was invited to contribute to magazines, published books and set up collaborations. This exciting career boost was balanced by the peace and quiet of the surroundings in which she worked. In the early 1920s Stein and Toklas had fallen in love with the French countryside. In 1922–3 they spent some time in Provence, in St-Rémy, and in 1924 they lost their hearts to the town of Belley in the South-east of France, "where [they] hope[d] to be as well situated as ever."[3] For years to come they would return to "the valley of the Rhône, the landscape that of all landscapes means the most to [Stein]."[4]

The rural surroundings and vibrant natural scene had a huge impact on Stein. She felt sheltered by the landscape and was struck by the stillness and sense of permanence she experienced there. The "feeling" she had in St-Rémy, Stein tells us in "Portraits and Repetition," was that of "light and air and air moving and being still."[5] Where the opposition between still life and dynamic life had been central to her 1910s work, her writings in the 1920s no longer see movement and stasis in contrast to each other. Indeed, for much of the decade she explores how she can think together change and permanence, time and space, concrete and abstract, and life and death. How, she appears to be wondering, can these apparent opposites hold each other?

Stein's explorations, the following chapter argues, not only were triggered by her sensuous enjoying of the French countryside, about which she remarked that it "moves but also stays," but they also kept track with the work of her friend Alfred North Whitehead, who spent the 1920s formulating an intricate philosophy of nature in which, as we will see, concrete and abstract, time and space, and change and permanence intersect.[6]

It is difficult to sum up Whitehead's project, not only because he did so many different things – his writings cover logic, education and speculative philosophy – and because the things he did are so complex, but also because, from the 1920s onwards, he kept working on a single problem, which each of his books tackled with a baffling willingness to begin again. That problem is much in line with Stein's favorite problem: how to think of nature, history and life, in all their diverging dimensions, as one "thing." The result of Whitehead's mode of beginning again, which Isabelle Stengers details beautifully in her stunning *Thinking with Whitehead*, is that his oeuvre is one of remarkable twists and bends while also showing great consistency. Recent years have witnessed a surge of attention for his work – indeed, the contemporary enthusiasm for Whitehead in myriads of fields is such that his position as an early twentieth-century thinker seems almost to be overlooked – but that attention has had to make up for decades of near scholarly silence.[7] Unlike James, Bergson and Benjamin, Whitehead is not part of the modernist pantheon. A century ago, nevertheless, the British thinker was set up for modernist fame. He had a successful academic career, teaching mathematics at Trinity and in London, and his 1925 book *Science and the Modern World* was labeled "the most important book published in the conjoint realms of science and philosophy since Descartes' Discourse on Method" in *The Criterion*, with reviewer Herbert Read pointing out the importance of art in Whitehead's scheme.[8] Whitehead himself, furthermore, considered his work to be, to a large extent, in line with that of Bergson and James. In the preface to *Process and Reality*, notably, he expresses his indebtedness "to Bergson, William James, and John Dewey."[9] Yet somehow Whitehead's fame never quite happened.

Whitehead's odd non-contemporaneity was lost neither on himself nor on Stein. When Stein met Whitehead, he was chiefly known as a mathematician and a logician. Between 1910 and 1913 he and Bertrand Russell had published their monumental three-volume work on symbolic logic, *Principia Mathematica*. By the time Stein wrote about their meeting in the early 1930s, Russell had become an international star. Reading the section about Whitehead in *The Autobiography of Alice B. Toklas*, where narrator Alice emphasizes that "it was Doctor Whitehead and not Russell who had had the ideas for their great book," I feel that Stein wants to put her friend in the spotlight she felt he deserved.[10] Whitehead had moved in 1924 to Harvard, where he had accepted the position of professor of philosophy and had started work on an intricate speculative project, which he himself labeled a philosophy of organism. Although he was much loved by his students, the works he wrote as a philosopher did not take the philosophical world by storm. Upon the publication of *Process and Reality* in 1929, he wrote a letter to his son in which he admitted he did "not expect a good reception from professional philosophers" since the book "deserts the ordinary way of putting things at the present moment."[11]

Stein, not surprisingly, lovingly pays tribute to Whitehead's non-contemporaneity. As she describes in *The Autobiography of Alice B. Toklas*, she met Whitehead in the most chaotic of times, when the world was about to change dramatically: the summer of 1914. At a dinner party in London, Stein and Toklas and Alfred North and Evelyn Whitehead "all became interested in each other," and the Whiteheads subsequently invited Stein and Toklas to spend a weekend at their house in Lockridge.[12] Because of the outbreak of World War One, that weekend turned into an extended stay of six weeks, during which Stein and Whitehead "walked endlessly around the country." Despite the world falling apart, "[i]t was beautiful weather and beautiful country, and Doctor Whitehead and Gertrude Stein never ceased wandering around in it and talking about all things."[13]

A distinct sense of permanence colors Stein's descriptions of the time she spent with Whitehead. There is no end to their walks; the landscape they roam is "still the same as in the days of Chaucer, with the green paths of the early Britons that could still be seen in long stretches;" and Whitehead is characterized in saintly terms as "[t]he gentlest and most simply generous of human beings."[14] More than a tribute, in fact, this anecdote also touches on the central question of Whitehead's thinking about nature in the 1920s, which is when Stein would have been reading his work. How is it that. in a world of constant change or passage, as Whitehead calls it, we can also encounter things that do not seem to move?

Notes

1. Stein, *Lectures in America*, 310, 308, 305.
2. Ibid., 311.
3. Stein, "Natural Phenomena," 168.
4. Stein, *The Autobiography of Alice B. Toklas*, 843. See Dydo, *Gertrude Stein: The Language that Rises*, 45, 325. For more on Stein and the Bugey area, see Dominique Saint-Pierre's excellent study *Gertrude Stein, le Bugey, la guerre: d'août 1924 à décembre 1944* (Paris: Editions Musnier Gilbert, 2009).
5. Stein, *Lectures in America*, 307.
6. Ibid., 269.
7. On the reception of Whitehead, see Nicholas Gaskill and A. J. Nocek, "An Adventure of Thought," introduction to *The Lure of Whitehead*, ed. Nicholas Gaskill and A. J. Nocek (Minneapolis: University of Minnesota Press, 2014).
8. Herbert Read, review of A. N. Whitehead, *Science and the Modern World*, *The New Criterion* 4 (June 1926): 581.
9. Whitehead, *Process and Reality*, xii.
10. Stein, *The Autobiography of Alice B. Toklas*, 807.
11. Whitehead quoted in Alan Van Wyk and Michel Weber, eds, *Creativity and Its Discontents: The Response to Whitehead's Process and Reality* (Frankfurt: Ontos, 2008), 5. They take the quotation from Victor August Lowe's biography of Whitehead, *Alfred North Whitehead: The Man and His Work*, 2 vols (Baltimore: Johns Hopkins University Press, 1985 and 1990).
12. Stein, *The Autobiography of Alice B. Toklas*, 805.
13. Ibid., 807, 812.
14. Ibid., 808.

Chapter 6

Landscapes

Before we really delve into Whitehead's thinking about nature I want to take a close look at how Stein presents her new take on movement in her lectures. As we may expect, her new views led to several, seemingly contradictory, projects. In "Portraits and Repetition" she boasts about having isolated a fundamental movement: a type of movement that has nothing to do with seeing, speaking, hearing or feeling, and that does not find itself in relation to anything else. "[A]ll that was necessary," she writes with respect to the 1928 portrait of George Hugnet with which she felt pleased, "was that there was something completely contained within itself and being contained within itself was moving, not moving in relation to anything not moving in relation to itself but just moving." Her writing seems severed from her daily life:

> But now to make you understand, that although I was as usual looking listening and talking perhaps more than ever at that time and leading a very complicated and perhaps too exciting every day living, never the less it really did not matter what I say or said or heard, or if you like felt, because now there was at last something that was more vibrant than any of all that and somehow some way I had isolated it and in a way had gotten it written. It was about that time that I wrote Four Saints.[1]

When we turn to the lecture "Plays," in which she writes more about the opera *Four Saints in Three Acts*, we find Stein taking a different course. Here, she emphasizes relations over movement. She is happy with the opera, she tells us, because "it did almost what I wanted, it made a landscape [. . .]." Essential to landscapes, as Stein sees them, is the fact that they are made up of relations; they are "not moving but being always in relation, the trees to the hills the hills to the fields the trees to each other any piece of it to any sky and then any detail to any other detail." It was because she was living in the landscape around Belley, furthermore, that she "slowly came to feel that [. . .] the landscape was the thing."[2] Why does Stein claim that she was creating some kind of absolute movement that had nothing to do with what she was feeling and at the same time working hard on a detailed exploration of spatial relations prompted by the sensuous experience of living in the Bugey area?

A closer look at the lectures and at the actual texts Stein references in them soon makes clear that the opposition she appears to establish does not really hold. It is difficult, for instance, to read the Hugnet portrait as "not moving in relation to anything." Relations and a distinct echo of Stein's daily life, rather, are at the heart of the text. Consider the lines she quotes in "Portraits and Repetition," taken from the middle of the portrait:

> George Genevieve Geronimo straightened it out without their finding it out.
> Grammar makes George in our ring which Grammar makes George in our ring.[3]

Stein puts the word "Grammar" on the same level as the three proper nouns that are at the heart of the portrait, making us read it as "grandma" and having us wonder about how these characters relate to each other. She also hints at a connection between grammar and her social circle ("our ring"), inviting us to see both as systems made up of different possible relations. As Dydo has pointed out, moreover, it is hard not to read the portrait in the context of the French poet's plans to translate Stein, which surely would bring up the question of Stein's idiosyncratic grammar, and his admiration of Stein's "attempts to free language from the constraints of thought and grammar."[4] Landscapes, moreover, do not really *not* move. The movement in a landscape, Stein tells us in "Plays," should be seen as "the movement of nuns very busy and in continuous movement but placid as a landscape has to be." *Four Saints in Three Acts*, she explains at the end of the lecture, "moves but it also stays."[5] There is a permanence and a predictability to Stein's landscape plays, but that does not stop her from using acts and scenes, devices to structure plot movement, even if she does without plot.

How, then, to make sense of Stein's new take on movement, embodied by the portraits that, supposedly, move yet do not relate and the landscape plays that relate and move without really moving?

Differently put, and borrowing Stengers's Whiteheadian metaphor of the thinker–mountaineer, where can we find a foothold to trust?[6] It is Whitehead's understanding of life that constitutes our ledge and from where a trajectory reveals itself.

Disturbing Life

Life, for Whitehead, is what upsets the predictable pattern of inheritance. In *Process and Reality*, he states that "an organism is 'alive' when in some measure its reactions are inexplicable by any tradition of pure physical inheritance." Life amounts to novelty: "it is the name for originality, and not for tradition." Life, furthermore, is not restricted to biological organisms. "A single occasion is alive," he explains, "when the subjective aim which determines its concrescence has introduced a novelty of definiteness not to be found in the inherited data of its primary phase."[7] Without going into full Whiteheadian detail yet, we can understand occasions, or events, as the stuff the world is made of. These occasions are constantly transforming, and their particular mode of transforming has the quality of life when it deviates from what it was before. Life, in other words, has a disturbing effect. "The novelty is introduced conceptually and disturbs the inherited 'responsive' adjustment of subjective forms. It alters the values, in the artist's sense of that term."[8] Value is again a complex Whiteheadian term but, in a nutshell, what he means by it is the quality that makes an occasion into what it is: "the intrinsic reality of an event."[9] In other words, it has nothing to do with judgment. "The artist," then, knows that the work she is making is not hers. She is rather contributing to its event, finding out its value as she continues. The dynamics of that value are the result of changes in present circumstances: "the reaction is dictated by the present, and not by the past."[10]

I see Stein as Whitehead's artist, exploring the value of her work, committed to its vitality. I take her present – which is actually a multiple present, as I am focusing not only on the texts Stein wrote in the 1920s but also on her 1930s comments on those texts – to be informed by Whitehead's work. For her portraiture to be alive, it has to change conceptually. If life stands in opposition to tradition, then Stein's portraits are lively because they insert a fissure in the tradition of portraiture.[11] At its most basic, that tradition demands that the relation between the portrait and who or what is portrayed matters. Stein, in many ways, subverts that demand, most conspicuously perhaps by misspelling Georges Hugnet's name as George Hugnet. When she tells us, then, that it "[i]t really does not make any difference who George Hugnet was or what he did or what I said," she can be seen to refuse portraiture's inheritance.[12] Moreover, the phrase she uses for the conceptual change of her portraiture – she felt that she had created "something that was more vibrant" – comes with Whiteheadian overtones. It is true that, as Jane Bennett points out, vibrancy has a long history of connoting life. The opposition between "dull matter (it, things) and vibrant life (us, beings) is a 'partition of the sensible,'" an unwritten law governing our experience.[13] Whitehead no doubt taps into that tradition when he uses the term vibrancy in *Science and the Modern World*. As Steven Meyer points out, both Stein and Whitehead "came to believe that the actual world, 'nature alive,' was ultimately a function of 'vibratory existence' and composed, at bottom, of 'entit[ies] constituted by . . . vibrations,' or *vibratory organisms*, in Whitehead's phrasing."[14] If vibratory organisms constitute one vantage by means of which Whitehead thinks about the fundamentals of a nature alive, then another is the idea of one underlying energy or rhythm. That shines through when Stein talks about her plays.

As with the new portraits, Stein presents her landscape plays in opposition to tradition. In their "bid for freedom" lies, in almost a clichéd modernist gesture, an ambition to make it new.[15] The tradition of Western drama, again at its most basic, centers on action. In Aristotle's words, action is "the end and purpose" of drama.[16] Upon entering the theater, we expect to see events unfold in time. That process is one of the things Stein claims she finds bothersome about plays. She feels as if there are two rhythms at play – the play's and the audience's – where there should be only one: "your emotion as a member of the audience is never going on at the same time as the action of the play."[17] This really goes back to her take on interpretation, which I have discussed in the chapters on history. Interpretation, as Stein sees it, should coincide with whatever is happening, and not take place as a delayed reflection on an antecedent reality.[18] The problem with the theater, for Stein, is that it does not invite these in-the-moment interpretations. It is so centered on plot that you find yourself anticipating what will happen or making sense of it afterwards: "your emotion concerning that play is always either behind or ahead of the play."[19] It is in order to solve this problem, and constitute a break with theatrical tradition, that Stein presents her plays as "placid" landscapes. "All these things might have been a story but as a landscape they were just there and a play is just there." Her landscape plays are simply there for you to look at. You do not have to worry about what will happen or what has happened. Any movement that is part of a landscape is "like a movement in and out with which anybody looking can keep in time."[20] The replacing of plot by placid movement and the projection of a vague synthetic experience may not sound like a very convincing inventive move, but that does not matter. As with the portraits, the value of Stein's breaking with tradition is to be found in dialogue with Whitehead's project.

When it moves "in and out," and thereby invites anyone to keep time ("anybody looking can keep in time"), a landscape moves like breath. Like Whitehead, who references Ezekiel in *Process and Reality*, Stein adopts and adapts the biblical image of breath as the source of creation.[21] Where *Tender Buttons*, as we have seen, feeds us "plenty of breath," the landscape plays "breathe" because Stein wants them to straddle the abstract and the concrete, unity and individuation. Breathing is a rhythm that all the bodies assembled in a theater share – of all the bodily rhythms it is the one most symbolic of life – yet it is also a highly individual rhythm. Together we breathe, yet we never breathe one breath. Stein's plays are lively, not only because they are *not* what you may expect, but more importantly because they try to do what Whitehead referred to as "prehending," and which amounts to a rhythm of life, or what he also refers to as "underlying energy" or "underlying activity."[22]

In thinking about how to define unity – both unities in nature and nature as unity – Whitehead came up with the concept of prehension in *Science and the Modern World*. "In [. . .] analogy with Spinoza," he explains, "his one substance is for me the one underlying activity of realisation individualising itself in an interlocked plurality of modes." Everything that happens, everything we see, and all the many many modes of existence, can be analyzed "into underlying activity of prehension, and into realised prehensive events."[23] Stein makes "presence" central to her landscapes: "things are there," she tells us, "and I put into the play the things that were there."[24] Such a notion of presence is also how Stengers reads Whitehead's prehension. It constitutes a "holding together": "[t]he whole ruminates in every part, and the various parts are henceforth 'presence.'"[25]

Vibratory things and breath as underlying energy enable us to see how Stein frames her 1920s work in Whiteheadian terms, but they do not yet explain why she was, at the same time, "folding up" and relating everything to everything. So, let's stop skipping ledges and unfold Whitehead's understanding of nature, and Stein's writing in response to it, foothold by foothold.

The Bifurcation of Nature

The idea of unity is so prevalent in Whitehead that he almost matches Stein's obsession with it. In his 1934 lectures *Nature and Life* he calls the unity of life and nature "the standing problem of philosophy and science," and he had been working on it at least since *The Concept of Nature* (1920).[26] What he means by it is that "nature," or science, and "life," or experience, are two separate frameworks we use to make sense of the world, and not one, as he thinks should be the case. When Whitehead looks at the history of science and philosophy he concludes that the dominant frameworks we use to make sense of the world treat nature as lifeless, a "bloodless dance of categories."[27] This strikes him as baffling since anyone who has ever experienced the beauty of a landscape – in *Science and the Modern World* Whitehead gives us the figure of Wordsworth haunted by "the brooding presence of the hills" – knows that nature is alive and "full-blooded," that "real facts are happening."[28] The odd discrepancy between cold theory and warm experience is what Whitehead calls the bifurcation of nature, and all his writings, from *The Concept of Nature* onwards, constitute a response to it.

In *The Concept of Nature* the bifurcation of nature receives its clearest outline. Here, Whitehead writes:

> What I am essentially protesting against is the bifurcation of nature into two systems of reality, which, in so far as they are real, are real in different senses. One reality would be the entities such as electrons which are the study of speculative physics. This would be the reality which is there for knowledge; although on this theory it is never known. For what is known is the other sort of reality, which is the byplay of the mind. Thus there would be two natures, one is the conjecture and the other is the dream.[29]

For Whitehead there is only one nature, and "[a]ll we know of nature is in the same boat, to sink or swim together."[30] He critiques the modern scientific paradigm not for getting things wrong, but for conquering our worldview. Unlike Bergson, Whitehead does not want to find access to a pure experience uncorrupted by an ever more efficient intellect.[31] In a specific scientific context, it pays off to look at the world as made up of entities such as electrons, yet the idea that such entities, which we cannot experience, constitute the real building blocks of our reality and that, by consequence, the redness of a fire is a mere sensation, makes no sense to Whitehead. "It seems an extremely unfortunate arrangement that we should perceive a lot of things that are not there."[32] In *The Concept of Nature* he seeks to construct a concept of nature that can hold both the so-called primary and secondary qualities, or, put more ambitiously still, a concept of nature to which everything we experience, all "entities disclosed in our sense-awareness," can belong.[33]

Stein's landscapes meet Whitehead's demand that both concrete and abstract are part of the same world. She may call them "placid" when she pits them against the action-driven Western theatrical tradition, but she also makes clear that they contain a lot of activity. With reference to the opera *Four Saints in Three Acts* she states that she "also wanted it to have the movement of nuns very busy and in continuous movement."[34] A phrase that captures what is at stake in these landscapes is that of a "buzzing world." In *Process and Reality* Whitehead writes that "[w]e find ourselves in a buzzing world, amid a democracy of fellow creatures," and in doing so pays tribute to William James's famous dictum of "the big, blooming, buzzing confusion" that is our infant experience.[35] Whitehead's buzzing world should be seen in opposition to the idea, upheld by "orthodox philosophy," that there are "solitary substances, each enjoying an illusory experience." His critique on solitary substances is a variation on his protesting against the bifurcation of nature. In *Science and the Modern World*, the book that followed on from *The Concept of Nature*, the problem of the bifurcation of nature has changed guise; it has now become the fallacy of misplaced concreteness.[36] Whitehead explains that the theory of primary and secondary qualities, which he holds responsible for our muddled modern understanding of the world, is rooted in the triumph of bits of matter:

> The answer [. . .] which the seventeenth century gave to the ancient question of the Ionian thinkers, "What is the world made of?" was that the world is a succession of instantaneous configurations of matter – or of material if you wish to include stuff more subtle than ordinary matter, the ether for example.[37]

By Whitehead's account, this mechanist understanding of the world, "which has reigned supreme ever since the seventeenth century," has led us to think of what are, in effect, abstractions – material configurations situated in a single location in space – as concrete realities, clothed in secondary qualities by the powers of our mind. "Nature," in this view, "is a dull affair, soundless, scentless, colourless; merely the hurrying of material, endlessly, meaninglessly."[38]

Nature as a buzzing world, by contrast, has myriads of relations between myriads of things. It includes both concrete organisms – the "birds and bees and butterflies" that Stein introduces in her buzzing square of grass in "Poetry and Grammar" – and abstract creations, like representations or theories.[39] As Didier Debaise explains, in *The Concept of Nature* Whitehead "breaks the distinction between the events of nature and the manner in which they are represented – factual states and representations – and places them directly on the same level, on the same plane. All is laid horizontally on the plane of nature."[40] This is also key to Stein's idea of the landscape, in which, as we have already seen, relations are key, connecting "any detail to any other detail." Two such details that Stein zooms in on in "Plays" are the magpie and the scarecrow. In insisting that "the scarecrows on the ground are the same thing as the magpies in the sky, they are a part of the landscape," she situates fact and representation on the same plane. Where magpies are actual birds, scarecrows represent human-like figures. You might be inclined to see this landscape as made up of two spheres, with a factual sky and a representational ground, but Stein would not be Stein if she did not complicate this: The magpies, she tells us, "look exactly like the birds in the Annunciation pictures the bird which is the Holy Ghost and rests flat against the side sky very high." The magpie, then, is both real and image, as is the scarecrow which, despite it being a representation, is also a very real thing chasing away the crows from the fields. Both, furthermore, have individual stories to tell, but Stein prefers to see them as part of the landscape: it could "be a story but it is a piece of the landscape."[41]

Stein telling us that her plays include both abstract/concrete scarecrows and concrete/abstract magpies in the 1935 lecture is one thing, but her actual attempts to write the abstract and concrete in and out of each other sent her off on some of her wildest adventures. What does it take to have everything in the same boat and to sink or swim together?

Whitehead's Event

For a philosopher it took the creation of a new concept. Whitehead's alternative for a world made up of individual bits of matter (which we never experience) and the (un-natural) impressions we take them to trigger is to look at nature in terms of the event. His concern, in *The Concept of Nature*, is with "the whole occurrence of nature [...] nature as an event." Nature, in other words, happens before our eyes: "It is nature as an event present for sense-awareness, and essentially passing. There is no holding nature still and looking at it." This does not mean that we can actually grasp the whole of nature. "This whole event," Whitehead posits, "is discriminated by us into partial events. We are aware of an event which is our bodily life, of an event which is the course of nature within this room, and of a vaguely perceived aggregate of other partial events."[42]

The event is Whitehead's response to time and space, as the framework where we tend to situate primary and secondary qualities in connection with each other. "The perceived redness of the fire and the warmth," Whitehead points out in *The Concept of Nature*, "are definitely related in time and in space to the molecules of the fire and the molecules of the body."[43] Existing theories of time and space, however, fail to do justice to nature in its concreteness.[44] Nature, for Whitehead, comes in chunks or "slabs," and where time and space as abstract systems in various ways delete the chunky character or slab-ness, the concept of the event knows how to retain it. For Whitehead, the event, or "the specific character of a place through a period of time," is apprehended nature at its most concrete. The event generates the textures both of space, since events are intertwined with other events occurring simultaneously "within the immediate general fact which is all nature now discernible," and of time, since "[e]very event extends over other events, and every event is extended over by other events."[45]

Whitehead's understanding of nature as event is in line with Bergson's theory of duration in that Whitehead, like Bergson, emphasizes process over permanence.[46] His object of study in *The Concept of Nature* is "nature as an event present for sense-awareness, and essentially passing."[47] It is here, "in this doctrine," that he declares himself "in full accord with Bergson," even if, unlike Bergson, he would never use the word time "since the measurable time of science and of civilized life generally merely exhibits some aspects of the more fundamental fact of the passage of nature."[48] A more important point of difference between the two process philosophers is that Whitehead refuses the Bergsonist hierarchy of experience. For Bergson, as we have already seen, duration is where true experience takes place. The abstractions that are unchangeable things located in space, by contrast, are the products of a highly efficient and pragmatic intellect that operates in opposition to duration. Abstraction enables repetition yet

> what is repeated is some aspect that our senses, and especially our intellect, have singled out from reality, just because our action upon which all the effort of our intellect is directed, can move only among

repetitions. Thus, concentrated on that which repeats, solely preoccupied in welding the same to the same, intellect turns away from the vision of time. It dislikes what is fluid, and solidifies everything it touches.

By Bergson's account, the repetitions and abstractions by which we think preclude life: "We do not *think* real time. But we *live* it, because life transcends intellect."[49] Whitehead, too, associates life with that which cannot be repeated. In *The Concept of Nature* he wants it to be clear that "the life of nature" is incompatible with repetition. "You cannot recognize an event; because when it is gone, it is gone." It is possible to witness "another event of analogous character, but the actual chunk of the life of nature is inseparable from its unique occurrence."[50] However, for Whitehead, abstraction is not a lie, and permanence not incompatible with the event.

In *The Concept of Nature* one of the examples by which Whitehead clarifies his concept of the event is "Cleopatra's Needle is on the Charing Cross Embankment."[51] It contrasts with the first example he gives – "Yesterday a man was run over on the Chelsea Embankment" – because it "seems to lack the element of time or transitoriness." Cleopatra's Needle being on the Charing Cross Embankment does not happen in the sense that an accident occurs. It appears to be simply there. And yet, Whitehead points out, we cannot truly consider the Needle on the Embankment as a timeless fixture. When he was a little boy, for example, it was not there. It appears as "a certain chunk in the transitory life of nature" for all those Londoners who pass it in their daily lives, but it all depends on how you look at it:

> If we define the Needle in a sufficiently abstract manner we can say that it never changes. But a physicist who looks on that part of the life of nature as a dance of electrons, will tell you that daily it has lost some molecules and gained others, and even the plain man can see that it gets dirtier and is occasionally washed.[52]

Still, for Whitehead, the molecular or aesthetic life of the Needle is not more real than the Needle as the landmark that we recognize when we walk along the Embankment.[53] What we recognize when we say "'Hullo, there's the Needle'" is not the Needle as event itself, but what Whitehead calls the "character" of an event.

The character of an event – or how an event is – depends on objects. By objects Whitehead does not mean things in general but those "elements in nature which do not pass." Objects, in other words, are static. Life, or duration, does not affect them, even though they are implicated in life. In *The Concept of Nature* objects are things we can recognize, things which "can 'be again.'"[54] They do not have to be bits of matter – color or sound, for example, can be considered objects in the Whiteheadian sense. A particular assemblage of objects makes an event into what it is. Objects, in other words, can be considered the "ingredient[s] in the character of some event." By means of a particularly circular definition, Whitehead emphasizes the mutual dependence that characterizes the relationship between objects and events:

> The ingression of an object into an event is the way the character of the event shapes itself in virtue of the being of the object. Namely the event is what it is, because the object is what it is; and when I am thinking of this modification of the event by the object, I call the relation between the two "the ingression of the object into the event." It is equally true to say that objects are what they are because events are what they are. Nature is such that there can be no events and no objects without the ingression of objects into events.[55]

As Stengers points out, this is "[a] pseudo-definition if ever there was one." It merely affirms what it pretends to explain: events are what they are because of objects, and vice versa. It is not, however, a definition without effect. For Stengers, it "simultaneously prohibits and incites."[56]

Whitehead's concept of nature includes both the abstract (the unchangeable object) and the concrete (the "chunk" of nature that is the event). The abstract is that aspect of nature that responds to our tendencies to recognize, name and judge. Yet for us to be able to recognize or name at all, there needs to be a concrete event, which passes never to return. The bind between object and event stops us looking for a ground below or beyond the object. In Stengers's words, "[i]t prohibits us from waiting, hoping for, or anticipating conditions that explain why and how an object can perform ingression into an event."[57] There is no pure nature, or a nature that is simply nature and not other things, for Whitehead. Just because it is more concrete does not imply that the event can explain the object. And, inversely, just because it is timeless does not mean that the object holds power over the event. Any attempt to disentangle the one from the other would lead us into the familiar direction of a bifurcating nature. Object and event go together.

The flipside of Whitehead's object/event tandem is, following Stengers, that we find ourselves "incited to pay attention to the diversity of the objects, gathered together by this common feature, '*There it is again.*'" An artist looking at the Needle may well claim that it is never the same because the light that falls on it is always changing, but when she passes the Needle on her daily walk, she will nevertheless recognize it as the same old thing. Her being an artist does not cancel her daily living. As Stengers sums it up, "[t]he artist's perception is not more authentic, it is different." The artist's claim that "it is never the same" is deliciously paradoxical (how can it be "it" when it is always different?) while also making perfect sense ("it" does not cancel out multiple perspectives). Stengers points out that "[T]he artist's testimony concerns the experience of a contrast but does not provide weapons to a contradiction."[58] In Stein's scheme of things, "this difference was not a contradiction but a combination."[59]

Whitehead knew that language could contain these multitudes. Perhaps surprisingly, since he rarely reflects on language, Whitehead appeals to the differentiating potential of language to help counter the bifurcation of nature in *The Concept of Nature*. Where common sense, shaped by modern science, tends to cling to the "simple-minded theory that an object is at one place at any definite time, and is in no sense anywhere else," language still harbors the dynamic plurality of objects.[60] Literature, Whitehead remarks, is attuned to the never-ending interplay of "ingressing" objects. "Every other sentence in a work of literature which is endeavouring truly to interpret the facts of experience," he adds, "expresses differences in surrounding events due to the presence of some object. An object is ingredient throughout its neighbourhood, and its neighbourhood is indefinite."[61] Because events are related to other events in space and time, objects have a never-ending playing field. "The difference they make," David A. Grandy explains, "triggers other differences ad infinitum."[62]

Before I explore Stein's solution to the challenge of having everything in the same boat in relation to her landscape play *Four Saints in Three Acts*, I want to pause briefly at her book *How to Write* because it speaks to the spreading difference that Whitehead encounters in literary language. For Stein, spreading difference had been a concern since *Tender Buttons*. In her 1920s writings she combines an interest in the concept of landscape, which she tends to use interchangeably with nature and sometimes even "play," with an explicit interest in language. Grammar, sentences and vocabulary become themes for Stein in the late 1920s. The volume *How to Write* (1931) collects these texts, written between 1927 and 1930. In tune with Whitehead's appreciation for the vast neighborhoods that literary language knows how to conjure, Stein explores an immense terrain of associations. She packs her meditations on the nature of language with spatial imagery and highlights the intertwining of abstract and concrete by having dogs run through her language-scape. Wittily, she uses the format of the "simple-minded" approach to rhetoric – *How to Write*, Sharon Kirsch has pointed out, "poses as a handbook on composition" – to show that it makes little sense, for example, to try to define what sentences are.[63] She may try to distinguish between unemotional sentences and emotional paragraphs herself, but she is, at the same time, more than happy to have her sentences rebel. Sentences, *How to Write* makes clear, thrive on all sorts of connections. "A sentence has wishes as an event," or it "hopes that you are very well and happy," or it "is made by coupling."[64] Ultimately, the only way you can learn about sentences is through actual sentences. If, for Whitehead, there is no object without event, Stein makes clear there is no sentence without sentences. Analogously, grammar cannot be equated with a neutral set of rules to apply or a system to uncover. Grammar is in the hands of grammarians, who can be called Arthur, as in "Arthur a Grammar," or Gertrude Stein ("I am a grammarian. I think of the differences there are"), or involve you ("It stops because you stop. Think of that.").[65] As Rachel Blau DuPlessis points out, Stein was well aware of "the role of gender asymmetry and power formation in discourse."[66] *How to Write* ends with "Forensics," in which, as Kirsch shows, Stein problematizes authority and authorship by a sequence of "shifting, unattached pronouns [that] introduce doubt about who is speaking and whose ideas belong to whom."[67] But Stein does more than spotlight unmoored pronouns. "Forensics" concludes on a sequence of incomplete staccato sentences, a stuttering that refuses the resolution of conflict that, for Aristotle, was the purpose of forensic rhetoric. Instead of resolution, Stein offers "[a] detachment of troops." She holds off judging and sends out linguistic troops – short statements, different voices, hurried thoughts and "[m]ore facts" – into an indefinite neighborhood.[68]

Stein's Saints

In contrast to Whitehead, Stein does not consider the event a particularly exciting concept. By her account, events amount to meaningless happenings strung together in the newspaper or in a radio broadcast, much like Benjamin's stifling mode of production modeled on the newspaper that I have discussed in the previous chapters. In "How Writing is Written" (1935) she makes it clear that events have very little to do with life, for which she uses the terms movement, excitement, vitality and existence:

> One thing which came to me is that the Twentieth Century gives of itself a feeling of movement, and has in its way no feeling for events. To the Twentieth Century events are not important. You must know that. Events are not exciting. Events have lost their interest for people. You read them more like a soothing syrup, and if you listen over the radio you don't get very excited. The thing has got to this place, that events are so wonderful that they are not exciting. Now you have to remember that the business of an artist is to be exciting. If the thing has its proper vitality, the result must be exciting. [. . .] People are interested in existence. Newspapers excite people very little. Sometimes a personality breaks through the newspapers – Lindbergh, Dillinger – when the personality has vitality. It wasn't what Dillinger *did* that excited anybody.

Stein may write off the event, but she was doing what Whitehead was doing in the sense that she became fascinated by what she calls "the static thing." "You can see it in my *Four Saints*," she continues in "How Writing is Written."

> Saints shouldn't do anything. The fact that a saint is there is enough for anybody. The *Four Saints* was written about as static as I could make it. The saints conversed a little, and it all did something. It did something more than the theatre which has tried to make events has done.[69]

Instead of feeding its audience a "soothing story syrup," the play gives us a Whiteheadian event: a performance with timeless figures as protagonists.

Much like Whitehead's Needle, Stein's saints are sites for the concrete and the abstract to meet.[70] They have histories but they also appear unaffected by time. Saint Therese and Saint Ignatius, the play's protagonists, are different from Stein's usual suspects in that, as Dydo puts it, they "came to her ready-made from outside, from history."[71] Yet Stein would not be Stein if she did not complicate the relation between outside world and literature. Her saints surpass their historical referents. "Saint Ignatius [who] was very well known" immediately brings to mind the famous Ignatius of Loyola, co-founder of the Jesuit order and author of *Spiritual Exercises*, but the fact that Stein, a couple of pages into the text, suddenly introduces a "Saint Ignatius Loyola" opens up the possibility that the first Saint Ignatius is not who we had taken him to be.[72] Similarly, Saint Therese, whom Stein positions "in a storm at Avila," clearly refers to Ignatius of Loyola's contemporary, Teresa of Ávila, whose *Way of Perfection* and *The Interior Castle* are classics in the tradition of Catholic mysticism.[73] Yet Stein may also have been thinking of the so-called "little flower," Thérèse de Lisieux. Named after Teresa of Ávila, Saint Thérèse was a young French nun who had died of tuberculosis in 1897 and whose heavily mediatized process of canonization was happening in the 1920s. The cult of Thérèse was fed by the photographs her sister had taken and these can be seen to appear in *Four Saints* when Stein writes "Saint Therese could be photographed having been dressed like a lady and then they taking out her head changed it to a nun and a nun a saint and a saint so."[74]

The becoming-saint that Stein alludes to when she comments on the Saint Therese photographs implies a long and formal process that makes it possible for a historical individual to be set apart, literally written into the canon and venerated as holy. Following Durkheim's 1912 analysis, "the division of the world into two domains, one containing all that is sacred and the other all that is profane" amounts to "the distinctive trait of religious thought," and this implies that saints can be considered go-betweens.[75] What they did – their miraculous lives and works – is rooted in the mundane, or concrete, yet their status is holy, or abstracted from everyday life. Once canonized, they no longer have to do anything, except for making the odd appearance in the mundane world. Stein's conceiving of her saints as "real saints" wittily complicates the division into two domains. As real saints, they are obviously abstractions, so they do not do anything: "[a] saint a real saint never does anything," she repeats in *Everybody's Autobiography*.[76] Yet for them to be real saints, they also have to be really there, in the actual world: "While I was writing the Four Saints I wanted one always does want the saints to be actually saints before them as well as inside them, I had to see them as well as feel them."[77] It should not surprise, therefore, that among the "many many saints" that Stein includes in the play, some share the names of the people close to her.[78] Saint Michael and Saint Sarah, for example, hint at her brother and sister-in-law, historical figures she could actually see as well as feel.

Four Saints in Three Acts itself highlights in different ways the double position of the saints. Not only is there the odd mixture of saints whose names refer to the Catholic tradition with saints modeled on people in Stein's circle, but Stein also often positions her main saint, Saint Therese, in between states. We encounter her "half in doors and half out of doors," "seated" and "not seated," "very nearly half inside and half outside the house," "left in complete" as well as "meant to be complete completely," and "left to right" in addition to "right to left."[79] This sets *Four Saints in Three Acts* apart from Stein's earlier saints plays, in which she tends to position the figures in her landscapes with precision – exactly there, exactly thus. Because of that detailed positioning, Lyn Hejinian compares Stein's landscapes to *tableaux vivants*, in which "episodes become qualities."[80] The examples she quotes from "A Saint in Seven" (1922) capture scenes we could imagine staging in a rainy, nineteenth-century salon: "[a] guardian of a museum holding a cane" or "[a] very stout girl with a basket and flowers summer flowers and the flowers are in front of a small tree."[81] I love Hejinian's comparison and I actually think it works even better for *Four Saints in Three Acts* than for the earlier landscapes. It may be harder to imagine yourself impersonating Saint Therese "seated" and "not seated" than as "a very stout girl," but the impossible double positions of the opera captures what the *tableau vivant* is all about, according to one of its most fervent theorists. The *tableau vivant*, according to Pierre Klossowski, does not give us "simply life imitating art." "The emotion sought after," rather, "was that of life giving itself as a spectacle to life, of life hanging in suspense."[82]

Tableaux Vivants

Tableaux vivants used to be popular parlor games in the nineteenth century. Participants would dress up and reproduce in elaborate detail a well-known painting or sculpture. An audience had to guess which. "The essential nature and attraction of the *tableau vivant* performance," Lynda Nead writes, "was the constant and provocative oscillation between stasis and movement." The idea was to keep still but the fun was in the desire for movement. It was, in sum, "as much an art of animation, of coming into movement, as it was an art of de-animation and stasis."[83] The French post-modernist Klossowski adds to the ambiguous nature of the game by complicating the relationship between original painting and reproduction. Klossowski may seem like an odd diversion from our Whiteheadian framework, but what Klossowski found in the *tableau vivant* is a quality that, by Deleuze's account, is central to the Whiteheadian event. As Scott Durham explains, the *tableau vivant*, on Klossowski's terms, arrests the process of actualization and thereby makes visible "qualities that were not apparent in the original [scene]."[84] These qualities are what Deleuze would call the virtual aspect of an event. Deleuze's understanding of the event is very much indebted to Whitehead. Indeed, in *The Fold: Leibniz and the Baroque*, he sees "a secret school" of event-thinkers at work in the history of philosophy, whose efforts, in the twentieth century, are taken up by Whitehead.[85] What Deleuze calls the virtual is in line with what Whitehead refers to as "Pure Potentials for the Specific Determination of Fact" in *Process and Reality*.[86]

In *Process and Reality* the timeless objects of *The Concept of Nature* have now become "Eternal Objects," but their function has not changed. They "can be described only in terms of [their] potentiality for 'ingression' into the becoming of actual entities." Ingression, Whitehead explains, "refers to the particular mode in which the potentiality of an eternal object is realized in a particular actual entity, contributing to the definiteness of that actual entity."[87] Like Stein, who wanted her saints to be actual – she wanted to "see" and "feel" them – Whitehead's eternal objects are involved in a making-actual that is not some kind of embodiment of a higher truth, but an individual occasion centered on feeling. "[E]ternal objects determine *how* the world of actual entities enters into the constitution of each one of its members via its feelings."[88] Klossowski's description of a *tableau vivant* as "life giving itself as a spectacle to life" captures the unbreakable bind between object (or timeless potentiality) and event (or fleeting actualization) that is key to Whitehead's project. Actual life is haunted by potential life. For Klossowksi, the *tableau vivant* succeeds in "draw[ing] out of the remembered gesture qualities that were not apparent in the original," but virtually present.[89] For Whitehead, potentiality becoming reality does not mean that it dies an actual death:

> Potentiality becomes reality; and yet it retains its message of alternatives which the actual entity has avoided. In the constitution of an actual entity: – whatever component is red, might have been green; and whatever component is loved, might have been coldly esteemed.[90]

Stein came to a similar insight when she saw a series of photographs mapping the transition from woman to nun. "[T]here is on the Boulevard Raspail," she tells us in "Plays," a place where they make photographs that have always held my attention. They take a photograph of a young girl dressed in the costume of her ordinary life and little by little in successive photographs they change it into a nun. These photographs are small and the thing takes four or five changes but at the end it is a nun and this is done for the family when the nun is dead and in memoriam.

This step-by-step visualization of a process seems to contrast sharply with Stein's criticism of entelechial models, as I have described it earlier. However, Stein still relates this model to death rather than life ("this is done for the family when the nun is dead and in memoriam") and what matters here is less the nature of the process of becoming than the message of alternative lives these pictures capture. For Stein, they visualize the residues of potentiality at work in actualization. They make her see the "ordinary young lady" in her Saint Therese:

> For years I had stood and looked at these when I was walking and finally when I was writing Saint Therese in looking at these photographs I saw how Saint Therese existed from the life of an ordinary young lady to that of the nun. And so everything was actual and I went on writing.[91]

In *Four Saints*, Stein weaves saintly alternatives in and out of each other. There are a lot of "coulds" and "mights" that invite the reader to see the saints differently. As the following example shows, Stein often practices a rhythm of adding and subtracting qualities, denying and affirming alternatives:

> Saint Ignatius could be in porcelain actually.
> Saint Ignatius could be in porcelain actually while he was young and standing.
> Saint Therese could not be young and standing she could be sitting.
> Saint Ignatius could be in porcelain actually actually in porcelain standing.
> Saint Therese could be admittedly could be in moving seating. Saint Therese could be in moving sitting.
> Saint Therese could be.
> Saint Ignatius could be.
> Saint Ignatius could be in porcelain actually in porcelain standing.[92]

She not only makes us see the saints as made up of very different types of occasions – porcelain statues, dynamically sitting, being – she also applies this halo of alternatives to the text itself. We are kept guessing at the setting. It could be the French countryside since the play starts with a diary-like fragment in which Stein writes that "[they] had intended if it were a pleasant day to go to the country," but then later in the play a Saint Eustace wonders "Might it be mountains if it were not Barcelona." The saints have fun with time, with a Saint Gallo pronouncing that it is "clock o' clock," and Stein reminding us that some holy days turn weekdays into Sundays ("All Saints make Sunday Monday Sunday Monday Sunday Monday set"). There is no exhausting the saints' alternatives since the precise quantity of saints in the play is kept indefinite:

> Saint Therese. How many saints are there in it.
> Saint Cecilia. How many saints are there in it.
> Saint Therese. There are as many saints as there are in it.
> Saint Cecilia. There are as many saints as there are saints in it.
> Saint Cecilia. How many saints are there in it.
> Saint Therese. There are many saints in it.[93]

And because the saints make the landscape that is the play, there is no exhausting the play's alternatives. To those asking how many acts the play contains, Stein, in an emphatically circular act, returns the question. What matters is that those who wonder, come and find out for themselves:

> How many acts are there in it. Acts are there in it.
> Supposing a wheel had been added to three wheels how many acts how many how many acts are there in it.
> Any Saint at all.
> How many acts are there in it.
> How many saints in all.
> How many acts are there in it.
> Ring around a rosey.
> How many acts are there in it.
> Wedded and weeded.
> Please be coming to see me.[94]

When Stein wrote the play in 1927, the phrase "Please be coming to see me" was potentiality rather than actuality. It would take another seven years until the play was turned into an opera production.[95] The story of Stein's collaboration with composer Virgil Thomson is told wonderfully by Steven Watson in his *Prepare for Saints*. For my story here, Stein's conceiving her play as an opera is more important than the details of its production and reception.

Opera

As speaks from Stein's 1922 play "Saints and Singing," the connection between saints and singing is not a new idea. Although Stein, by Thomson's account, was not "by nature what we would call musical," her turn to music makes perfect conceptual sense.[96] Abstraction is easier to attain via music than it is via language. Language is inescapably referential, will always be involved in stories. Music, by contrast, "cannot narrate, cannot speak what took place in time past."[97] Singing, and the idea of the lyric that she explores in the 1928 text "A Lyrical Opera Made By Two To Be Sung," then, can be considered strategies for Stein to fuse together concrete and abstract. That is not exactly how she explains it herself, however. In "Portraits and Repetition" she relates the early 1920s pieces to an interest in melody. Looking back on "Four Religions, Capital Capitals, Saints in Seven and a great many other things," she sees "a very greatly increased melody" because she was focused on a smooth going together of movement and stasis, which had enraptured her during her stay in Provence. She refers to it as "the feeling [she] then had there in Saint Remy of light and air and air moving and being still."[98] Reading these texts in this optic makes for an almost pastoral reading experience.[99] In "Saints and Singing," for example, harmony sets the tone. Stein concludes the play's sentimental four-line introduction with the statement "We have been baffled by harmony" and then explores the secluded, creative togetherness that being in nature, religious experience and singing share: "And wind sounds like rain, wind when it is turning. How a little nature makes religion, and how a little religion makes creation makes a saint in singing and now rush and hush. We are not going to meeting."[100] That sense of hushed withdrawal is absent from *Four Saints in Three Acts*, which moves beyond the connection between saints and singing. As its subtitle states, it is "An Opera To Be Sung."

Stein and Thomson's plans to make an opera not only should be seen in the context of Stein's interest in artistic collaborations, but also should be viewed as a decision to contribute to the tradition of opera – to keep it alive by insisting on fissure. Coming out of the nineteenth century, that tradition was haunted by the idea of the *Gesamtkunstwerk* or "the total work of art," an idea of which the ambitions far transcended opera. Wagner's mid-nineteenth-century concept, as many critics have noted, captures both the horror and the hope of the modern project. As Matthew Wilson Smith puts it:

On one hand: the Gesamtkunstwerk is modernity's leviathan. Its worst moments are its moments of entry into the world. Its moments of fullest realization are also the moments of history's greatest horror.

On the other: the Gesamtkunstwerk is modernity's polestar. It is an uncompromising wish for a joyful community to be realized in this life, in this world. It is a longing for unity amidst fragmentation, for collectivity amidst alienation. It is inherently restless and potentially revolutionary, and while it is inescapably ideological its longings can never be entirely contained within the bounds of ideology. It is the shape of radical hope.

On one hand and on the other – can both hands be right?[101]

Thomson, in overseeing the production of *Four Saints in Three Acts*, insisted on the other hand. His decision to work with Black performers turned Stein's play into the first American opera with an all-Black cast, giving shape to "a joyful community in this life." In the early 1930s, this was a radical move. As Watson points out, "[a]s a general rule, the further up the ladder of high culture, the greater the resistance to black performers."[102] There were Black opera companies and Black performers were regularly cast in minstrel shows and revues, but prior to Thomson no one had invited Black singers to perform an opera that had nothing to do with Black life.[103] As Susan Holbrook and Thomas Dilworth point out, "[i]n the racist culture of the time, his decision is revolutionary."[104]

Thomson informed Stein of his production ideas rather than consulting with her, yet his decision to go against the grain of institutional conventions is very much in tune with the libretto's textual logic. Stein approaches opera as *Gesamtkunstwerk* to work out her new, Whitehead-inspired, take on collectivity. In *Science and the Modern World*, Whitehead introduces the idea of prehension, by which he responds to the modern drama of individuation: the inability to see our lives in relation to other lives and surroundings. Whitehead holds the bifurcation of nature, or the fallacies of misplaced concreteness and single location, responsible for a lamentable individualism. When he strips it down, the situation of our mistaking abstractions for concrete realities hits him as "quite unbelievable" and yet the entire modern system of knowledge production is based on that mistake. "Every university in the world organizes itself in accordance with it. No alternative system of organizing the pursuit of scientific truth has been suggested. It is not only reigning, but it is without a rival."[105] It has helped install an ideology in which the individual has become the prime entity. As Whitehead points out, the birth of modern science in the seventeenth century not only ran parallel to developments in philosophy, with Locke's distinction between primary and secondary qualities and Descartes's theory of body and mind as key contributions, but also should be seen as keeping pace with a social tendency towards individualism, "issued from the moral discipline of the Middle Ages." The result of these concordant developments was that modern science "gave stability and intellectual status to a point of view which has had very mixed effects upon the moral presuppositions of modern communities." On the one hand, it triggered an unseen efficiency in taking control of life; in the eighteenth century rationalism surpasses "the hysteria of remote barbaric ages." On the other hand, the increasing stress on individual entities, and on the producing, buying and selling of such entities in the nineteenth century, has led to "private worlds of morals" in which the most important shared values are those of self-respect and of "making the most of your own individual opportunities."[106] The inheritance of this situation is a twofold evil: the lack of attention to the relation between individual organisms and their environment, and our tendency to ignore the worth of the environment as such.

For Whitehead, individuation always concerns the holding together, or prehension, of an event. And however individual that process of holding together may be, it always finds itself in relation to other events, near and far – much like Stein's landscape is "being always in relation, the trees to the hills the hills to the fields the trees to each other any piece of it to any sky and then any detail to any other detail."[107] Whitehead came up with the term prehension when he was looking for a word that does justice to the nebulous aspects of the process of knowing. He considered the dominant scientific vantage "too narrow for the concrete facts which are before it for analysis." There is more to see than science enables us to. In perception, we always "take account of things of which at the time we have no explicit cognition." Since the terms perception and apprehension fail to do justice to this uncognitive dimension of the process of knowing, he opted for "the word 'prehension' for *uncognitive apprehension.*"[108] Whiteheadian prehension is not just an extended mode of perception. Whitehead disagrees with Berkeley, for whom the perceiving mind constitutes the unity in which things become real things. "For Berkeley's mind," he writes, "I substitute a process of prehensive unification." This implies that what is realized is not the things, but the prehension, the "gathering of things into a unity." This unity is always "a *here* and a *now,*" with the things in the unity relating to other situations and historical moments.[109]

When Whitehead introduces the idea of prehension in *Science and the Modern World*, a plurality of perspectives opens up. If the problem in *The Concept of Nature* was that Cleopatra's Needle could be "again," the emphasis has now shifted from the happening of the event to individual "'holding together' of the gathering it constitutes." Rather than perspectives, Whitehead prefers to call these many possible holding-togethers "modes," in tune with Spinoza. "His one substance," he writes with reference to Spinoza, "is for me the one underlying activity of realisation individualising itself in an interlocked plurality of modes." As Stengers points out, what is at stake here is indeed "the question of individualization." Whitehead's mode – the prehension's *how* that constitutes the event – makes it impossible for an individual to be deduced from its community. There is never mere deduction or "simple fusion," in Whitehead. An event cannot choose its mode of prehension, "but it must be prehended, and it must be prehended 'severally,' in a determinate mode each time."[110]

The fringes of knowledge, which Whitehead sought to include in considering the world in terms of prehensions, are also at the origin of Stein's playwriting. As I have already pointed out, Stein considered including "what everybody did not always know" as key to her first play, "What Happened. A Five Act Play." In *Lectures in America*, she tells us that "naturally what I wanted to do in my play was what everybody did not always know nor always tell. By everybody I do of course include myself [. . .]."[111] Stein wanted to show what was happening if you look at things through a lens other than that of a dominant narrative framework. Opera is by no means a marginal framework, but Stein makes it clear from the start that she is not interested in sticking closely to operatic conventions. The very title of her play indicates that there is more to her opera than it can hold: there are "four saints" for only "three acts." These acts, as familiar conventions, are furthermore introduced as "idle":

> Why should every one be at home why should every one be at home
>   why should every one be at home.
> Why should every one be at home.
> In idle acts.
> Why should everybody be at home.
> In idle acts.[112]

Since we know that Stein wanted her saints to be doing as little as possible, the "idle acts" also hint at the static quality of the world that she had become fascinated by. Yet Stein would not be Stein if she did not also subvert a straightforward static scheme: the preposition "in" can be taken as the negation of idle and "acts" can also be read as a verb. The refrain "Why should every one be at home," furthermore, echoes Whitehead's fallacy of single location. It is not because things ("ones" or "bodies") do not seem to move, Stein seems to be saying, that they are bound to one location (a home). If the fallacies of misplaced concreteness and single location make the world into a dull, cerebral place, Stein makes clear that that is not the world of her saints. "To know to know to love her so" is the very first line of the opera, and it makes manifest that there is no knowing without feeling – or, differently, that opera, as the artform harnessed to feeling, can also be a vehicle to make claims about knowing.[113]

The most obvious way in which Stein develops her take on knowing as prehension is by means of the "four saints." Instead of giving us four individual saints that together constitute a group, which would put the stress on the individual, Stein starts the opera by presenting us with a manifold "holding together" of four saints. Four saints, in these first pages, is the event, and it is prehended again and again. There is no original group of four, only aspects or modes of four saints. The modes in which four saints is prehended include language play ("for saints"), the question of amount ("Four Saints are never three. Three Saints are never four."), the text that Stein is working on ("Four saints an opera in three acts"), an open constellation of historical figures (at one point there is the claim "Four saints were not born at one time although they knew each other," but at the end of this section of the opera we also get more than twenty names), and a constellation of selves, with Saint Therese emerging in manifold right before the first of the first acts.[114] As event, furthermore, four saints is emphatically connected to other situations. These range from details pertaining to Stein's daily life – she inserts, for instance, the diary-like entry "We had intended if it were a pleasant day to go to the country it was a very beautiful day and we carried out our intention" – to quizzical reflections on the saints' relation to their natural surroundings ("The difference between saints forget me nots and mountains have to have to have to at a time").[115] When "Act One" shifts the emphasis to Saint Therese and Saint Ignatius, this does not imply a return to the individual as static and limited entity. Both, rather, should be seen as events happening parallel to the enfolding four saints event. Saint Therese, like four saints, has many different modes. Apart from positioned in between states, we encounter Saint Therese as, for example, a sequence of photographs, candy ("Saint Therese saints make sugar with a flavor"), "a young girl being widowed," and uninterested in hypothetical questions concerning mass destruction ("If it were possible to kill five thousand chinamen by pressing a button would it be done. / Saint Therese not interested"). All these modes constitute a *Gesamtkunstwerk* not because they add up to a totality, but because their range is indefinite: there is no limit to prehensions. Or, as Saint Chavez puts it, four saints is "[i]n consideration of everything."[116]

If all this makes *Four Saints in Three Acts* sound like a very abstract event, then let's return to its subtitle, "An Opera To Be Sung." There is more to this text than a philosophical exploration of the event, Stein indicates. Its aim is actual sound: the ingression of sound as eternal object into performance. According to event-thinker par excellence Gilles Deleuze, there is little that better embodies the concept of the event than a concert. "A concert is being performed tonight," he writes in *The Fold*:

> It is the event. Vibrations of sound disperse, periodic movements go through space with their harmonics or submultiples. The sounds have inner qualities of height, intensity, and timbre. The sources of the sounds, instrumental or vocal, are not content only to send the sounds out: each one perceives its own, and perceives the others while perceiving its own. These are active prehensions that are expressed among each other, or else prehensions that are prehending each other.[117]

While readers cannot simply will a performance of *Four Saints in Three Acts* to happen, we can, as the text prompts, "Imagine imagine it imagine it in it."[118]

Life histories

Four Saints in Three Acts as event, finally, is the foothold that enables us to understand the paradox we set out from: Stein's new take on movement exemplified by landscape-plays-that-relate-yet-hardly-move and portraits-that-move-yet-do-not-relate. Stein wanted us to see the latter, let us remember, as "something that was more vibrant," and as "something completely contained within itself and being contained within itself was moving, not moving in relation to anything not moving in relation to itself but just moving."[119] The fact that, in my reading of the George Hugnet portrait, I could not help but see "relations," or references to Stein's life and her relationship to Hugnet, does not, now, mean that the portrait is not also a self-contained entity. All events,

Whitehead posits in *Science and the Modern World*, have a double nature:

> Each event corresponds to two [...] patterns; namely, the pattern of aspects of other events which it grasps into its own unity, and the pattern of its aspects which other events severally grasp into their unities. [...] There is thus an intrinsic and an extrinsic reality of an event, namely, the event as in its own prehension, and the event as in the prehension of other events.[120]

The charm of the opera is that Stein showcased a rollercoaster of prehensions, together constituting an open *Gesamtkunstwerk*. The four saints were joyfully prehended by language, history and experience. The portraits are different not because they are not prehended by outside events, but because Stein shifts emphasis; she chooses to explore the "intrinsic reality" of an event.

Whitehead's framing of events in terms of pattern offers us a way into discovering how Stein goes about constructing these intrinsic realities. "An actual event," Whitehead sums up, "is an achievement for its own sake, a grasping of diverse entities into a value by reason of their real togetherness in that pattern, to the exclusion of other entities." Self-identity, in other words, is a pattern that endures.[121] This pattern, furthermore, is active on every level of the event, informing both parts and whole: "The event, in its own intrinsic reality, mirrors in itself, as derived from its own parts, aspects of the same patterned value as it realises in its complete self." The pattern is also how we should understand Stein's enigmatic "thing contained within itself." The event, Whitehead continues, "thus realises itself under the guise of an enduring individual entity, with a life-history contained within itself."[122] Pattern does not, however, equal life.

As Meyer points out, Whitehead was thinking about how pattern relates to life as early as in his 1919 *An Enquiry Concerning the Principles of Natural Knowledge*. "What is life?" seems too metaphysical a question for a book that wants to answer the question "What are the ultimate data of science?," and yet Whitehead concludes his enquiry by means of a reflection on life as such, referencing both Bergson's *élan vital* burdened by matter and romantic poetry's fascination with death haunting life.[123] Working towards this poetic conclusion, he argues that it is no use tying life to objects. "[I]ndividual life *is*, beyond the mere object." We should not, therefore, talk about living objects, but see objects as "bearing" or "expressing" life. That does not imply that life is a mysterious essence that somehow preys on objects that it can use to manifest itself. Indeed, it is "too obstinately concrete" to be even located in a single instant, let alone in an other-worldly force. In *An Enquiry*, life equals rhythm. "[W]herever there is some rhythm," Whitehead states matter-of-factly, "there is some life [. . .]." More than fifteen years before the publication of *Nature and Life*, he formulates a first answer to the question of how nature and life relate to each other: "The rhythm is then the life in the sense in which it can be said to be included in nature." Rhythm is not rhythm without pattern. "A rhythm involves a pattern and to that extent is always self-identical." No rhythm, however, "can be a mere pattern."

> [T]he rhythmic quality depends equally upon the differences involved in each exhibition of the pattern. The essence of rhythm is the fusion of sameness and novelty; so that the whole never loses the essential unity of the pattern, while the parts exhibit the contrast arising from the novelty of their detail. A mere recurrence kills rhythm as surely as does a mere confusion of differences. A crystal lacks rhythm from excess of pattern, while a fog is unrhythmic in that it exhibits a patternless confusion of detail.[124]

Event and rhythm should both be seen as contributing to life. Neither "has" it. The event is the factor that brings in unity and the unique novelty that is inherent to its passage, and rhythm supplies a mode of recurrence.[125]

For Stein, pattern and rhythm meant formalist fun. In connection with her "tremendously important" discovery of things contained by themselves, she mentions not only the George Hugnet portrait, but also her portrait of Bernard Faÿ. Surprisingly, perhaps, she gives clear hints that she wants us to read these portraits in the context of formalist writing. Right after quoting a couple of lines from the Faÿ portrait, she tells us that it mattered so much "because it made [her] realize what poetry really is."[126] She also adds that "[t]his has something to do with what Edgar Allan Poe is." Poe's take on poetry, famously, is that the poem should be written "solely for the poem's sake." In *The Poetic Principle* he defined poetry as *"The Rhythmical Creation of Beauty,"* only incidentally concerned with "outside" things such as "Duty" or "Truth."[127] While we should take Stein's insight into the reality of poetry with a grain of salt – she hardly converts to art for art's sake – it stands out that "Bernard Faÿ" is an exercise in using pattern to create rhythm.

The pattern in "Bernard Faÿ" is all about combinations of three: "one two three and after unity."[128] This may be inspired by Faÿ's striking last name, consisting of only three letters, or we may also pause at the fact that Faÿ was a devout Catholic and see Stein's fascination with three as related to the symbolic unity of the Father, the Son and the Holy Ghost. Those considerations, however, are of little importance, since what matters here is the internal make-up of the poem. To emphasize form over reference, Stein opts for a linguistic threesome: articles. "A is an article" is how the poem starts. If this sentence contains only two articles, a third is soon added ("the"), upon which Stein starts exploring different combinations of ones, twos and threes:

> A an article. A an article.
> A the same.
> A and the. A and the.[129]

While "A an article. A an article" gives us two sets of one (A) or two (A + an), the line "A the same" adds a third, but differently. "A and the. A and the" repeat the doubling, but now we have the three articles in one sentence, with "an" hiding in "and." While there is no third sentence following, we can take "A the same" to be the first sentence, on which the double "A and the" follows. As a whole, furthermore, the poem is loosely composed of three parts, with parts and whole effectively mirroring each other. There are three references to "part three" and if the opening sentence marks part one, then the sentences "Articles are a an and the" and "An article is a and an and the" can be taken as marking parts two and three.[130] Ones, twos and threes are not limited to articles but, in different ways, mark the whole of the poem. Always, Stein makes sure not to make the pattern stifling. Take the sentences Stein quotes in "Portraits and Repetition":

> Patience is amiable and amiably
> What is amiable and amiably.
> Patience is amiable and amiably.
> What is impatience.
> Impatience is amiable and amiably.[131]

Patience (one) equals amiable and amiably (two), which together makes three. This is repeated, but there is also room for variation, with "impatience" taking the place of "Patience." In contrast to Patience, impatience cannot be taken for a proper name, until, of course, it turns into the capitalized "Impatience." "Thank you for all three," Stein writes at the end of the portrait, to have it followed by

"The making of never stop. Or the making of stop or stopped."[132] This antepenultimate line embodies the advice it gives us – never to stop making – by adding alternatives: are we to never stop making threes, making "never stops," or making stops? All this, again, is an ironic attempt to stop the poem.

In "Portraits and Repetition" Stein tells us she found this focus on an entity's life history, this "creat[ing] something out of something without adding anything," to be "very exciting," until she "slowly got a little tired."[133] As we have seen, Stein often uses the term exciting to spotlight her interest in life. "If the thing has its proper vitality," she reminded us in "How Writing Is Written," "the result must be exciting." The next thing she wrote, by her own account, was *The Autobiography of Alice B. Toklas*. It is tempting to think that Stein felt prompted by the Whiteheadian notion of a life history to experiment with the tradition of life writing, but she makes it clear that it was an "entirely different" project from what she had been doing. The difference was triggered by two experiences that caused Stein to think about how others saw her work. The first is "some poetry [she] had been writing, Before the Flowers of Friendship Faded Friendship Faded" and the second is Stein "going to hear Bernard Fay lecture about Franco-American things."[134] "Before the Flowers of Friendship Faded Friendship Faded" is the title Stein gave her translations of Georges Hugnet's poems of "Enfances." Stein and Hugnet had fallen out over money and the issue of the poet's and translator's names in the planned bilingual publication. The text, in other words, is more related to the literary field than to a compositional challenge Stein had set herself.[135] Faÿ's lectures, second, had sparked an interest "in the relation of a lecturer to his audience." This, too, caused Stein to think about what she calls "the outside," or the world of audiences, publishers and reviewers. Up until writing *The Autobiography of Alice B. Toklas*, she had set her own literary challenges ("I had always had nothing but what was inside me while I was writing"). In thinking about the demands and expectations of an audience, she "suddenly began, to feel the outside inside and the inside outside." This, she adds, "was perhaps not so exciting but it was very interesting."[136]

I cannot read Stein's claim that what she was doing in the 1930s "was perhaps not so exciting but it was very interesting" as a minor remark. For me, it signals the end of Stein's fascination with life as I have tried to map it in this book. "Interest" comes with different connotations than excitement and the texts she writes change in tone and form as she ponders the issue of how outside and inside relate to each other. Of course, as always, Stein's new project is not a total break with what she had been doing before and Stein duly modifies her remark by adding that the new stuff was "quite exciting" after all. Indeed, I have drawn on quite a few of the texts she wrote in order to make sense of her fascination with life. In their own right, however, Stein's interesting texts ask for a different story than the one I have told here.

Notes

1. Stein, *Lectures in America*, 310, 311.
2. Ibid., 265, 262. For more on the notion of the landscape in Stein's work, see Marianne DeKoven, "Gertrude Stein's Landscape Writing," *Women's Studies: An Interdisciplinary Journal* 9.3 (1982): 221–39; Elliott L. Vanskike, "'Seeing Everything as Flat': Landscape in Gertrude Stein's *Useful Knowledge* and *The Geographical History of America*," *Texas Studies in Language and Literature* 35.2 (1993): 151–67; Jessica Berman, *Modernist Fiction, Cosmopolitanism, and the Politics of Community* (Cambridge: Cambridge University Press, 2001); Bowers, "The Composition that All the World Can See," 121–44; Voris, *The Composition of Sense in Gertrude Stein's Landscape Writing*.
3. Stein, *Lectures in America*, 310, and Gertrude Stein, "George Hugnet," *Portraits and Prayers*, 66.
4. Dydo, *Stein Reader*, 539.
5. Stein, *Lectures in America*, 269.
6. In *The Concept of Nature*, Whitehead writes: "The complete foothold of the mind in nature is represented by the pair of events, namely the present duration which marks the 'when' of awareness and the percipient event which marks the 'where' of awareness and the 'how' of awareness" (*The Concept of Nature*, 70). Stengers explains that "foothold does not designate the act of taking hold, but what the mind or knowledge requires from nature, what it needs to be offered by nature if its operations are not to be illusory (*Thinking with Whitehead*, 66–7). I love the metaphor because it works beautifully for the literary critic as well. Texts can mean so many different things. It is up to the critic–mountaineer to make them tell a particular story, and he or she can do that only by using the text's words and phrases as footholds.
7. Whitehead, *Process and Reality*, 104.
8. Ibid., 104.
9. Whitehead, *Science and the Modern World*, 93.
10. Whitehead, *Process and Reality*, 105.
11. On Stein in relation to the tradition of portraiture, see Ulla Haselstein "Gertrude Stein's Portraits of Matisse and Picasso," *New Literary History: A Journal of Theory and Interpretation* 34.4 (2003). See also Ulla

Haselstein's monograph *Gertrude Steins Literarische Porträts* (Konstanz: Konstanz University Press, 2019).
12. Stein, *Lectures in America*, 310.
13. Bennett, *Vibrant Matter*, vii.
14. Meyer, *Irresistible Dictation*, 201. Meyer quotes from Whitehead, *Science and the Modern World*, 36.
15. Whitehead, *Process and Reality*, 104.
16. Aristotle, *Poetics*, trans. I. Bywater, in *The Complete Works of Aristotle*, ed. Jonathan Barnes, vol. 2 (Princeton, NJ: Princeton University Press, 1984), 4975.
17. Stein, *Lectures in America*, 244.
18. This does not mean that interpretation cannot go on after the initial event.
19. Stein, *Lectures in America*, 244.
20. Ibid., 268–9.
21. Whitehead writes: "The miracle of creation is described in the vision of the prophet Ezekiel: 'So I prophesied as he commanded me, and the breath came into them, and they lived, and stood up upon their feet, an exceeding great army.'" Whitehead turns this image into "the breath of feeling," which he explains as that transformation that "creates a new individual fact" and that is not "wholly traceable to the mere data" (*Process and Reality*, 85).
22. Whitehead, *Science and the Modern World*, 105.
23. Ibid., 87–8.
24. Stein, *Lectures in America*, 267.
25. Stengers, *Thinking with Whitehead*, 155.
26. Alfred North Whitehead, *Nature and Life* (Cambridge: Cambridge University Press, 2011), 53.
27. Ibid., 44.
28. Whitehead, *Science and the Modern World*, 83; Whitehead, *Nature and Life*, 44.
29. Whitehead, *The Concept of Nature*, 21.
30. Ibid., 95.
31. In *Process and Reality* (209) Whitehead writes he does not believe the "accusation" that the intellect necessarily "ignore[s] the fluency" and "analyse[s] the world in terms of static categories."
32. Whitehead, *The Concept of Nature*, 19.
33. Stengers, *Thinking with Whitehead*, 38.
34. Stein, *Lectures in America*, 269.
35. Whitehead, *Process and Reality*, 50.
36. Stengers, *Thinking with Whitehead*, 113.
37. Whitehead, *Science and the Modern World*, 50.
38. Ibid., 54.
39. Stein, *Lectures in America*, 330.
40. Didier Debaise, *Nature as Event: The Lure of the Possible*, trans. Michael Halewood (Durham, NC: Duke University Press, 2017), 32–3.

41. Stein, *Lectures in America*, 268.
42. Whitehead, *The Concept of Nature*, 10.
43. Ibid., 22.
44. See *The Concept of Nature* for Whitehead's discussion of existing theories of time and space.
45. Whitehead, *The Concept of Nature*, 35, 39. Whitehead's concept of the event has been of great influence on Deleuze. In *The Fold* he pays tribute to Whitehead's concept thus: "With Whitehead's name there comes for the third time an echo of the question, What is an event? He takes up the radical critique of the attributive scheme, the great play of principles, the multiplication of categories, the conciliation of the universal and the individual, and the transformation of the concept into a subject: an entire hubris [. . .] an event does not just mean that 'a man has been run over.' The Great Pyramid is an event, and its duration for a period of one hour, thirty minutes, five minutes . . ., a passage of Nature, of God, or a view of God" (Gilles Deleuze, *The Fold: Leibniz and the Baroque*, trans. Tom Conley (London: Athlone Press, 1993), 76).
46. This is not how Graham Harman reads Whitehead. See Harman's chapter "Whitehead and Schools X, Y and Z" in *The Lure of Whitehead*, ed. Nicholas Gaskill and A. J. Nocek (Minneapolis: University of Minnesota Press, 2014). Harman (231–2) claims we should distinguish between, on the one hand, Whitehead and Latour, and, on the other, "such figures as Henri Bergson, Manuel DeLanda, William James, Gilbert Simondon, and Isabelle Stengers." If we unite these two traditions, he argues, "we completely miss what ought to be a pivotal debate in present-day Continental philosophy. For whereas School X opposes the traditional philosophy of enduring substance with a relational but ultimately punctiform model of entities, School Y opposes substance in the name of an uncensored form of raw, pulsating, nonstop flux-and-flow action in which becoming is continuous and individual states or moments do not really exist."
47. Whitehead, *The Concept of Nature*, 10.
48. Ibid., 36.
49. Bergson, *Creative Evolution*, 46.
50. Whitehead, *The Concept of Nature*, 108.
51. The other two examples are "Yesterday a man was run over on the Chelsea Embankment" and "There are dark lines in the Solar Spectrum" (*The Concept of Nature*, 106). Debaise gives a lucid analysis of Whitehead's three examples (*Nature as Event*, 30–5).
52. Whitehead, *The Concept of Nature*, 106, 107.
53. Ibid., 108.
54. Ibid., 92.
55. Ibid., 93.
56. Stengers, *Thinking with Whitehead*, 81.
57. Ibid., 79, 81.

58. Ibid., 82, 76.
59. Stein, *Lectures in America*, 244.
60. Whitehead, *The Concept of Nature*, 93.
61. Ibid., 93.
62. David A. Grandy, *The Speed of Light: Constancy + Cosmos* (Bloomington: Indiana University Press, 2009), 81.
63. Kirsch, "How to Read *How to Write*," 110.
64. Stein, *How to Write*, 115.
65. Ibid., 110, 111.
66. Rachel Blau DuPlessis, "Woolfenstein, the Sequel," in *Primary Stein: Returning to the Writings of Gertrude Stein*, ed. Janet Boyd and Sharon J. Kirsch (Lanham, MD: Lexington Books, 2014), 40.
67. Kirsch, "How to Read *How to Write*," 121.
68. Stein, *How to Write*, 395.
69. Stein, "How Writing is Written," 157–8.
70. Only a few of Stein's texts have "saints" in the title, including "Saints in Seven," "Saints and Singing," *Four Saints in Three Acts* and "Talks to Saints or Stories of Saint Remy" – but the fact that she repeatedly uses those as examples in her lectures, from the 1926 "An Acquaintance with Description" to the *Lectures in America*, is proof of how important she considers them. Individual saints, furthermore, make an appearance in a number of her 1920s works.
71. Dydo, *The Language that Rises*, 199.
72. Gertrude Stein, *Four Saints in Three Acts*, in *Writings: 1903–1932*, ed. Harriet Scott Chessman and Catharine R. Stimpson (New York: Library of America, 1998), 624.
73. Ibid., 613.
74. Ibid., 615. Stein further complicates any historical references when, a couple of pages later, she writes "Scene five Saint Therese had a father photographically. Not a sister" (*Four Saints*, 626).
75. Emile Durkheim, *The Elementary Forms of Religious Life*, trans. Karen E. Fields (New York: The Free Press, 1995), 34.
76. Stein, *Everybody's Autobiography*, 109.
77. Ibid., 109; Stein, *Lectures in America*, 268.
78. Stein, *Four Saints*, 625.
79. Ibid., 612, 614, 620.
80. Lyn Hejinian, *The Language of Inquiry* (Berkeley: University of California Press, 2000), 115.
81. Gertrude Stein, "A Saint in Seven," in *A Primer for the Gradual Understanding of Gertrude Stein*, ed. Robert Bartlett Haas (Los Angeles: Black Sparrow Press, 1971), 76.
82. Pierre Klossowski, *The Revocation of the Edict of Nantes* (New York: Grove, 1969), 100.
83. Lynda Nead, *The Haunted Gallery: Painting, Photography, Film c. 1900* (New Haven, CT: Yale University Press, 2007), 72.

84. Scott Durham, *Phantom Communities: The Simulacrum and the Limits of Postmodernism* (Stanford, CA: Stanford University Press, 1998), 77.
85. Deleuze, *The Fold*, 76.
86. In "The New Whitehead? An Ontology of the Virtual in Whitehead's Metaphysics" Keith Robinson argues that Whitehead's "distinction between the actual and the potential . . . resembles the Deleuzian distinction between the actual and the virtual" (*Symposium* 10.1 (Spring 2006): 72).
87. Whitehead, *Process and Reality*, 23.
88. Ibid., 148.
89. Durham, *Phantom Communities*, 77.
90. Whitehead, *Process and Reality*, 149.
91. Stein, *Lectures in America*, 268.
92. Stein, *Four Saints*, 618–19.
93. Ibid., 608.
94. Ibid., 648.
95. The opera had a wonderful opening performance at the Hartford Atheneum on February 8, 1934, and ran successfully in New York as well as Chicago. Steven Watson's *Prepare for Saints: Gertrude Stein, Virgil Thomson and the Mainstreaming of American Modernism* (New York: Random House, 1998) gives an erudite account of the collaboration between Thomson and Stein.
96. Thomson quoted in Watson, *Prepare for Saints*, 41.
97. Jean-Jacques Nattiez, *Music and Discourse: Toward a Semiology of Music*, trans. Carolyn Abbate (Princeton: Princeton University Press, 1990), 128.
98. Stein, *Lectures in America*, 307.
99. On Stein and the pastoral, see the conclusion to Ann Marie Mikkelsen's *Pastoral, Pragmatism and Twentieth-Century American Poetry* (New York: Palgrave Macmillan, 2011).
100. Gertrude Stein, "Saints and Singing," in *A Stein Reader*, ed. Ulla E. Dydo (Evanston, IL: Northwestern University Press, 1993), 383, 387.
101. Matthew Wilson Smith, *The Total Work of Art: From Bayreuth to Cyberspace* (New York: Routledge, 2007), 8.
102. Watson, *Prepare for Saints*, 201.
103. When Carl Van Vechten pointed out that the opera had nothing to do with Black life, Thomson replied: "Think how many opera stars have blacked up to sing Amonasro and Aida. Why can't my colored singers white up for Four Saints?" (quoted in Watson, *Prepare for Saints*, 200).
104. Susan Holbrook and Thomas Dilworth, eds, *The Letters of Gertrude Stein and Virgil Thomson: Composition as Conversation* (Oxford: Oxford University Press, 2010), 197.
105. Whitehead, *Science and the Modern World*, 54.

106. Ibid., 194, 195, 196.
107. Gertrude Stein, *Lectures in America*, 265.
108. Whitehead's thinking on uncognitive knowing brings to mind James's notion of "knowledge of acquaintance." James distinguishes between "knowledge of acquaintance" and "knowledge-about." He writes: "Our earliest thoughts are almost exclusively sensational. They give us a set of *whats,* or *thats,* or *its*; of subjects of discourse in other words, with their relations not yet brought out" (James, *Psychology*, 22).
109. Whitehead, *Science and the Modern World*, 66, 69.
110. Stengers, *Thinking with Whitehead*, 155, 189.
111. Stein, *Lectures in America*, 260.
112. Stein, *Four Saints*, 611.
113. Ibid., 608.
114. Ibid., 608, 610, 612.
115. Ibid., 610.
116. Ibid., 616, 613, 635.
117. Deleuze, *The Fold*, 91.
118. Stein, *Four Saints*, 611.
119. Stein, *Lectures in America*, 310.
120. Whitehead, *Science and the Modern World*, 103.
121. "Thus though each event is necessary for the community of events, the weight of its contribution is determined by something intrinsic in itself. We have now to discuss what that property is. Empirical observation shows that it is the property which we may call indifferently retention, endurance or reiteration. This property amounts to the recovery, on behalf of value amid the transitoriness of reality, of the self-identity which is also enjoyed by the primary eternal objects" (Whitehead, *Science and the Modern World*, 104).
122. Ibid., 104.
123. Steven Meyer reads the book's beautiful conclusion in the light of the death-in-combat of Whitehead's son Eric, to which the book is dedicated: "At the conclusion of *An Enquiry Concerning the Principles of Natural Knowledge* Whitehead returned to literature in order to articulate his sense of the rhythmic foundation of life, and for solace. [. . .] In [the three concluding paragraphs] Whitehead expresses a keen sense that the music of his son's life needs to perish with the 'relapse' of the élan vital into matter" (*Irresistible Dictation*, 205).
124. Alfred North Whitehead, *An Enquiry Concerning the Principles of Natural Knowledge* (Cambridge: Cambridge University Press, 1919), 196, 197, 198.
125. "An event considered as gaining its unity from the continuity of extension and its unique novelty from the inherent character of 'passage,' contributes one factor to life, and the pattern exhibited within the event, which as self-identical should be a rigid recurrence, contributes the other factor to life" (Whitehead, *An Enquiry*, 198).

126. Stein, *Lectures in America*, 311.
127. Edgar Allan Poe, "The Poetic Principle," in *The Works of Edgar Allan Poe*, The Raven Edition, vol. 5. Available at: <https://www.gutenberg.org/files/2151/2151-h/2151-h.htm#chap5.11> (last accessed September 3, 2021).
128. Gertrude Stein, "Bernard Faÿ," *Portraits and Prayers* (New York: Random House, 1934), 42.
129. Stein, "Bernard Faÿ," 41.
130. Ibid., 42.
131. Ibid., and Stein, *Lectures in America*, 311.
132. Stein, "Bernard Faÿ," 45.
133. Stein, *Lectures in America*, 311.
134. Ibid., 312.
135. On the history of "Before the Flowers of Friendship Faded Friendship Faded," see Dydo, *The Language That Rises*, 301–23.
136. Stein, *Lectures in America*, 312.

Now That Is All

I wrote this book because I wanted to know how to make sense of the many references to life and liveliness in Stein's texts. What I hope to have mapped is a dynamic modernist understanding of life. Life, for Stein and other late nineteenth- and early twentieth-century writer–thinkers, amounts to a differential force that counters tradition with novelty, stasis with movement. Life, I have wanted to show, is at the heart of the modernist project to make new how we write, how we think about ourselves in relation to others, how we experience time and how we relate to our surroundings.

Stein famously invites us to see life as a "thing," which incessantly moves and changes. Framing life as a "thing" is a vintage Stein move. It is both a funny quip – life is too vast a concept to be a thing – and a sincere vantage – it really works to read Stein through the lens of "this thing life." Seeing life as a thing, as I have shown in the first two chapters, brings life down to earth, to endless biological diversity and to the flux of historical experience. Where the question of how a scientific perspective of life relates to the actual experience of life may sound like an issue moored in romanticism, Stein's working through it gives it a distinct modernist slant. She does not lament the perceived loss of a spontaneous or intuitive life, triggered by scientific and technological developments, but sets up a hermeneutic experiment, trying to understand the life of all Americans. In doing so, she comes up with an impossible literary form, a vast typological description of all Americans, out of which emerges a long series of portraits. Stein's attempt "to make portraits of this thing [life]," in the 1910s, is where her work meets the cinema. In Chapters 3 to 5 I have traced the ways in which Stein's texts intersect with the discourse on early modernist film and theories about the nature of time and memory. The magic of film was that, for the first time, it was possible to preserve movement, to store it like a thing. For some, this meant that death could be outwitted – and I confess to feeling shocked and moved when I first saw Stein in real life, in a home movie clip from 1927.[1] Stein's texts relate to early twentieth-century film, not because she was particularly interested in the medium, but because, in her own way, she was thinking through the new relations between experience, memory and tradition that the cinema made possible. Life as thing, finally, also connects the abstract and the concrete. That, I argue in Chapter 6, is where Stein's texts intersect with the work of Alfred North Whitehead, for whom the bifurcation of nature, or the practice of taking nature apart in concrete or abstract, or matter and experience, equaled a modern disaster. In dialogue with Whitehead's work, Stein works against bifurcations and weaves together anecdote and language play, movement and stasis, detail and theory. When, with her opera *Four Saints in Three Acts*, she rethinks the *Gesamtkunstwerk*, she puts into practice Whitehead's insight that life, first and foremost, implies a working against tradition.

Although much of Stein's writing is firmly rooted in her daily living – as we have seen she always "of course include[s]" herself – I have not discussed Stein's experiments with autobiography, of which the most famous is *The Autobiography of Alice B. Toklas*, which she wrote in 1932 and which brought her unexpected fame.[2] While it may seem odd that a book about a writer's interest in life leaves out the writer's actual life writing, the life that I have wanted to spotlight is an impersonal life. What that implies is beautifully summed up by Gilles Deleuze, in "Immanence: A Life." Deleuze turns to a scene in Charles Dickens's *Our Mutual Friend* to make us see what he means by "a singular life":

> No one has described what *a* life is better than Charles Dickens if we take the indefinite article as an index of the transcendental. A disreputable man, a rogue, held in contempt by everyone, is found as he lies dying. Suddenly, those taking care of him manifest an eagerness, respect, even love, for his slightest sign of life. Everybody bustles about to save him, to the point where, in his deepest coma, this wicked man himself senses something soft and sweet penetrating him. But to the degree that he comes back to life, his saviors turn colder, and he becomes once again mean and crude. Between his life and his death there is a moment that is only that of *a* life playing with death.

This scene seems far removed from any of Stein's texts that I have discussed, but Deleuze is quick to modify the exemplary quality of the Dickensian encounter between individual life and universal death. "*A* life," he continues, "is everywhere, in all the moments that a given living subject goes through and that are measured by given lived objects."[3] Such moments and objects, which have an independence from the subjects that think they are theirs, are central to the texts that I have discussed, from the different modes of doing things in *The Making of Americans*, over Orta's dancing and the objects, food and rooms in *Tender Buttons*, to the landscape in Stein's 1920s texts.

To a certain extent, Stein's interest in life changes in the 1930s. This change, I am well aware, does not amount to a break in her oeuvre. After all, for my story about Stein's interest in life in her early texts, I have drawn heavily on her mid-1930s lectures. As it speaks from the titles of the texts she wrote in the 1930s, furthermore, the concept certainly continued to hold appeal. In the first half of the decade she wrote not only *The Autobiography of Alice B. Toklas*, but also "Marguerite A Novel Of High Life," "A Little Love Of Life" and "The Superstitions Of Fred Anneday, Annday, Anday A Novel Of Real Life." Even if, apart from the narrative *The Autobiography of Alice B. Toklas*, the style of these texts is not markedly different from that of *Four Saints in Three Acts*, they do signal a new perspective in that Stein establishes a connection between life and literary genre. Building on her experiment with the format of the opera, she becomes interested in the question of how to rethink the ways in which the autobiography, the novel and the love poem have framed life. In addition, the success of *The Autobiography of Alice B. Toklas* sharpens an interest in the relationship between writer and audience, which Stein had started thinking about when she was working on "Composition as Explanation" in 1926. In a sense, Stein returns to two problems that were important to her when she first started writing: how to write history and how to think of yourself in relation to others. This return was more than likely triggered by the publication of *The Making of Americans* in 1925 and her writing of *A Novel of Thank You* to mark the occasion. Differently than in the 1900s, she no longer refuses storytelling. While I would love to really think through those connections, it is a different project. For now, I have said all I can about Stein and this thing life.

Notes

1. See "Gertrude Stein home movie, circa 1927," Beinecke, <https://www.youtube.com/watch?v=wX4NMuJGOsY> (last accessed September 28, 2021).
2. Stein, *Lectures in America*, 290.
3. Gilles Deleuze, "Immanence: A Life," in *Pure Immanence: Essays on A Life*, trans. A. Boyman (New York: Zone Books), 28–9.

Bibliography

Adams, Henry. *The Education of Henry Adams*. Boston and New York: Houghton Mifflin Company, 1918. Available at: <https://openlibrary.org/books/OL13446110M/The_education_of_Henry_Adams> (last accessed September 3, 2021).

Albéra, François and Maria Tortajada, eds. *Cinema Beyond Film: Media Epistemology in the Modern Era*. Amsterdam: Amsterdam University Press, 2010.

Altieri, Charles. "Reading Bradley after Reading Laforgue: How Eliot Transformed Symbolist Poetics into a Paradigmatic Modernism." *Modern Language Quarterly* 72.2 (2011): 225–52.

Aristotle. *Metaphysics*. Translated by W. D. Ross. In *The Complete Works of Aristotle*, edited by Jonathan Barnes, vol. 2. Princeton, NJ: Princeton University Press, 1984.

Aristotle. *Nicomachean Ethics*. Translated by W. D. Ross. In *The Complete Works of Aristotle*, edited by Jonathan Barnes, vol. 2. Princeton, NJ: Princeton University Press, 1984.

Aristotle. *Poetics*. Translated by I. Bywater. In *The Complete Works of Aristotle*, edited by Jonathan Barnes, vol. 2. Princeton, NJ: Princeton University Press, 1984.

Ashbery, John. "The Impossible." In *Critical Essays on Gertrude Stein*, edited by M. J. Hoffman, 104–7. Boston: G. K. Hall, 1986.

Ashbery, John. *Selected Prose*, edited by Eugene Richie. Ann Arbor: University of Michigan Press, 2004.

Ashton, Jennifer. Introduction to Gertrude Stein, *Matisse Picasso and Gertrude Stein with Two Shorter Stories*, 1–7. Mineola, NY: Dover Publications, 2000.

Ayers, David, Benedikt Hjartarson, Tomi Huttunen and Harri Veivo, eds. *Utopia: The Avant-Garde, Modernism and (Im)possible Life*. Berlin: Walter de Gruyter, 2015.

Bambach, Charles. *Heidegger, Dilthey and the Crisis of Historicism*. Ithaca, NY: Cornell University Press, 1995.

Bay-Cheng, Sarah. *Mama Dada: Gertrude Stein's Avant-Garde Theater*. New York: Routledge, 2005.

Beer, Gillian. *Darwin's Plots: Evolutionary Narrative in Darwin, George Eliot and Nineteenth-Century Fiction*. Cambridge: Cambridge University Press, 2000.
Benjamin, Walter. "Little History of Photography." In *Selected Writings: 1913–1934*, vol. 2, part 2, edited by Howard Eiland, Michael W. Jennings and Gary Smith, 507–30. Cambridge, MA: Belknap Press of Harvard University Press, 2005.
Benjamin, Walter. "On Some Motifs in Baudelaire." In *Selected Writings: 1938–1940*, vol. 4, edited by Howard Eiland and Michael W. Jennings, 313–55. Cambridge, MA: Belknap Press of Harvard University Press, 2006.
Benjamin, Walter. "The Storyteller: Observations on the Works of Nikolai Leskov." In *Selected Writings: 1935–1938*, vol. 3, edited by Howard Eiland and Michael W. Jennings, 143–66. Cambridge: Belknap Press of Harvard University Press, 2002.
Benjamin, Walter. "On the Concept of History." In *Selected Writings: 1938–1940*, vol. 4, edited by Howard Eiland and Michael W. Jennings, 389–400. Cambridge, MA: Belknap Press of Harvard University Press, 2006.
Benjamin, Walter. "The Work of Art in the Age of Its Technological Reproducibility, Second Version." In *Selected Writings: 1935–1938*, vol. 3, edited by Howard Eiland and Michael W. Jennings, 101–33. Cambridge, MA: Belknap Press of Harvard University Press, 2002.
Benjamin, Walter and Theodor Adorno. *The Complete Correspondence 1928–1940*, edited by Henri Lonitz and translated by Nicholas Walker. Cambridge, MA: Harvard University Press, 1999.
Bennett, Jane. *Vibrant Matter: A Political Ecology of Things*. Durham, NC: Duke University Press, 2010.
Bergson, Henri. *Creative Evolution*. Translated by Arthur Mitchell. Mineola, NY: Dover Publications, 1998.
Bergson, Henri. *The Creative Mind: An Introduction to Metaphysics*. Translated by Mabelle L. Andison. New York: Citadel, 1992.
Bergson, Henri. *Matter and Memory*. Translated by N. M. Paul and W. S. Palmer. New York and London: Zone Books and MIT Press, 1988.
Bergson, Henri. *The Two Sources of Morality and Religion*. Translated by R. Ashley Audra and Cloudesley Brereton, with the assistance of W. Horsfall Carter. Garden City: Doubleday & Anchor, 1954 [1935].
Berman, Jessica. *Modernist Fiction, Cosmopolitanism, and the Politics of Community*. Cambridge: Cambridge University Press, 2001.
Bernstein, Charles. *A Poetics*. Cambridge, MA: Harvard University Press, 1992.
Blencowe, Claire. "Destroying Duration: The Critical Situation of Bergsonism in Benjamin's Analysis of Modern Experience." *Theory, Culture & Society* 25.4 (2008): 139–58.
Boring, Edwin G. *A History of Experimental Psychology*. New York and London: D. Appleton Century Company, 1929.

Bowers, Jane Palatini. "The Composition that All the World Can See." In *Land/Scape/Theater*, edited by Elinor Fuchs and Una Chaudhuri, 121–44. Ann Arbor: University of Michigan Press, 2002.

Brannigan, Erin. *Dancefilm: Choreography and the Moving Image*. New York and Oxford: Oxford University Press, 2011.

Bridgman, Richard. *Gertrude Stein in Pieces*. New York: Oxford University Press, 1970.

Bristow, Jennie. *The Sociology of Generations: New Directions and Challenges*. London: Palgrave MacMillan, 2016.

Bulhof, Ilse. *Wilhelm Dilthey: A Hermeneutic Approach to the Study of History and Culture*. The Hague: Martinus Nijhoff, 1980.

Burckhardt, Jakob. *Weltgeschichtliche Betrachtungen*, ed. R. Marx. Stuttgart: Kröner, 1955.

Bürger, Peter. *Theory of the Avant-Garde*. Translated by Michael Shaw. Minneapolis: University of Minnesota Press, 1984.

Burns, Edward, ed. *The Letters of Gertrude Stein and Carl Van Vechten*. 2 vols. New York: Columbia University Press, 1986.

Burwick, Frederick and Paul Douglass, eds. *The Crisis in Modernism: Bergson and the Vitalist Controversy*. Cambridge: Cambridge University Press, 1992.

Bush, Clive. *Halfway to Revolution: Investigation and Crisis in the Work of Henry Adams, William James and Gertrude Stein*. New Haven, CT: Yale University Press, 1991.

Campbell, Scott M. and Paul W. Bruno, *The Science, Politics, and Ontology of Life-Philosophy*. London and New York: Bloomsbury, 2013.

Carson, Luke. *Consumption and Depression in Gertrude Stein, Louis Zukofsky and Ezra Pound*. Basingstoke: Macmillan, 1999.

Cecire, Natalia. "Ways of Not Reading Gertrude Stein." *ELH* 82.1 (2015): 281–312.

Chessman, Harriet Scott. *The Public is Invited to Dance: Representation, The Body and Dialogue in Gertrude Stein*. Stanford, CA: Stanford University Press, 1989.

Chow, Juliana. "Motion Studies: Vitalism in Gertrude Stein's Work." *Arizona Quarterly: A Journal of American Literature, Culture and Theory* 69.4 (2013): 77–109.

Clement, Tanya E. "'A thing not beginning and not ending': using digital tools to distant-read Gertrude Stein's *The Making of Americans*." *Literary and Linguistic Computing* 23.3 (2008): 361–81.

Colebrook, Claire. *Deleuze and the Meaning of Life*. London: Continuum, 2010.

Costello, Diarmuid. "Aura, Face, Photography: Re-Reading Benjamin Today." In *Walter Benjamin and Art*, edited by Andrew Benjamin, 164–84. London and New York: Continuum, 2005.

Crary, Jonathan. *Suspensions of Perception: Attention, Spectacle and Modern Culture*. Cambridge, MA: MIT Press, 2001.

Curnutt, Kirk. "Inside and Outside: Gertrude Stein on Identity, Celebrity, and Authenticity." *Journal of Modern Literature* 23.2 (1999): 291–308.
Daly, Ann. *Done into Dance: Isadora Duncan in America*. Middletown, CT: Wesleyan University Press, 1995.
Darwin, Charles. *The Descent of Man and Selection in Relation to Sex*. New York: D. Appleton and Company, 1872. Available at: <https://openlibrary.org/books/OL6586780M/The_descent_of_man_and_selection_in_relation_to_sex> (last accessed September 3, 2021).
Darwin, Charles. *The Origin of Species by Means of Natural Selection; or, The Preservation of Favored Races in the Struggle for Life*. New York: Hurst, 1872. Available at: <https://openlibrary.org/books/OL7230649M/The_Origin_of_Species_by_Means_of_Natural_Selection> (last accessed September 3, 2021).
Davis, Phoebe Stein. "'Even Cake Gets to Have Another Meaning': History, Narrative, and 'Daily Living' in Gertrude Stein's World War II Writings." *MFS: Modern Fiction Studies* 44.3 (1998): 568–607.
Debaise, Didier. *Nature as Event: The Lure of the Possible*. Translated by Michael Halewood. Durham, NC: Duke University Press, 2017.
DeKoven, Marianne. "Gertrude Stein's Landscape Writing." *Women's Studies: An Interdisciplinary Journal* 9.3 (1982): 221–39.
Deleuze, Gilles. "Bergson's Conception of Difference." In *Desert Islands and Other Texts, 1953–1974*, edited by David Lapoujade and translated by Michael Taormina, 32–51. Los Angeles: Semiotext(e), 2004.
Deleuze, Gilles. *Cinema 1: The Movement Image*. Translated by Hugh Tomlinson and Barbara Habberjam. London: Continuum, 2005.
Deleuze, Gilles. *The Fold: Leibniz and the Baroque*. Translated by Tom Conley. London: Athlone Press, 1993.
Deleuze, Gilles. "Immanence: A Life." In *Pure Immanence: Essays on A Life*. Translated by A. Boyman, 25–33. New York: Zone Books.
Deleuze, Gilles and Félix Guattari. *What Is Philosophy?* Translated by Hugh Tomlinson and Graham Burchell. New York: Columbia University Press, 1994.
De Mul, Jos. *The Tragedy of Finitude: Dilthey's Hermeneutics of Life*. Translated by Tony Burrett. New Haven, CT: Yale University Press, 2014.
Dewey, John. *The Influence of Darwin on Philosophy and Other Essays in Contemporary Thought*. New York: Henry Holt and Company, 1910. Available at: <https://archive.org/details/cu31924012730820> (last accessed September 3, 2021).
Diepeveen, Leonard. *Modernist Fraud: Hoax, Parody, Deception*. Oxford: Oxford University Press, 2019.
Dilthey, Wilhelm. *Contributions to the Study of Individuality*. Translated by Erdmann Waniek. In *Understanding the Human World*, edited by Rudolf A. Makkreel and Frithjof Rodi, 211–84. Vol. 2 of *Selected Works*. Princeton, NJ: Princeton University Press, 2010.

Dilthey, Wilhelm. *Die Geistige Welt: Einleitung in die Philosophie Lebens. Erste Hälfte: Abhandlungen zur Grundlegung der Geisteswissenschaften*. Gesammelte Schriften 5, edited by G. Mische. 2nd edn. Stuttgart: B. G. Teubner / Göttingen: Vandenhoeck & Ruprecht, 1957.

Dilthey, Wilhelm. *Die Geistige Welt: Einleitung in die Philosophie Lebens. Zweite Hälfte: Abhandlungen zur Poetik, Ethik und Pädagogik*. Gesammelte Schriften 6. Edited by G. Mische. 3rd edn. Stuttgart: B. G. Teubner / Göttingen: Vandenhoeck & Ruprecht, 1958.

Dilthey, Wilhelm. *Drafts for a Critique of Historical Reason*. Translated by Rudolf A. Makkreel and William H. Oman. In *The Formation of the Historical World in the Human Sciences*, edited by Rudolf A. Makkreel and Frithjof Rodi, 213–314. Vol. 3 of *Selected Works*. Princeton, NJ: Princeton University Press, 2002.

Dilthey, Wilhelm. *Ideas for a Descriptive and Analytic Psychology*. Translated by Rudolf A. Makkreel and Donald Moore. In *Understanding the Human World*, edited by Rudolf A. Makkreel and Frithjof Rodi, 115–210. Vol. 2 of *Selected Works*. Princeton, NJ: Princeton University Press, 2010.

Dilthey, Wilhelm. "The Rise of Hermeneutics." Translated by Fredric R. Jameson and Rudolf A. Makkreel. In *Hermeneutics and the Study of History*, edited by Rudolf A. Makkreel and Frithjof Rodi, 235–58. Vol. 4 of *Selected Works*. Princeton, NJ: Princeton University Press, 1996.

Doane, Mary Ann. *The Emergence of Cinematic Time: Modernity, Contingency, the Archive*. Cambridge, MA: Harvard University Press, 2002.

Doyle, Laura. "The Flat, the Round, and Gertrude Stein: Race and the Shape of Modern(ist) History." *Modernism/modernity* 7.2 (2000): 249–71.

Driesch, Hans. *The History and Theory of Vitalism*. Translated by C. K. Ogden. London: Macmillan, 1914.

Driesch, Hans. *The Science and the Philosophy of the Organism: The Gifford Lectures 1907*, vol. 1. London: Adam and Charles Black, 1908. Available at: <https://openlibrary.org/books/OL23410462M/The_science_and_philosophy_of_the_organism> (last accessed September 3, 2021).

Duffy, Enda. *The Speed Handbook*. Durham, NC, and London: Duke University Press, 2009.

DuPlessis, Rachel Blau. "Woolfenstein, the Sequel." In *Primary Stein: Returning to the Writings of Gertrude Stein*, edited by Janet Boyd and Sharon J. Kirsch, 37–56. Lanham, MD: Lexington Books, 2014.

Durham, Scott. *Phantom Communities: The Simulacrum and the Limits of Postmodernism*. Stanford, CA: Stanford University Press, 1998.

Durkheim, Emile. *The Elementary Forms of Religious Life*. Translated by Karen E. Fields. New York: The Free Press, 1995.

Duttlinger, Carolin. "Between Contemplation and Distraction: Configurations of Attention in Walter Benjamin." *German Studies Review* 30.1 (2007): 33–54.

Dworkin, Craig. *Reading the Illegible*. Evanston, IL: Northwestern University Press, 2003.

Dydo, Ulla, ed. *A Stein Reader*. Evanston, IL: Northwestern University Press, 1993.

Dydo, Ulla with William Rice. *Gertrude Stein: The Language that Rises, 1923–1934*. Evanston, IL: Northwestern University Press, 2003.

Elder, R. Bruce. *Harmony + Dissent: Film and Avant-Garde Art Movements in the Early Twentieth Century*. Waterloo, Ontario: Wilfrid Laurier University Press, 2010.

Emerson, Ralph Waldo. "History." In *Essays and Lectures*, edited by Joel Porte, 235–56. New York: Library of America, 1983.

Epstein, Jean. "On Certain Characteristics of *Photogénie*." In *French Film Theory and Criticism: A History/Anthology*, vol. 1: 1907–1929, edited by Richard Abel, 314–18. Princeton, NJ: Princeton University Press, 1988.

Ermarth, Michael. *Wilhelm Dilthey: The Critique of Historical Reason*. Chicago: University of Chicago Press, 1978.

Felski, Rita. *Doing Time: Feminist Theory and Postmodern Culture*. New York: New York University Press, 2000.

Felski, Rita. *The Gender of Modernity*. Cambridge, MA: Harvard University Press, 1995.

Felski, Rita. "Introduction," special issue, "Everyday Life," *New Literary History* 33.4 (2002): 607–22.

Foster, Hal. *The Return of the Real: The Avant-Garde at the End of the Century*. Cambridge, MA: MIT Press, 1996.

Foucault, Michel. *The Order of Things: An Archaeology of the Human Sciences*. London: Routledge, 2002.

Franken, Claudia. *Gertrude Stein, Writer, Thinker*. Münster: LIT, 2000.

Fraser, Mariam, Sarah Kember and Celia Lury, eds. *Inventive Life: Approaches to the New Vitalism*. London: Sage, in association with *Theory, Culture & Society*, 2006.

Frost, Elisabeth. *The Feminist Avant-Garde in American Poetry*. Iowa City: University of Iowa Press, 2003.

Garelick, Rhonda K. *Electric Salome: Loie Fuller's Performance of Modernism*. Princeton, NJ, and Oxford: Princeton University Press, 2007.

Gasché, Rodolphe. "The Deepening of Apperception: On Walter Benjamin's Theory of Film." *Mosaic* 41.4 (2008): 27–38.

Gaskill, Nicholas and A. J. Nocek. "An Adventure of Thought." Introduction to *The Lure of Whitehead*, edited by Nicholas Gaskill and A. J. Nocek, 1–40. Minneapolis: University of Minnesota Press, 2014.

Georges-Michel, Michel. "Henri Bergson Talks to Us About Cinema." Translated by Louis-Georges Schwartz. *Cinema Journal* 50.3 (2011): 79–82.

Gigante, Denise. *Life: Organic Form and Romanticism*. New Haven, CT: Yale University Press, 2009.

Gillies, Mary Ann. *Henri Bergson and British Modernism*. Montreal: McGill University Press, 1996.

Gleber, Anke. *The Art of Taking a Walk: Flanerie, Literature and Film in Weimar Culture*. Princeton, NJ: Princeton University Press, 1999.

Goble, Mark. *Beautiful Circuits: Modernism and the Mediated Life*. New York: Columbia University Press, 2010.
Goldstein, Amanda Jo. *Sweet Science: Romantic Materialism and the New Logics of Life*. Chicago: University of Chicago Press, 2017.
Gontarski, S. E., Paul Ardoin, Laci Mattison, eds. *Understanding Bergson, Understanding Modernism*. London: Bloomsbury, 2013.
Grandy, David A. *The Speed of Light: Constancy + Cosmos*. Bloomington: Indiana University Press, 2009.
Griffiths, Alison. *Shivers Down Your Spine: Cinema, Museums and the Immersive View*. New York: Columbia University Press, 2008.
Grosz, Elizabeth. *Becoming Undone: Darwinian Reflections on Life, Politics and Art*. Durham, NC: Duke University Press, 2011.
Grosz, Elizabeth. *The Nick of Time: Politics, Evolution and the Untimely*. Crows Nest: Allen and Unwin, 2004.
Gunning, Tom. "The Art of Succession: Reading, Writing, and Watching Comics." *Critical Inquiry* 40.3 (2014): 36–51.
Gunning, Tom. "Attractions: How They Came into the World." In *The Cinema of Attractions Reloaded*, edited by Wanda Strauven, 31–40. Amsterdam: Amsterdam University Press, 2006.
Gunning, Tom. "The Birth of Film Out of the Spirit of Modernity." In *Masterpieces of Modernist Cinema*, edited by Ted Perry, 13–40. Bloomington and Indianapolis: Indiana University Press, 2006.
Gunning, Tom. "The Cinema of Attraction: Early Film, Its Spectator and the Avant-Garde." In *Early Cinema: Space Frame Narrative*, edited by Thomas Elsaesser, 56–62. London: BFI, 1990.
Gunning, Tom. "Light, Motion, Cinema!: The Heritage of Loïe Fuller and Germaine Dulac." *Framework* 46.1 (2005): 106–29.
Guthrie, James R. *Above Time: Emerson's and Thoreau's Temporal Revolutions*. Columbia: University of Missouri Press, 2001.
Gutkowski, Emanuela. "Gertrude Stein and Jules Laforgue: A Comparative Approach." *European Journal of American Culture* 22.1 (2003): 125–38.
Hansen, Miriam Bratu. *Cinema and Experience: Siegfried Kracauer, Walter Benjamin and Theodor Adorno*. Berkeley and Los Angeles: University of California Press, 2002.
Hardt, Michael and Antonio Negri. *Empire*. Cambridge, MA: Harvard University Press, 2000.
Harman, Graham. "Whitehead and Schools X, Y and Z." In *The Lure of Whitehead*, edited by Nicholas Gaskill and A. J. Nocek. Minneapolis: University of Minnesota Press, 2014.
Harrington, Austin. "Dilthey, Empathy and Verstehen: A Contemporary Reappraisal." *European Journal of Social Theory* 4.3 (August 2001): 311–29. Available at <https://doi.org/10.1177/13684310122225145> (last accessed September 27, 2021).
Haselstein, Ulla. *Gertrude Steins Literarische Porträts*. Konstanz: Konstanz University Press, 2019.

Haselstein, Ulla. "Gertrude Stein's Portraits of Matisse and Picasso." *New Literary History: A Journal of Theory and Interpretation* 34.4 (2003): 723–43.

Haselstein, Ulla. "*Tender Buttons:* Stein et ses portraits des choses." In *Carrefour Stieglitz*, edited by Jay Bochner and Jean-Pierre Montier, 339–48. Rennes: Presses Universitaires de Rennes, 2012.

Hejinian, Lyn. *The Language of Inquiry*. Berkeley: University of California Press, 2000.

Helm, Bertrand. *Time and Reality in American Philosophy*. Amherst: University of Massachusetts Press, 1985.

Hemingway, Ernest. *A Moveable Feast*. Harmondsworth: Penguin, 1966. Available at: <https://openlibrary.org/books/OL24214522M/A_Moveable_feast> (last accessed September 3, 2021).

Highmore, Ben. "Awkward Moments: Avant-Gardism and the Dialectics of Everyday Life." In *European Avant-Garde: New Perspectives*, edited by Dietrich Scheunemann, 245–64. Amsterdam: Rodopi, 2000.

Highmore, Ben. *Everyday Life and Cultural Theory: An Introduction*. London: Routledge, 2002.

Highmore, Ben. *The Everyday Life Reader*. London: Routledge, 2002.

Highmore, Ben. *Ordinary Lives: Studies in the Everyday*. London: Routledge, 2011.

Hitchcock, F. H. "Letter to Gertrude Stein, 9 April 1909." In *The Flowers of Friendship: Letters Written to Gertrude Stein*, edited by Donald Gallup, 43. New York: Knopf, 1953.

Hoffman, Michael J. *Critical Essays on Gertrude Stein*. Boston: G. K. Hall, 1986.

Holbrook, Susan and Thomas Dilworth, eds. *The Letters of Gertrude Stein and Virgil Thomson: Composition as Conversation*. Oxford: Oxford University Press, 2010.

Holmberg, Jan. "Ideals of Immersion in Early Cinema." *Cinémas: revue d'études cinématographiques / Cinemas: Journal of Film Studies* 14.1 (2003): 129–47.

Horkheimer, Max. "On Bergson's Metaphysics of Time." Translated by Peter Thomas and Stuart Martin. *Radical Philosophy* 131 (2005 [1934]): 9–19.

Iggers, Georg G. "The Intellectual Foundations of Nineteenth-Century 'Scientific' History: The German Model." In *The Oxford History of Historical Writing*, vol. 4: *1800–1945*, edited by Stuart Macintyre, Juan Maiguashca and Attila Pók, 41–58. Oxford: Oxford University Press, 2011.

Jaeger, Hans. "Generations in History: Reflections on a Controversial Concept." *History and Theory* 23.3 (1985): 273–92.

James, Henry. "The Art of Fiction." In *Literary Criticism*, edited by Leon Edel, vol. 1. New York: Library of America, 1984.

James, William. "Does 'Consciousness' Exist?" In *Writings: 1902–1910*, edited by Bruce Kuklick, 1141–58. New York: Library of America, 1987.

James, William. *A Pluralistic Universe and Other Essays in Popular Philosophy*. In *Writings: 1902–1910*, edited by Bruce Kuklick, 625–820. New York: Library of America, 1987.
James, William. *Psychology: Briefer Course*. In *Writings: 1878–1899*, edited by Gerald E. Myers, 1–444. New York: Library of America, 1992.
James, William. "The Thing and Its Relations." In *Writings: 1902–1910*, edited by Bruce Kuklick, 782–96. New York: Library of America, 1987.
James, William. *The Will to Believe and Other Essays in Popular Philosophy*. In *Writings: 1878–1899*, edited by Gerald E. Myers, 445–704. New York: Library of America, 1992.
James, William. "A World of Pure Experience." In *Writings: 1902–1910*, edited by Bruce Kuklick, 1159–82. New York: Library of America, 1987.
Jameson, Fredric. Translator's note to "The Rise of Hermeneutics," by Wilhelm Dilthey. Translated by Fredric Jameson. *New Literary History* 3.2 (1972): 229–44.
Jay, Martin. *Songs of Experience: Modern American and European Variations on a Universal Theme*. Berkeley: University of California Press, 2005.
Johnson, Curtis. *Darwin's Dice: The Idea of Change in the Thought of Charles Darwin*. Oxford: Oxford University Press, 2015.
Jones, Donna V. *The Racial Discourses of Life Philosophy: Négritude, Vitalism and Modernity*. New York: Columbia University Press, 2010.
Kahan, Benjamin. *Celibacies: American Modernism & Sexual Life*. Durham, NC: Duke University Press, 2013.
Kelley, Donald R. *Fortunes of History: Historical Inquiry from Herder to Huizinga*. New Haven, CT: Yale University Press, 2003.
Kern, Stephen. *The Culture of Time and Space 1880–1918*. Cambridge, MA: Harvard University Press, 1983.
King, Rob. "Laughter in an Ungoverned Sphere: Actuality Humor in Early Cinema and Web 2.0." In *New Silent Film*, edited by Paul Flaig and Katherine Groo, 294–314. New York: Routledge, 2016.
Kirsch, Sharon J. "How to Read *How to Write*." In *Primary Stein: Returning to the Writing of Gertrude Stein*, edited by Janet Boyd and Sharon J. Kirsch, 109–24. Lanham, MD: Lexington Books, 2014.
Kloppenberg, James. *Uncertain Victory: Social Democracy and Progressivism in European and American Thought, 1870–1920*. Oxford: Oxford University Press, 1986.
Klossowski, Pierre. *The Revocation of the Edict of Nantes*. New York: Grove, 1969.
Kolocotroni, Vassiliki, Jane Goldman and Olga Taxidou, eds. *Modernism: An Anthology of Sources and Documents*. Edinburgh: Edinburgh University Press, 1998.
Kracauer, Siegfried. *Theory of Film: The Redemption of Physical Reality*. Princeton, NJ: Princeton University Press, 1997.
Kracauer, Siegfried and Paul Oskar Kristeller. *History: The Last Things before the Last*. Princeton, NJ: Marcus Wiener, 1995.

Krieger, Murray. *Ekphrasis: The Illusion of the Natural Sign*. Baltimore and London: Johns Hopkins University Press, 1992.

Lang, Abigail. "Stein and Cinematic Identity." In *Gertrude Stein in Europe: Reconfigurations Across Media, Disciplines, and Traditions*, edited by Sarah Posman and Laura Luise Schultz, 145–64. London: Bloomsbury, 2015.

Langbauer, Laurie. "Cultural Studies and the Politics of the Everyday." *Diacritics* 22.1 (1992): 47–65.

Lash, Scott. "Life (Vitalism)." *Theory Culture & Society* 23 (2006): 323–9.

Latour, Bruno. "An Attempt at a 'Compositionist Manifesto.'" *New Literary History* 41.3 (2010): 471–90.

Latour, Bruno. *We Have Never Been Modern*. Translated by Catherine Porter. Cambridge, MA: Harvard University Press, 1993.

Latour, Bruno. "What Is Given in Experience?," Foreword to Isabelle Stengers, *Thinking with Whitehead: A Free and Wild Creation of Concepts*. Cambridge, MA: Harvard University Press, 2011.

Leick, Karen. *Gertrude Stein and the Making of an American Celebrity*. New York: Routledge, 2009.

Lessing, Gotthold Ephraim. *Laocoon: An Essay upon the Limits of Painting and Poetry*. Translated by Ellen Frothingham. New York: Dover, 2005.

Lewis, Wyndham. *Time and Western Man*, edited by Paul Edwards. Santa Rosa, CA: Black Sparrow Press, 1993.

Lindsay, Vachel. *The Art of the Moving Picture*. New York: Random House, 2000 [1915].

Lorange, Astrid. *How Reading is Written: A Brief Index to Gertrude Stein*. Middletown, CT: Wesleyan University Press, 2014.

Lyon, Janet. *Manifestoes: Provocations of the Modern*. Ithaca, NY: Cornell University Press, 1999.

McCabe, Susan. *Cinematic Modernism: Modernist Poetry and Film*. Cambridge: Cambridge University Press, 2005.

Macpherson, Kenneth. Letter, June 24, 1927. *The Flowers of Friendship: Letters Written to Gertrude Stein*, edited by Donald Gallup. New York: Alfred A. Knopf, 1953.

Mannheim, Karl. "The Problem of Generations." In *Essays on the Sociology of Knowledge,* edited by Paul Kecskemeti, 276–320. London: Routledge, 2007 [1952].

Marcus, Laura. *The Tenth Muse: Writing about Cinema in the Modernist Period*. Oxford: Oxford University Press, 2007.

Marey, Etienne-Jules. *Du mouvement dans les fonctions de la vie*. Paris: Germer Baillière, 1868.

Mellow, James R. *Charmed Circle: Gertrude Stein & Company*. New York: Praeger, 1974.

Meyer, Steven. *Irresistible Dictation: Gertrude Stein and the Correlations of Writing and Science*. Stanford, CA: Stanford University Press, 2001.

Mikkelsen, Ann Marie. *Pastoral, Pragmatism and Twentieth-Century American Poetry*. New York: Palgrave Macmillan, 2011.

Morris Jr, Roy. *Gertrude Stein Has Arrived: The Homecoming of a Literary Legend*. Baltimore: Johns Hopkins University Press, 2019.

Moses, Omri. "Gertrude Stein's Lively Habits." *Twentieth-Century Literature* 55.4 (2009): 445–84.

Moses, Omri. *Out of Character: Modernism, Vitalism, Psychic Life*. Stanford, CA: Stanford University Press, 2014.

Mülder-Bach, Inka and Gail Finney. "History as Autobiography: The Last Things before the Last." *New German Critique* 54 (Autumn 1991): 139–57.

Münsterberg, Hugo. *The Photoplay: A Psychological Study*. New York and London: D. Appleton and Company, 1916.

Murphet, Julian. "Gertrude Stein's Machinery of Perception." In *Literature and Visual Technologies*, edited by Julian Murphet and L. Rainford, 67–81. London: Palgrave Macmillan, 2003.

Murphy, Tim. *The Politics of Spirit: Phenomenology, Genealogy, Religion*. Albany: State University of New York Press, 2010.

Nattiez, Jean-Jacques. *Music and Discourse: Toward a Semiology of Music*. Translated by Carolyn Abbate. Princeton, NJ: Princeton University Press, 1990.

Nead, Lynda. *The Haunted Gallery: Painting, Photography, Film c. 1900*. New Haven, CT: Yale University Press, 2007.

Ngai, Sianne. *Ugly Feelings*. Cambridge, MA: Harvard University Press, 2005.

Nickels, Joel. *Poetry of the Possible: Spontaneity, Modernism and the Multitude*. Minneapolis and London: University of Minnesota Press, 2012.

Normandin, Sebastian and Charles T. Wolfe, eds. *Vitalism and the Scientific Image in Post-Enlightenment Life-Science, 1800–2010*. Dordrecht: Springer, 2013.

Noys, Benjamin. "The Poverty of Vitalism (and the Vitalism of Poverty)." Paper presented at To Have Done with Life: Vitalism and Anti-vitalism in Contemporary Philosophy Conference; June 17–19, MaMa, Zagreb, Croatia. Available at: <https://www.academia.edu/689255/The_Poverty_of_Vitalism_and_the_Vitalism_of_ Poverty_> (last accessed September 3, 2021).

Oettermann, Stephan. *The Panorama: History of a Mass Medium*. Translated by Deborah Lucas Schneider. New York: Zone Books, 1997.

Olson, Liesl. "Gertrude Stein, William James and Habit in the Shadow of War." *Twentieth-Century Literature* 49.3 (2003): 328–59.

Ortega y Gasset, José. *The Modern Theme*. Translated by James Cleugh. New York, Evanston, IL, and London: Harper & Row, 1961.

Owensby, Jacob. *Dilthey and the Narrative of History*. Ithaca, NY: Cornell University Press, 1994.

Parsons, Deborah L. *Streetwalking the Metropolis: Women, the City and Modernity*. Oxford: Oxford University Press, 2000.

Pearson, Keith Ansell. Introduction to *Henri Bergson: Key Writings*, edited by Keith Ansell Pearson and John Mullarky, 1–48. New York: Continuum, 2001.
Poe, Edgar Allan. "The Poetic Principle." In *The Works of Edgar Allan Poe*, The Raven Edition, vol. 5. Available at: <https://www.gutenberg.org/files/2151/2151-h/2151-h.htm#chap5.11> (last accessed September 3, 2021).
Porte, Rebecca Ariel. "Long Dull Poems: Stein's *Stanzas in Meditation* and Wordsworth's *The Prelude*." In *Primary Stein: Returning to the Writings of Gertrude Stein*, edited by Sharon J. Kirsch and Janet Boyd, 183–98. Lanham, MD: Lexington Books, 2014.
Posman, Sarah. "Breed That." *Jacket2* (March 2015). Available at: <https://jacket2.org/reviews/breed> (last accessed September 3, 2021).
Posman, Sarah. "'More Light! – Electric Light': Stein in Dialogue with the Romantic Paradigm in *Doctor Faustus Lights the Lights*." In *Primary Stein: Returning to the Writings of Gertrude Stein*, edited by Sharon J. Kirsch and Janet Boyd, 138–98. Lanham, MD: Lexington Books, 2014.
Posman, Sarah and Laura Luise Schultz. "One Who Was Networking." Introduction to *Gertrude Stein in Europe: Reconfigurations Across Media, Disciplines and Traditions*, edited by Sarah Posman and Laura Luise Schultz, 1–22. London: Bloomsbury, 2015.
Preston, Carrie J. "The Motor in the Soul: Isadora Duncan and Modernist Performance." *Modernism/Modernity* 12.2 (2005): 273–89.
Rabinbach, Anson. *The Human Motor: Energy, Fatigue and the Origins of Modernity*. Berkeley and Los Angeles: University of California Press, 1992.
Rabinovitz, Lauren. "Department Stores." In *Encyclopedia of Early Cinema*, edited by Richard Abel, 176–7. London and New York: Routledge, 2005.
Rado, Lisa. *Modernism, Gender and Culture: A Cultural Studies Approach*. New York: Routledge, 1997.
Randall, Bryony. *Modernism, Daily Time and Everyday Life*. Cambridge: Cambridge University Press, 2007.
Read, Herbert. Review of A. N. Whitehead, *Science and the Modern World*. *The New Criterion* 4 (June 1926): 581–7.
Retallack, Joan. *The Poethical Wager*. Berkeley and Los Angeles: University of California Press, 2003.
Reynolds, Kimberley. *Radical Children's Literature: Future Visions and Aesthetic Transformations in Juvenile Fiction*. Basingstoke: Palgrave Macmillan, 2007.
Richardson, Joan. *A Natural History of Pragmatism: The Fact of Feeling from Jonathan Edwards to Gertrude Stein*. Cambridge: Cambridge University Press, 2007.
Richardson, Robert D. *William James: In the Maelstrom of American Modernism*. New York: Houghton-Mifflin, 2006.

Ricoeur, Paul. *Interpretation Theory: Discourse and the Surplus of Meaning*. Fort Worth: Texas Christian University Press, 1976.

Robinson, Keith. "The New Whitehead? An Ontology of the Virtual in Whitehead's Metaphysics." *Symposium* 10.1 (Spring 2006): 69–80.

Rodowick, D. N. "The Last Things before the Last: Kracauer and History." *New German Critique* 41 (Spring/Summer 1987): 109–39.

Rose, Bernice, ed. *Picasso, Braque and Early Film in Cubism*. New York: Pace Wildenstein, 2007.

Rousseau, George. "The Perpetual Crisis of Modernism and the Traditions of Enlightenment Vitalism: with a Note on Mikhail Bakhtin." In *The Crisis in Modernism: Bergson and the Vitalist Controversy*, edited by Frederick Burwick and Paul Douglass, 15–97. Cambridge: Cambridge University Press, 1992.

Royce, Josiah. "Is There a Science of Education?" *Educational Review* 1.1 (1891): 18. Available at: <https://royce-edition.iupui.edu/wp-content/uploads/2018/10/1891-Royce-Is-There-a-Science-of-Education.-I.pdf> (last accessed September 3, 2021).

Rowe, John Carlos. *Afterlives of Modernism: Liberalism, Transnationalism and Political Critique*. Hanover, NH: Dartmouth College Press, 2011.

Ruddick, Lisa. *Gertrude Stein: Body, Text, Gnosis*. Ithaca, NY: Cornell University Press, 1990.

Sachs, Joe. *Aristotle's Physics: A Guided Study*. New Brunswick, NJ, and London: Rutgers University Press, 1998.

Sadoul, Georges. *L'Invention du cinema*. Paris: Denoël, 1950.

Sadoul, Georges. *Louis Lumière*. Paris: Seghers, 1964.

Saint-Pierre, Dominique. *Gertrude Stein, le Bugey, la guerre: d'août 1924 à décembre 1944*. Paris: Editions Musnier Gilbert, 2009.

Schaefer, Heike. "'Making a Cinema of It.' Seriality and Presence in Gertrude Stein's Early Portraits." In *American Literature and Immediacy: Literary Innovation and the Emergence of Photography, Film and Television*, 116–42. Cambridge: Cambridge University Press, 2020.

Scherr, Rebecca. "Tactile Erotics: Gertrude Stein and the Aesthetics of Touch." *Lit: Literature Interpretation Theory* 18.3 (2007): 193–212.

Schleifer, Ronald. *Modernism and Time: The Logic of Abundance in Literature, Science and Culture 1880–1930*. Cambridge: Cambridge University Press, 2000.

Schleifer, Ronald. *Rhetoric and Death: The Language of Modernism and Postmodern Discourse Theory*. Urbana: University of Illinois Press, 1990.

Schnädelbach, Herbert. *Philosophy in Germany 1831–1933*. Translated by Eric Matthews. Oxford: Oxford University Press, 1984.

Schoenbach, Lisi. *Pragmatic Modernism*. Oxford: Oxford University Press, 2012.

Schuster, Joshua. *The Ecology of Modernism: American Environments and Avant-Garde Poetics*. Tuscaloosa: University of Alabama Press, 2015.

Schuster, Joshua. "The Making of 'Tender Buttons': Gertrude Stein's Subjects, Objects and the Illegible." *Jacket2* (April 21, 2011). Available at: <https://jacket2.org/article/making-tender-buttons> (last accessed September 3, 2021).
Schwartz, Louis-Georges. "Cinema and the ~~Meaning~~ of Life." *Discourse* 28.2/3 (2006): 7–27.
Shaviro, Steven. *Without Criteria: Kant, Whitehead, Deleuze and Aesthetics*. Cambridge, MA: MIT Press, 2009.
Shelley, Percy Bysshe. *Selected Poems and Prose*, edited by Jack Donovan and Cian Duffy. London: Penguin, 2016.
Simpson, William M. R., Robert C. Koons and Nicholas J. Teh, eds. *Neo-Aristotelian Perspectives on Contemporary Science*. New York: Routledge, 2018.
Skinner, B. F. "Has Gertrude Stein a Secret?" *Atlantic Monthly* 53 (1934): 50–7. Available at: <https://www.bfskinner.org/publications/pdf-articles/> (last accessed September 3, 2021).
Smith, Matthew Wilson. *The Total Work of Art: From Bayreuth to Cyberspace*. New York: Routledge, 2007.
Sontag, Susan. *Against Interpretation and Other Essays*. London: Penguin, 2009.
Spahr, Juliana. *Everybody's Autonomy: Connective Reading and Collective Identity*. Tuscaloosa: University of Alabama Press, 2001.
Stack, George J. *Nietzsche and Emerson: An Elective Affinity*. Athens: Ohio University Press, 1992.
Stein, Gertrude. "Ada." In *Geography and Plays*, 14–16. Mineola, NY: Dover Publications, 1999.
Stein, Gertrude. "Bon Marche Weather." In *A Stein Reader*, edited by Ulla Dydo, 149–50. Evanston, IL: Northwestern University Press, 1993.
Stein, Gertrude. *The Autobiography of Alice B. Toklas*. In *Writings: 1932–1946*, edited by Harriet Scott Chessman and Catharine R. Stimpson, 653–916. New York: Library of America, 1998.
Stein, Gertrude. "Composition as Explanation." In *Writings: 1903–1932*, edited by Harriet Scott Chessman and Catharine R. Stimpson, 520–9. New York: Library of America, 1998.
Stein, Gertrude. *Everybody's Autobiography*. New York: Exact Change, 1993.
Stein, Gertrude. "Flirting at the Bon Marche." In *Writings: 1903–1932*, edited by Harriet Scott Chessman and Catharine R. Stimpson, 304. New York: Library of America, 1998.
Stein, Gertrude. *Four Saints in Three Acts*. In *Writings: 1903–1932*, edited by Harriet Scott Chessman and Catharine R. Stimpson, 608–50. New York: Library of America, 1998.
Stein, Gertrude. *The Geographical History of America or The Relation of Human Nature to the Human Mind*. In *Writings: 1932–1946*, edited by Harriet Scott Chessman and Catharine R. Stimpson, 356–488. New York: Library of America, 1998.

Stein, Gertrude. *Geography and Plays*. Mineola, NY: Dover Publications, 1999.

Stein, Gertrude. *How to Write*, edited by Patricia Meyerowitz. New York: Dover Publications, 1975 [1931].

Stein, Gertrude. "How Writing Is Written." In *How Writing is Written: The Previously Uncollected Writings of Gertrude* Stein, edited by R. B. Haas, vol. 2, 151–60. Los Angeles: Black Sparrow Press, 1974.

Stein, Gertrude. *Ida: A Novel*, edited by Logan Esdale. New Haven, CT: Yale University Press, 2012.

Stein, Gertrude. *Lectures in America*. In *Writings: 1932–1946*, edited by Harriet Scott Chessman and Catharine R. Stimpson, 191–336. New York: Library of America, 1998.

Stein, Gertrude. *The Making of Americans: Being a History of a Family's Progress*. Normal, IL: Dalkey Archive Press, 1995.

Stein, Gertrude. "Many Many Women." In *Matisse, Picasso and Gertrude Stein, with Two Shorter Stories*, 117–98. Mineola, NY: Dover Publications, 2000.

Stein, Gertrude. "Matisse." In *Writings: 1903–1932*, edited by Harriet Scott Chessman and Catharine R. Stimpson, 278–81. New York: Library of America, 1998.

Stein, Gertrude. *Matisse, Picasso and Gertrude Stein, with Two Shorter Stories*. Mineola, NY: Dover Publications, 2000.

Stein, Gertrude. *Narration: Four Lectures*. Chicago: University of Chicago Press, 2010.

Stein, Gertrude. "Orta Or One Dancing." In *Writings: 1903–1932*, edited by Harriet Scott Chessman and Catharine R. Stimpson, 285–303. New York: Library of America, 1998.

Stein, Gertrude. *Painted Lace and Other Pieces, 1914–1937*, vol. 5 of *The Yale Edition of the Unpublished Writings of Gertrude Stein*. New Haven, CT: Yale University Press, 1955.

Stein, Gertrude. *Paris France*. New York: Liveright, 1970.

Stein, Gertrude. "Picasso." In *Writings: 1903–1932*, edited by Harriet Scott Chessman and Catharine R. Stimpson, 282–4. New York: Library of America, 1998.

Stein, Gertrude. *Portraits and Prayers*. New York: Random House, 1934.

Stein, Gertrude. *Q.E.D.* In *Writings: 1903–1932*, edited by Harriet Scott Chessman and Catharine R. Stimpson, 1–64. New York: Library of America, 1998.

Stein, Gertrude. "Rue de Rennes." *Two: Gertrude Stein and her Brother and Other Early Portraits, 1908–1912*, vol. 1 of *The Yale Edition of the Unpublished Writings of Gertrude Stein*. New Haven, CT: Yale University Press, 1951.

Stein, Gertrude. "A Saint in Seven." In *A Primer for the Gradual Understanding of Gertrude Stein*, edited by Robert Bartlett Haas, 75–80. Santa Barbara, CA: Black Sparrow Press, 1971.

Stein, Gertrude. *Tender Buttons*, edited by Seth Parlow. San Francisco: City Lights Books, 2014.
Stein, Gertrude. *Three Lives*. In *Writings: 1903–1932*, edited by Harriet Scott Chessman and Catharine R. Stimpson, 65–274. New York: Library of America, 1998.
Stein, Gertrude. *Two: Gertrude Stein and her Brother and Other Early Portraits, 1908–1912*, vol. 1 of *The Yale Edition of the Unpublished Writings of Gertrude Stein*. New Haven, CT: Yale University Press, 1951.
Stein, Gertrude. *Wars I Have Seen*. London: Brilliance Books, 1984.
Stein, Gertrude. "What Happened: A Play in Five Acts." In *Geography and Plays*, 205–9. Mineola, NY: Dover, 1999.
Steiner, George. *Real Presences: Is There Anything in What We Say?* London: Faber, 1989.
Steiner, Wendy. *Exact Resemblance to Exact Resemblance: The Literary Portraiture of Gertrude Stein*. New Haven, CT, and London: Yale University Press, 1978.
Stengers, Isabelle. "A Constructivist Reading of *Process and Reality*." In *The Lure of Whitehead*, edited by Nicholas Gaskill and A. J. Nocek, 43–64. Minneapolis: University of Minnesota Press, 2014.
Stengers, Isabelle. *Thinking with Whitehead: A Free and Wild Creation of Concepts*. Translated by Michael Chase. Cambridge, MA: Harvard University Press, 2011.
Steuer, Daniel. "A Book That Won't Go Away: Otto Weininger's *Sex and Character*." In *Sex and Character: An Investigation of Fundamental Principles*. Translated by Ladislaus Löb, edited by Daniel Steuer with Laura Marcus, xi–xlvi. Bloomington: Indiana University Press, 2005.
Symons, Arthur, *The Symbolist Movement in Literature*. London: William Heinemann, 1899. Available at: <https://openlibrary.org/books/OL6907922M/The_symbolist_movement_in_literature> (last accessed September 3, 2021).
Taylor, Clyde. *The Mask of Art: Breaking the Aesthetic Contract - Film and Literature*. Bloomington and Indianapolis: Indiana University Press, 1998.
Toulmin, Stephen Edelston and June Goodfield. *The Discovery of Time*. Chicago: University of Chicago Press, 1982.
Tracy, Ryan. "Writing in Cars with Gertrude Stein and Jacques Derrida, or, The Age of Autotheory." *Arizona Quarterly: A Journal of American Literature, Culture, and Theory* 76.1 (2020): 15–37.
Vanskike, Elliott L. "'Seeing Everything as Flat': Landscape in Gertrude Stein's *Useful Knowledge* and *The Geographical History of America*." *Texas Studies in Language and Literature* 35.2 (1993): 151–67.
Van Wyk, Alan and Michel Weber, eds. *Creativity and Its Discontents: The Response to Whitehead's Process and Reality*. Frankfurt: Ontos, 2008.
Vesterman, William. *Dramatizing Time in Twentieth-Century Fiction*. New York: Routledge, 2014.

Von Helmholtz, Hermann. *Handbuch der physiologischen Optik*. Leipzig: Leopold Voss, 1867.
Voris, Linda. *The Composition of Sense in Gertrude Stein's Landscape Writing*. New York: Palgrave Macmillan for Springer Nature, 2016.
Wagers, Kelley. "Gertrude Stein's 'Historical Living.'" *Journal of Modern Literature* 31.3 (2008): 22–43.
Wahl, Jean. "Miss Stein's Battle." In *Critical Essays on Gertrude Stein*, edited by M. J. Hoffman, 83–4. Boston: G. K. Hall, 1986.
Wald, Priscilla. *Constituting Americans: Cultural Anxiety and Narrative Form*. Durham, NC: Duke University Press, 1995.
Walker, Jayne L. *The Making of a Modernist: Gertrude Stein from* Three Lives *to* Tender Buttons. Amherst: University of Massachusetts Press, 1984.
Wasser, Audrey. *The Work of Difference: Modernism, Romanticism and the Production of Literary Form*. New York, Fordham University Press, 2016.
Watson, Dana Cairns. *Gertrude Stein and the Essence of What Happens*. Nashville: Vanderbilt University Press, 2005.
Watson, Steven. *Prepare for Saints: Gertrude Stein, Virgil Thomson and the Mainstreaming of American Modernism*. New York: Random House, 1998.
Weininger, Otto. *Sex and Character: An Investigation of Fundamental Principles*. Translated by Ladislaus Löb, edited by Daniel Steuer with Laura Marcus. Bloomington: Indiana University Press, 2005.
Whitehead, Alfred North. *Adventures of Ideas*. Cambridge: Cambridge University Press, 1933.
Whitehead, Alfred North. *The Concept of Nature*. Cambridge: Cambridge University Press, 2015 [1920].
Whitehead, Alfred North. *An Enquiry Concerning the Principles of Natural Knowledge*. Cambridge: Cambridge University Press, 1919.
Whitehead, Alfred North. *Nature and Life*. Cambridge: Cambridge University Press, 2011 [1934].
Whitehead, Alfred North. *Process and Reality: An Essay in Cosmology*, edited by David Ray Griffin and Donald W. Sherburne. New York: The Free Press, 1978.
Whitehead, Alfred North. *Science and the Modern World*. New York: The Free Press, 1967 [1925].
Wicks, Robert L. *Schopenhauer's "The World as Will and Representation": A Reader's Guide*. London: Continuum, 2011.
Will, Barbara. *Gertrude Stein, Modernism and the Problem of "Genius"*. Edinburgh: Edinburgh University Press, 2000.
Williams, Keith. *H. G. Wells, Modernity and the Movies*. Liverpool: Liverpool University Press, 2007.
Wilson, Leigh. *Modernism and Magic: Experiments with Spiritualism, Theosophy and the Occult*. Edinburgh: Edinburgh University Press, 2015.

Wolfe, David W. *Tales from the Underground: A Natural History of Subterranean Life*. Cambridge, MA: Basic Books, 2001.
Wordsworth, William. *The Major Works*, edited by Stephen Gill. Oxford: Oxford University Press 2008.
Yeats, William Butler. *The Collected Poems of W. B. Yeats*, edited by Richard J. Finneran. New York: Scribner, 1996.

Index

abstractions and concreteness
  as gendered concepts, 16, 73, 132–3
  in landscape plays by GS, 177,
    179–80, 185, 186–7, 192, 196–7
  and life, 38, 41, 45–6, 51, 210
  in other texts by GS, 74–5,
    132–3, 146
  theoretical biography, 73, 74–5
  Whitehead, 19–20, 179–80, 181–3,
    193–4, 199, 210
actual, concept of the (Bergson), 30,
  95, 118–19
actualities, 93, 95, 126, 130–1,
  160–1, 191
actualization *see* entelechy
Adams, Henry, 34, 43
Altieri, Charles, 63
America (USA), 36–8, 45–6, 62–3, 69,
  73–4, 76, 193
American Civil War, 37
American Historical Foundation, 45
Aristotle
  entelechy, 92–3, 94, 95–6
  Nicomachean Ethics, 8, 69–70
  other mentions, 76, 176
art
  aura, 115, 120, 151, 153, 155, 161
  Dilthey, 51, 52–3
  and generation(s)/entelechy, 87, 90,
    96–9
  and modernism, 14–15, 106, 117,
    129, 160
  Whitehead, 175, 184
Ashton, Jennifer, 131
Atget, Eugène, 120
audiences
  of cinema, 7, 151–2, 154–5
  of dance, 145
  GS's interest in, 20, 201, 211
  of plays, 141–2, 159, 176
  unreturned gaze, 115–16, 120, 151
autobiography, 46, 62, 196, 210,
  211, 221
The Autobiography of Alice B. Toklas
  (GS), 20, 37, 39, 114, 150, 152,
  171, 201, 210, 211
avant-garde, 2–3, 13–17, 154

Baltimore, 42, 46, 48
Barnes, Djuna, 66
becoming (duration), 95–7, 115, 120,
  124, 126, 181, 187
Beer, Gillian, 36
Belley, Bugey, France, 169, 174
Benjamin, Walter
  on Bergson, 4, 97, 106–7, 118–20
  "Little History of Photography",
    120–1
  memory, 112, 114, 116–21,
    123–4
  "On Some Motifs in Baudelaire",
    112, 115, 116–17, 118–19,
    123–4, 149
  "Short Speech on Proust", 121
  "The Storyteller", 114–15, 119
  "The Work of Art in the Age of
    Technological Reproducibility",
    114, 115, 123, 149, 150–2, 154–5
  other mentions, 7, 43, 102, 144
Bennett, Jane, 176
Bergson, Henri
  becoming (duration), 95–7, 120,
    124, 126, 181
  Benjamin on, 4, 97, 106–7, 118–20

Creative Evolution, 10, 94–5, 97, 124
The Creative Mind, 34
élan vital, 5, 10, 30, 92, 94, 95, 198
intuition, 11, 30, 95, 120, 124,
    127, 144
Matter and Memory, 118–19, 124,
    125, 126
memory, 118–20, 124–7
movement of thought, 146
Time and Free Will, 124, 127
*The Two Sources of Morality and
    Religion*, 7, 11, 119, 127
and Whitehead, 4, 178, 181–2
Berkeley, George, 194
Bernstein, Charles, 66
biography, 20, 46, 51, 52, 64
    theoretical biography, 72–3, 74, 78
Blencowe, Claire, 118
Blumenbach, Johan Friedrich, 93
Bon Marché department store, 141,
    147–9
breathing, 154, 177
Bridgman, Richard, 63
Bulhof, Ilse, 50
Burckhardt, Jakob, 44–5
Bürger, Peter, *Theory of the Avant-
    Garde*, 13–15
Burwick, Frederick, 93
Bush, Clive, 72

Cage, John, 160
Carson, Luke, 100
Cecire, Natalia, 60
Certeau, Michel de, 15
character
    of an event (Whitehead), 181, 182–3
    The Making of the Americans (GS),
        69–70, 74, 76–7
    in portraits by GS, 130, 133, 135, 174
    Weininger, 71–5, 78
    in other texts by GS, 10, 62, 64,
        66, 159
cinema, 19, 121–36
    attendance at, by GS, 83–5, 101,
        105, 158
    audiences, 7, 151–2, 154–5
    history of, 104–5
    and life, 83–5, 104, 106, 121–5,
        153–4, 157–8

and memory, 112, 114, 116–21,
    123–8, 134–5, 209
and movement, 83–5, 102–6, 121–6,
    134–5, 142–3, 146, 209–10
and perception, 122, 123, 142,
    143, 150
and portraits by GS, 122–3, 125–7
and storytelling/narrative, 115–16,
    121, 130, 133–4, 136, 160–1
and time, 84–5, 101–7, 122, 130,
    134–5, 160–1, 209
unreturned gaze, 115–16, 120, 151
urban spaces for women, 141, 147
cinematic compositions, 83–4
classification, 8, 9, 29, 97–9, 102–3;
    see also typology
Clement, Tanya, 60
Cleopatra's Needle, 182, 184, 195
Colebrook, Claire, 6
collective life
    vs. individual life, 7–8, 17, 29–30,
        37, 68–9, 132, 135, 157
    and memory, 112, 114, 118–19
    in plays by GS, 141–2, 150, 161
    in portraits by GS, 141, 144, 147–9
    universality of death, 38, 210
    see also generation(s)
community, 64, 68–9, 151, 193, 195
complete history, 19, 87
    The Making of Americans (GS),
        7, 30, 37, 49–50, 62, 67–8, 69,
        73–4, 76–9, 83, 114, 209
composition, 16–20
    cinematic compositions, 83–4
    "Composition as Explanation" (GS),
        17, 18–19, 87–8, 91–2, 96–102,
        133, 211
    death of the (GS), 97–8, 100, 102
    How to Write, 117, 184–5
    other mentions, 113, 151, 160
Comte, Auguste, 88
concreteness *see* abstractions and
    concreteness
consciousness, 39, 43, 45, 123–4, 194
constructivism, 31, 60–1
containers/containment, 169, 173
contemporaneity, 90–2, 101–7, 171
contingency, 128–30, 134–5, 160–1
continuous life, 113–21, 133–5

continuous movement, 95, 102–6, 126, 134–5, 174, 179
continuous present, 99–101; *see also* present moment
Costello, Diarmuid, 120
Crary, Jonathan, 126
creativity
  Dilthey, 52–3
  and generation/entelechy, 90–101
  and life (GS), 17, 19, 20, 39, 46, 92, 96–101
  and modernity, 115, 118, 120, 134
  other mentions, 61, 186, 192
crowds, 141, 147–9

dance, 142–7
Darwin, Charles, 29, 30, 33, 35–40
death
  of the composition (GS), 97–8, 100, 102
  and modernity/modernism, 2, 5, 9, 14, 100, 102, 118, 123, 209–10
  in other texts by GS, 65, 76–7, 84, 152, 154
  universality of, 38, 210
  Whitehead, 189–90, 198
Debaise, Didier, 180
Deleuze, Gilles, 1, 4, 51–2, 134–5
  "Bergson's Conception of Difference", 11
  The Fold: Leibniz and the Baroque, 189, 197
  "Immanence: A Life", 210
  What Is Philosophy? (with Guattari), 6
Dewey, John, 16, 33
Dickens, Charles, 210
differentiation
  American identity, 46, 63
  and composition, 17, 84, 87–8, 90–2, 96, 100–1, 184–5
  and life (Bergson), 4, 10–11, 92, 94–5
  and life (evolution), 33, 39
  and life (GS), 1, 3–4, 97, 118, 132, 209
  and life (Whitehead), 13, 184
  and repetition, 40–2, 48, 84–5, 102–3

Dilthey, Wilhelm, 48–53
  "Contributions to the Study of Individuality", 52–3, 75–8
  Geisteswissenschaften, 10, 30, 50
  hermeneutics, 7, 10–11, 48–53, 62, 64–5, 75–8
  "Ideas for a Descriptive and Analytic Philosophy", 48
  Lebensphilosophie, 4
  Life of Schleiermacher, 52
  "The Rise of Hermeneutics", 64–5
  other mentions, 29, 40, 68, 89
Dilworth, Thomas, 193
Doane, Mary Anne, 130, 161
Douglass, Paul, 93
Driesch, Hans, 5, 92, 93, 94–5
Dulac, Germaine, 142–3
Duncan, Isadora, 142, 143–4, 145, 146, 147
DuPlessis, Rachel Blau, 185
duration (becoming), 95–7, 115, 120, 124, 126, 181, 187
Durham, Scott, 189
Durkheim, Émile, 187
Dydo, Ulla, 127, 144, 147, 159, 174
dynamic lives (living portraits), 152–6
dynamic unity, 12, 30, 69

élan vital, 5, 10, 30, 92, 94, 95, 198
Elder, R. Bruce, 157
Eliot, T. S., 2
Emerson, Ralph Waldo, 45–6, 47
Enlightenment, 35, 88
entelechy, 5, 89–102, 124, 134, 188–90
  Aristotle, 92–3, 94, 95–6
Epstein, Jean, 154
Erfahrung (experience in tradition), 112, 115, 116, 118–21, 133–4, 144
Erlebnis (isolated experience), 112, 119, 120, 121, 124, 133, 144
Ermarth, Michael, 48
events
  GS unexcited by concept of, 185–6
  objects as (Whitehead), 181–5, 189, 195, 198–9
  in plays by GS, 196, 197

everybody/everyone
  crowds, 141, 147–9
  Deleuze on Dickens, 210
  GS's aim to write of, 2, 7, 10, 134, 150, 195
  The Making of Americans (GS), 7, 67–71, 73, 74, 77
  "Orta Or One Dancing" (GS), 145, 146
  World War One generation, 17, 88, 97, 100, 102, 171
everyday life/everything
  as gendered concepts, 15–16, 132–5, 144
  GS's aim to write of, 13, 15–16, 38, 42, 177, 184, 187
  The Making of Americans (GS), 49–50
  see also objects
evolutionary theories, 29, 30, 33–40, 89, 94–5
excessive poetics, 39, 66, 70
excitement, 30, 36–40, 104, 150, 158–9, 186, 201–2

familiarity *see* strange familiarity
family histories, 69–71
fascism, 4, 119
Faÿ, Bernard, 199–201
female experience, 16, 114, 132–6, 141–7
feminist theory, 15–16, 18
First World War, 17, 88, 97, 100, 102, 171
formalism, 53, 199–200
Foster, Hal, 14–15
Foucault, Michel, 8, 9
Four Saints in Three Acts (GS), 173, 174, 179, 186–8, 190–1, 192–3, 195–8, 210
Frankfurt School, 129
freedom, 7–8, 11, 127, 151–2, 160–1
French symbolism, 63–4
Freud, Sigmund, 124
Fuller, Loïe, 142–3, 146

Gadamer, Hans-Georg, 76
gaze, unreturned, 115–16, 120, 151

Geisteswissenschaften (human sciences), 10, 30, 50
gender, 15–16, 71–2, 73, 114, 132–6, 141–7, 185
generation(s), 87–107
  overview, 84–5, 87–92
  Aristotle's entelechy, 92–3, 94, 95–6
  formed by World War One, 17, 88, 97, 100, 102, 171
  non-contemporaneity, 90–2, 101–7
  and plays by GS, 142, 162
  and storytelling (GS), 84, 103, 117–18, 133–4, 150
  Tender Buttons, 149–50, 156
genius, 2, 43, 53, 71–2, 75, 78
German Historical School, 40, 44–5, 47, 64, 88
Gesamtkunstwerk (total work of art), 192–3, 197, 198, 210
God, 36, 38, 44
Goodfield, June, 35–6
grammar, 65–6, 78, 174, 184–5;
  see also paragraphs, GS's use of; sentences, GS's use of
Grandy, David A., 184
Grosz, Elizabeth, 33–4, 37
Guattari, Félix, 6
Gunning, Tom, 104–5, 130, 143
Guthrie, James, 35

Haeckel, Ernst, 38
Hegel, G. W. F., 43, 44–5, 68
Heidegger, Martin, 89
Hejinian, Lyn, 188
Helm, Bertrand, 35
Helmholtz, Hermann von, 126–7, 128
Herder, Johann Gottfried, 35–6
hermeneutics, 40–3, 48–53, 60–79
  Dilthey, 7, 10–11, 48–53, 62, 64–5, 68, 75–8
  James, 40–3
  The Making of Americans (GS), 7, 31, 49–50, 60, 62, 67–8, 69–70, 72, 74, 76–9, 209
  "Melanctha" (GS), 31, 62–7, 69
Highmore, Ben, 15
historicism, 43, 44–8, 68, 128

history, 35–40, 42–8, 50–3, 88–90, 119–21
  of cinema, 104–5
  cinema's impact on concept of, 84–5, 106, 128–30, 133, 135–6
  "Composition as Explanation" (GS), 19, 96–102, 133, 211
  life histories, 197–202
  "Melanctha" (GS), 66
  of objects, 156
  in plays by GS, 186–7, 196, 198
  Three Lives (GS), 63–4
  see also complete history
Holbrook, Susan, 193
Hugnet, George(s), 173, 174, 176, 197, 201

idealism, 43, 44–5, 48, 52, 68, 129
  ideal types, 64, 71, 73
  life philosophy's opposition to, 29–30, 61
Iggers, Georg, 45
Ignatius, Saint, in GS's play, 186–7, 190, 196
Ignatius of Loyola, 186–7
immigration, 46, 63, 64, 69
individual life
  biography, 20, 46, 51, 52, 64, 72–3, 74, 78
  vs. collective life, 7–8, 17, 29–30, 37, 68–9, 132, 135, 157
  in collective portraits by GS, 141, 144, 148–9
  and history, 43, 44–6, 47, 50–3
  and universality of death, 38, 210
individuation, 71, 177, 193–5, 196
industrialization (series production), 84, 101–3, 112
insistence, 40, 42, 48, 63, 103
interpretation *see* hermeneutics
intuition, 11, 30, 95, 120, 124, 127, 144, 209
isolation, experience in (*Erlebnis*), 112, 119, 120, 121, 124, 144

James, Henry, 46–7
James, William, 40–3
  Dilthey influenced by, 47, 48–9
  on experience, 12, 16, 29–30, 41–3, 49
  radical empiricism, 11–12, 30, 42–3
  other mentions, 67–8, 179
Jameson, Frederic, 48
Janik, Allan, 73
Johnson, Curtis, 40
Joyce, James, 69, 116

Kant, Immanuel, 8–9, 48
Keats, John, 156
Kirsch, Sharon, 117, 185
Kloppenberg, James, 42
Klossowski, Pierre, 188–9
knowledge and science
  overview, 8–10, 12–13, 30, 33–6, 44–8, 49–50
  evolutionary theories, 29, 30, 33–40, 89, 94–5
  logic, 51–2, 64, 75, 97–9, 102, 171
  moving picture experiments, 122, 123, 142, 143
  prehension, 177, 193–7, 198
  in texts by GS, 67, 76–8
  see also hermeneutics
Kracauer, Siegfried, 128, 133, 142

Laforgue, Jules, 63–4
landscape plays, 159, 173–4, 176–7, 179–80, 186–8, 190–8, 210
landscapes, 7, 19, 169–72, 173–4, 178, 192
language, 8–9, 39, 49, 65–6, 78, 174, 184–5, 192; *see also* paragraphs, GS's use of; sentences, GS's use of
Latour, Bruno, 13, 17, 19, 61
Lebenswelt, 128–9, 133
Lectures in America (GS), 38, 40–2, 48, 77–8, 103, 117
  "The Gradual Making of the Making of Americans", 67, 76, 129
  "Pictures", 104
  "What Is English Literature?" 46, 66
  see also "Portraits and Repetition" (GS)
Lefebvre, Henri, 15
Leskov, Nikolai, 119

Lessing, Gotthold Ephraim, 106
Lewis, Wyndham, 5
life, 1–20, 29–31, 33–53, 209–11
  and cinema, 83–5, 104, 106, 121–5, 153–4, 157–8
  continuous life, 113–21, 133–5
  and differentiation (Bergson), 4, 10–11, 92, 94–5
  and differentiation (GS), 1, 3–4, 97, 118, 132, 209
  and differentiation (Whitehead), 13, 184
  evolutionary theories, 29, 30, 33–40, 89, 94–5
  and movement, 1, 3, 11–12, 30, 46, 48, 83–5, 92, 95–6, 102–5, 117–18, 122–3, 186
  in plays by GS, 150, 158–62, 176–7
  in portraits by GS, 77, 83, 113–14, 132–3, 146, 149, 152–4, 175–6, 209
  vitalism, 4–10, 73, 76, 93–5, 97, 99, 119
  see also collective life; hermeneutics; nature
life philosophy, 29–31, 34–5, 61, 62, 72
Lindsay, Vachel, 154
listening *see* storytelling; talking and listening
liveliness
  breathing, 154, 177
  and creativity, 19, 97–8
  life nexus, 78, 130
  and movement, 1, 11, 30, 48, 102–3, 122
  reading GS's texts, 2, 16
  and tradition, 175, 209–10
logic, 51–2, 64, 75, 97–9, 102, 171
looking
  GS's mode of, 150, 152, 155, 161, 195
  and memory (GS), 125, 126–8
  new ways of seeing movement, 122, 123, 142, 143
  "seeing typically", 52–3, 75, 78
  unreturned gaze, 115–16, 120, 151
Lorange, Astrid, 60
Lumière brothers, 122, 130, 143
Lyell, Charles, 36

McCabe, Susan, 112
The Making of Americans (GS)
  as complete history, 7, 30, 37, 49–50, 62, 67–8, 69, 73–4, 76–9, 83, 114, 209
  portrait elements, 76–9, 83–4, 114, 129–30, 131–2
  as typological project, 49, 70–1, 73–5, 76, 78, 87, 209
  other mentions, 31, 46, 60, 72, 116, 211
manifesto, tradition of the, 2, 17
Mannheim, Karl, 89, 90–1, 97
Marcus, Laura, 157
Marey, Jules-Etienne, 122, 124
Marinetti, Filippo Tommaso, 2
masculinity, 16, 71–2, 75, 78, 141, 144
"Melanctha" (GS), 31, 62–7, 69
Melancthon, Philipp, 31, 64
memory, 116–21, 123–8
  Benjamin, 112, 114, 116–21, 123–4
  Bergson, 118–21, 124–7
  and cinema, 112, 114, 116–21, 123–8, 134–5, 209
  collective memory, 112, 114, 118–19
  and dance, 146
  The Making of Americans (GS), 131–2
  "Many Many Women" (GS), 132–3
Meyer, Steven, 13, 40, 176
modernism
  overview, 1–4, 13–14, 38
  GS as modernist, 15–16, 29, 69, 106, 118, 157, 176, 209
  vitalism, 4–10, 73, 76, 93–5, 97, 99, 119
modernity
  overview, 9–13, 17
  collective experience, 150–1, 161–2
  shocks, 102–3, 112, 114–15, 121
  and tradition, 112–16, 120–1, 127, 130, 132–3, 141
  see also Gesamtkunstwerk (total work of art)
morality, 38, 69–70, 71, 194
Moretti, Franco, 60
Moses, Omri, 7

movement
  and cinema, 83–5, 102–6, 121–6, 134–5, 142–3, 146, 209–10
  continuous, 95, 102–6, 126, 134–5, 174, 179
  dance, 142–7
  dynamic lifes (living portraits), 152–4
  in landscape plays by GS, 170, 172, 173–4, 177, 179, 192, 198
  and liveliness/life, 1, 3, 11–12, 30, 46, 48, 83–5, 92, 95–6, 102–5, 117–18, 122–3, 186
  moving paragraphs, 117, 146
  tableaux vivants, 188–9
  of time, 34–5, 84–5, 87–8
  transport, 3, 76, 84, 95, 127, 130
  see also stasis/stillness
Mul, Jos De, 52
Münsterberg, Hugo, 157–8
music *see* opera
Muybridge, Eadweard, 122

narrative
  biography as, 51
  in cinema, 130, 133–4, 160–1
  in early texts by GS, 50, 62, 65, 69–70, 84, 113
  in plays by GS, 161, 176–7, 195
natural history *see* evolutionary theories
nature
  naturalness, 97–9, 143
  in plays by GS, 192, 195, 196
  Whitehead, 12–13, 170, 172, 176, 177–84, 194, 198–9, 210
Nead, Lynda, 188
New Criticism, 53, 61
newspapers, 115, 186
Newtonian framework, 30, 33–4, 35
nexuses, 51–3, 62, 78, 87, 130
Nickels, Joel, 157
Nietzsche, Friedrich, 10, 11, 36, 38–9
non-contemporaneity, 90–2, 101–7, 171
Noys, Benjamin, 5

Oakland, California, 143
objects
  carafe, as example of, 3–4, 153, 169
  as events (Whitehead), 181–5, 189, 195, 198–9
  sound/concerts, 197
  as things, 30, 98, 115, 152–6, 161, 209
Ogden, C. K., 5
Olson, Liesl, 15
"one thing", GS's concept of, 3, 49, 83, 103, 113
open society (Bergson), 7–8, 11, 120, 127
opera, 192–7, 211; *see also Four Saints in Three Acts* (GS)
Ortega y Gasset, José, 88–9
otherness, 64–7, 69, 98

panoramas, 19, 76–8, 104–6
paragraphs, GS's use of, 99–101, 117, 133, 146, 185
Paris, 2, 141, 143, 147, 158
perception, 105, 112, 119, 121, 123–7, 150, 154–5; *see also* looking; prehension; sensation
permanence, 169, 170, 171, 172, 174, 181, 184, 186
photography, 115–16, 120–5, 128–9, 142, 187, 189–90, 196
Picasso, Pablo, 2, 39, 113–14, 117
Pinder, Wilhelm, 89–90, 97
Platonism, 41, 73
plays, 141–2, 150, 158–62
  landscape plays, 159, 173–4, 176–7, 179–80, 186–8, 190–8, 210
Poe, Edgar Allan, 149, 199
portraits
  "Ada" (GS), 114
  "Bernard Faÿ" (GS), 199–201
  breaking traditions of, 175–7
  and cinema, 122–3, 125–7
  crowds/collective portraits, 141, 144, 147–9
  dynamic lifes (living portraits), 152–6
  early portraits by GS, 101–3, 112–14, 209
  of Hugnet (GS), 173, 174, 176, 197
  "A Long Gay Book" (GS), 129–30, 131, 147
  The Making of Americans (GS), 76–9, 83–4, 114, 129–30, 131–2

"Many Many Women" (GS), 39, 129, 131–5, 147
"Matisse" (GS) and "Picasso" (GS), 39, 113–14, 117
"Orta Or One Dancing" (GS), 142, 144–7, 148
self-portraits by GS, 134, 150, 152
Tender Buttons (GS), 152–7
Two (GS), 144
"Portraits and Repetition" (GS), 1, 69, 83–5, 87, 91, 101–3, 113, 116, 117–18, 125, 127, 129–30, 131, 150, 169, 173, 174, 192, 195, 200–1
post-modernism, 61, 189–90
post-structuralism, 33, 61–2
potentialities, 92–6, 99, 126, 189–91, 193
prehension, 177, 193–7, 198
present moment, 99–101
  cinema, 135–6, 160
  memory, 118–19, 127–8, 132
  Whitehead, 175, 181, 189, 194–5
  other mentions, 14, 17, 41, 42, 43, 63, 77–8
process
  becoming (duration), 95–7, 115, 120, 181, 187
  captured in photograph series, 189–90, 196
  and plays by GS, 162
  tableaux vivants, 188–9
  see also composition; events
process philosophy, 3, 11
Proust, 69, 116–17, 119, 121, 124, 128
psychology
  Dilthey, 48–9, 52, 53, 65, 68–9
  GS's interest in, 7, 39, 49, 67–8, 71–4, 149
  James, 12, 42, 49, 67–8

Rabinovitz, Lauren, 141
race, 63, 64, 66–7, 71, 193
racism, 66–7, 71
Radcliffe College, 68, 71, 157
radical empiricism, 11–13, 30–1, 42–3; *see also* James, William; Whitehead, A. N.

Randall, Bryony, 15–16
Ranke, Leopold von, 43, 44, 45, 47, 88
Read, Herbert, 171
reading and readers, 16–17, 60–1, 65
reason, role of, 15, 35, 36, 38, 43
repetition, 40–2, 48, 84–5, 102–3, 169, 181–2; *see also* "Portraits and Repetition" (GS)
resemblances, 3, 63, 122, 125, 127–8, 131
Retallack, Joan, 160
Ricoeur, Paul, 51
Riegl, Alois, 90
romanticism
  philosophy, 35–6, 45, 50, 53, 89, 90, 97, 209
  poetry, 2, 156–7, 198
  and war, 99, 100, 102
  Wordsworth, 9, 20, 178
Rousseau, George, 93
Royce, Josiah, 68–9, 71
Russell, Bertrand, 171

Sachs, Joe, 93, 96
Sadoul, Georges, 122
Saint Remy, Provence, 169–70, 192
saints, literary depictions of, 64, 186–8, 190, 196–7
Scherr, Rebecca, 155
Schleiermacher, Friedrich, 50, 64–5
Schoenbach, Lisi, 15–16
Schopenhauer, Arthur, 40–1
Schuster, Joshua, 16
Schwartz, Louis-Georges, 121–3
science *see* knowledge and science
Second World War, 39
Sedgwick, Ellery, 39
sensation
  experience as, 41, 49, 51–2, 74, 144
  and memory, 116, 131–2
  multi-sensory, 16, 133, 160, 170, 173, 174
  sense-awareness (Whitehead), 178–9, 181
  of smell, 131, 133
  of sound, 160, 197
  of touch, 154–5
  see also looking

sentences, GS's use of, 117, 146, 185, 200
series production
  industrialization, 84, 101–3, 112
  newspapers, 115, 186
sexuality, 73–4, 134, 145
Shaviro, Steven, 60
Shelley, Percy Bysshe, 2
shocks of modernity, 102–3, 112, 114–15, 121
shops, 141, 147–9
sight, sense of *see* looking
Skinner, B. F., 39
smell, sense of, 131, 133
Smith, Matthew Wilson, 192–3
society
  Benjamin, 119–20, 151–2
  open society (Bergson), 7–8, 11, 120, 127
  in texts by GS, 2, 62–7, 69, 99
  other mentions, 35, 43, 68–9, 90–1
Sontag, Susan, 61
sound, sense of, 160, 197
Spencer, Herbert, 34, 43
Spinoza, Benedict de, 195
Stack, George J., 47
stasis/stillness
  objects as static events, 181–5, 189, 195, 198–9
  in opera, 192, 195–6
  permanence, 169, 170, 171, 172, 174, 181, 184, 186
  tableaux vivants, 188–9
Stein, Gertrude *("GS" in this index)*
  overview, 1, 11, 13, 15–16, 209–11
  "Ada", 114
  The Autobiography of Alice B. Toklas, 20, 37, 39, 114, 150, 152, 171, 201, 210, 211
  "Before the Flowers of Friendship Faded", 201
  "Bernard Faÿ", 199–201
  "Bon Marche Weather", 147, 148–9
  "Composition as Explanation", 17, 18–19, 87–8, 91–2, 96–102, 133, 211
  Everybody's Autobiography, 33, 187
  "A Family of Perhaps Three", 147

"Flirting at the Bon Marche", 147, 148
"Four Dishonest Ones", 147
Four Saints in Three Acts, 173, 174, 179, 186–8, 190–1, 192–3, 195–8, 210
"Galeries Lafayette", 147, 148
"The Gentle Lena", 63, 64
The Geographical History of America or The Relation of Human Nature to the Human Mind, 96
"G.M.P", 61, 129, 131, 147
"The Good Anna", 63, 64
"The Gradual Making of the Making of Americans", 67, 76, 129
How to Write, 117, 184–5
"How Writing is Written", 186, 201
Lectures in America see Lectures in America (GS); "Portraits and Repetition" (GS)
"A Long Gay Book", 129–30, 131, 147
"A Lyrical Opera Made By Two To Be Sung", 192
The Making of Americans see The Making of Americans (GS)
"Many Many Women", 39, 129, 131–5, 147
"Marry Nettie", 2
"Matisse", 113–14, 117
"Melanctha", 31, 62–7, 69
Narration: Four Lectures, 46, 47
A Novel of Thank You, 211
"Orta Or One Dancing", 142, 144–7, 148
Paris France, 2–3
"Picasso", 39, 113–14, 117
"Pictures", 104
"Plays", 150, 158–9, 160, 162, 173, 174, 180, 189–90
"Poetry and Grammar", 156, 180
"Portraits and Repetition" *see* "Portraits and Repetition" (GS)
Q.E.D., 30, 46, 62–3
"Rue de Rennes", 147, 149
"A Saint in Seven", 188
"Saints and Singing", 192

"Saving the Sentence", 3
Stanzas in Meditation, 20
Tender Buttons, 3, 131, 150, 152–7, 158, 161, 169, 177
Three Lives, 30, 31, 46, 62–7, 69
Two, 144
Wars I Have Seen, 29, 30, 33, 39, 40
"What Happened. A Five Act Play", 150, 159–60, 161, 195
"What Is English Literature?" 46, 66
see also portraits
Steiner, Wendy, 152
Stengers, Isabelle, 17–18, 170, 183–4, 195
Steuer, Daniel, 72
stillness *see* stasis/stillness
stories *see* narrative
storytelling
  Benjamin, 114–19, 121
  and cinema, 115–16, 121, 130, 133–4, 136, 160–1
  in early texts by GS, 42, 62–6, 69–70, 84, 113
  in plays and later texts by GS, 161, 176–7, 195, 211
  talking and listening, 48, 61, 75, 103, 125–6, 150
strange familiarity
  of objects, 150, 152–3, 161
  in plays by GS, 158–60, 161–2
Symons, Arthur, 64

tableaux vivants, 188–9
talking and listening, 48, 61, 75, 103, 125–6, 150
Taylor, Clyde, 98
Teresa of Ávila, 187
theater, 157–9, 160, 161; *see also* plays
theoretical biography, 72–3, 74, 78
Therese, Saint, in GS's play, 187–8, 190, 196–7
Thérèse de Lisieux, 187, 190
things/objects, 30, 98, 115, 152–6, 161, 209
  carafe, as example of, 3–4, 153, 169
thinking, 6, 8–9, 18, 144, 146–7, 181–2
Thomson, Virgil, 191, 192–3

Three Lives (GS), 30, 46, 62–7
  "The Gentle Lena", 63, 64
  "The Good Anna", 63, 64
  "Melanctha", 31, 62–7, 69
time
  overview, 3, 5, 34–6, 40, 42–3, 118, 120
  becoming (duration), 95–7, 115, 120, 124, 126, 181, 187
  and cinema, 84–5, 101–7, 122, 130, 134–5, 160–1, 209
  "Composition as Explanation" (GS), 87–8, 91–2, 96–102, 133
  and events (Whitehead), 181–4
  and generation(s), 87–92
  The Making of Americans (GS), 76–9
  movement of, 34–5, 84–5, 87–8
  non-contemporaneity, 90–2, 101–7, 171
  and objects, 156
  permanence, 169, 170, 171, 172, 174, 181, 184, 186
  in plays by GS, 141–2, 162, 176–7, 186, 191
  see also present moment
Toklas, Alice B., 114; *see also The Autobiography of Alice B. Toklas* (GS)
Toulmin, Stephen, 35–6
tradition, 112–36
  and cinema/photography, 106, 112–16, 120–30, 134–5, 142, 144, 146, 150–2
  liveliness in opposition to, 175–7, 179, 201, 209–10
  and memory, 112, 114, 116–21, 123–8, 132–5
  and storytelling, 114–19, 121, 133–4, 136
transport, 3, 76, 84, 95, 127, 130
typology, 52–3, 69–75
  The Making of Americans (GS), 49, 70–1, 73–5, 76, 78, 87, 209
  "seeing typically" (Dilthey), 52–3, 75, 78
  other mentions, 29, 125–6
Tzara, Tristan, 2

unconscious, the, 123–4, 194
understanding *see* hermeneutics
United States of America (USA), 36–8, 45–6, 62–3, 69, 73–4, 76, 193
unity
  dynamic unity, 12, 30, 69
  of nature and life (Whitehead), 12–13, 177, 178–9, 194, 198–9
  "one thing", GS's concept of, 3, 49, 83, 103, 113
  trinity, 199–200
  other mentions, 41, 45
  see also complete history; wholeness

vanguard collectives, 2, 13
virtual, concepts of the, 41, 106, 126, 128, 189
  Bergson, 30, 95, 118–19, 121, 124, 125
vitalism, 4–10, 73, 76, 93–5, 97, 99, 119

Wagner, Richard, 192
Wahl, Jean, 29
Walker, Jayne L., 66
wars, 17, 37, 39, 88, 96–7, 99–102, 104, 171
Wasser, Audrey, 6
Waterloo panorama, 104
Watson, Steven, 191, 193
Weininger, Otto, 31, 71–5, 78
Whitehead, A. N.
  abstractions and concreteness, 19–20, 179–80, 181–3, 193–4, 199, 210
  and Bergson, 4, 178, 181–2
  The Concept of Nature, 177–84, 189, 195
  An Enquiry Concerning the Principles of Natural Knowledge, 199
  events, 181–5, 189, 195, 198–9
  nature, 12–13, 170, 172, 176, 177–84, 194, 198–9, 210
  Nature and Life, 178
  prehension, 177, 193–5, 198
  Principia Mathematica, 171
  Process and Reality, 171, 175, 177, 179, 189
  Science and the Modern World, 170–1, 176, 177, 178, 179, 193, 195, 198
  other mentions, 8, 18, 60
Whitman, Walt, 156–7
wholeness
  Dilthey, 49, 50, 65, 76
  "idea of a whole thing" (GS), 29, 30, 66, 76–9, 113, 117; *see also* complete history
  and typology, 49, 71–2, 74, 76
  other mentions, 39, 95, 121, 177, 181
Will, Barbara, 71
Wilson, Leigh, 104
Wordsworth, William, 9, 20, 178
World War One, 17, 88, 97, 100, 102, 171
World War Two, 39

Yeats, W. B., 2

EU representative:
Easy Access System Europe
Mustamäe tee 50, 10621 Tallinn, Estonia
Gpsr.requests@easproject.com

www.ingramcontent.com/pod-product-compliance
Lightning Source LLC
Chambersburg PA
CBHW070345240426
43671CB00013BA/2404